Ciderlore

Ciderlore

Cider in the Three Counties

by

Fiona Mac

Logaston Press

LOGASTON PRESS
Little Logaston Woonton Almeley
Herefordshire HR3 6QH

First published by Logaston Press 2003
Copyright text © Fiona Mac 2003
Copyright illustrations © as per detailed in the Acknowledgements 2003

ISBN 1 904396 10 0

Set in Times and New Baskerville by Logaston Press
and printed in Great Britain by
Bell & Bain Ltd

*This book is dedicated to all the cider makers and cider drinkers
who shared with me these stories and memories of cider in the
three counties of Herefordshire, Gloucestershire and Worcestershire.
Every effort has been made to corroborate these tales
but as they are taken from living memory,
it is as likely that some are as full of fiction as truth!*

Good cider 'tis a drink divine
Better by far than all your wine.
Good in grief, good in joy,
Good for maid, man and boy.

Anon., 19th century

Eve gave Adam an apple
Adam gave Eve a kiss
Eve gave Adam her body
Adam gave Eve his

Dennis Gould, Aelington Mill

Contents

Author's and Publisher's Note

The few months leading up to the publication of this book in the autumn of 2003 has seen abrupt change for cider drinkers in the counties of Herefordshire, Gloucestershire and Worcestershire. Bulmers, the biggest producer of cider in the Three Counties—indeed the UK as a whole—ran into financial problems and for a while the predictions for the future of the company were changing weekly. It was only with the acceptance by the majority of Bulmers shareholders of the sale of the firm to the brewers Scottish and Newcastle that a fairly firm line could be drawn and a decision made to stop rewriting the company's history in this book.

But it has not only been Bulmers which has undergone change in the past year, small scale cider producers who have found a new market for their quality ciders and perrys through improved marketing and packaging also suffered significant losses. Core Food and Drink, the purpose-built regional centre of excellence at Pershore, funded by the cider industry and Advantage West Midlands to help local cider makers improve their skills and also to provide state of the art technical facilities and a bottling plant for use by small producers, closed early in 2003. Simultaneously another bottling plant being used by small scale producers at Three Choirs Vineyards also stopped contract bottling as the wine trade filled its spare capacity, leaving such producers without access to bottling facilities essential to the successful marketing of their ciders and perrys.

These events, along with the constant changes in the industry as it moves into the 21st century, with the rise in numbers of small scale producers, the growth of organic production, and the threat to contract fruit growers posed by the problems at Bulmers, have meant constant revision to the text. But it must be appreciated that in a modern, relentlessly changing industry this book will, of necessity, only represent a snapshot of cider and cider making in the Three Counties.

Acknowledgements

The Author would like to thank the following individuals who have helped make this book a reality: Ian Austen my IT wizard for his unflagging support throughout; Duncan Murch for keeping me going when all was black; Gills Williams for cheering me on from afar; the Cider Museum for the use of a quiet office to write in and unlimited access to their archives over many months; the E.F. Bulmer Foundation for keeping my van on the road to do the research; my long suffering editor Andy Johnson, for commissioning me to write the thing, then sticking with me when it took three years; and my PA Pauline Oliver for deciphering my handwriting into typed text.

For interviews, liquid refreshment and encouragement I would like to thank (in alphabetical order), BBC Hereford and Worcester, Charles Bennett, James Bissett, Jonathan Blair, Ray Boddington, Charlie Bower, Ted Bruning, Gillian Bulmer, Giles Bulmer, P. 'Butler' Symonds, Mr. D. Charles, Common Ground, Bob Cooke, Jonathan and Tom Crump, Rachel Datlin, Susie and Ivor Dunkerton, Matt Dunwell, Mike Edwards the 'Asham poet, Chris Fairs, Stella Forden-Cove, The Formation Drinking Team at the Barrels, Jim and Lincon Franklin, Eric Freeman, Dennis Gould, David Griffiths, Denis and Ivor Gwatkins, Major Robert and Mr. Robin Haig, Paul Hands, Thony Handy, Ed Hargrave, Dereck Hartland, Mike Henney, John Howes, Roger Jackson, Kenelm and Mike Johnson, Brian Jones, Paul Keetch MP, David Kitton, Keith and Zaz Knight, Andrew Lea, Janet Legge, Sheila Leitch, the Leominster Morris Side, Mick Lewis, R&H Lothian, Janet MacKay, Rosemary Manns, James Marsden, Charles Martell, Rory McLure, Kevin Minchew, Peter Mitchell, Geoff and Sue Morris, Felicity Norman, Jean Nowell, Cedric Olive, Tom Oliver, Lucy Powell, Pete Smithies, Heather Tarplee, Bill Taylor, George Thomas, Margaret Thompson, John Thynne-Russell B.E.M., Alan Tringham, Kate Tudge, Geoff Warren, Terry Watts, Margaret Wilce, Ray Williams, Bill Wood, John Worle, Albert Wrixen plus anyone else I may have left out in my stupefied haze.

For use of illustrations I would like to thank the following: The Museum of Cider in Hereford for those on pp. *xiv*, 20, 52, 62, 78 (both),

79, 87, 89, 197, 198, 199 and 200; Bulmers for those on pp. 25, 26, 27, 49, 64, 80 (both), 81, 82, 85, 92, 101, 103, 134, 146, 150, 151, 153 and 190; Logaston Press for those on pp. 12, 24 (both) with additional thanks to Gloucester Folk Museum for their assistance, 29, 42, 44, 45, 181 and 182; Ian Priddy for those on pp. 19, 60, 116, 117, 147 and 148; Dunkertons for those on pp. 74, 75, 156 (both) and 157; Westons for those on pp. 109, 111 (top and bottom left), 112, 113 and 114; Kevin Minchew for those on pp. 161, 171, 172 and 173; Jim Franklin for those on pp. 30, 31 and 32; Mike Johnson for those on pp. 18 and 158 (both); Denis Gwatkins for those on pp. 9 and 10; Brian Jones for those on pp. 14 and 15; The British Library for those on pp. 57 and 58; The *Hereford Times* for those on pp. 28 and 183; Dereck Hartland for that on p. 16; Mr. Charles for that on p. 34; Pete Smithies for that on p. 37; Keith Knight for that on p. 55; Michael Howes for that on p. 111 (bottom right); Long Ashton Research Station for that on p. 122; Paul Keetch MP for that on p. 142; Jean Nowell for that on p. 170; Worcester Record Office and the Church of England Record Centre for that on p. 176; Matthew Clark Brands Ltd for that on p. 178—and myself for those on pp. 185 and 188. In addition I would like to thank Bulmers and Dunkertons for the images used on the cover.

The Jubilee Barrel

There's many a bev'ridge in the ages of Man,
Some that have shortened -
Some lengthened his span;
But of all that are found in the span of the earth
'Tis the juice of the apple
That has greatest worth.

Yet, 'tis not just the juice - no matter how sweet;
'Tis the barrel that holds it
That makes it complete,
To which one must add not sugar alone
But the skill of a Master
With all that he's known.

There on his throne for twenty-five years
Reigned the fifth of the Georges
Through joys and through tears.
'His Jubilee then let all celebrate.'
Thus quoth the Master -
His tale I relate.

Ten great barrels each one had contained
Of gallons one hundred
Of rum long since drained,
But not so long since that each of the ten
Dripped a tenth of a gallon
To be used yet again.

And of the ten barrels the one that was best
Had proof that its rum
Topped the strength of the rest
This one was proclaimed 'The Jubilee Cask'
To hold the best cider
That any might ask.

They took the best apples the Master could find
From the very best trees
And orchards designed
For the very best cider to delight all who'd come
To sit at the barrel
That once had held rum.

The apples were shredded and laid in the mats;
The juice from the press
Poured into the vats.
From the vats to the barrel it went with a will
To mix with the rest
Of the young Master's skill.

That gallon of rum that he'd dripped from the rest
Was still not enough
If this would be best.
Cane sugar syrup - 'twas twice the amount,
Not a score pounds but forty,
If you'd have the count.

The 'Jubilee cask' was left to ferment
And its time of maturing
In stables was spent.
'Twas a place shunned by many through fear of a horse
So the Master was certain
It could safe run its course.

The months quickly passed and the Jubilee Day
Was almost upon them
And not far away,
When the young Master's father said 'Son, the time's come
That I taste of the cider
You mixed with the rum!'

The Master said 'Father, I knew not you knew.'
But the father said 'Son,
Things around here are few,
If any, that get past my ear and my eye,
So go tap that barrel
And I'll give it a try.'

The cider was brought for the father to taste
Who gave to the Master
This warning with haste:
'This is not how I taught you, you stupid young fool -
The man who drinks this
Will fall off his stool.'

'His legs will betray him and likely his brain.
I have taught you my skills
And it's all been in vain!'
But the barrel was broached on the Jubilee Day
And many were those
Who fell by the way!

The years have passed by and the 'Jubilee Cask'
Is forgotten by most
Though some, when you ask,
Wil tell you the strength of the contents was such
'Twas mixed with eight barrels
Ere you dare taste or touch!

Mike Edwards, Asum's (Evesham's) Poet, March 1998

Written for the 'young Master' himself—'Buster' Mustoe

Harvest workers of the 1930s, one quenching his thirst from a costrell

1   OF FRUIT, CIDER MAKERS AND RATS

The art of cider making in the three counties of Herefordshire, Gloucestershire and Worcestershire is upheld by arcane knowledge from the mists of time. The Celts, Romans, Saxons, Greeks and Scandinavian peoples all have pantheons that feature apple legends and apple lore and considered apples sacred. The gender of the apple is predominately female—when an apple is cut in half crosswise it displays two five pointed stars, symbolic of woman. To the Celts the apple was the food of the gods and cider was used in ritual to induce altered states of consciousness, which anyone who has drunk it will agree does not take very long!

In Christian symbolism the apple is ambivalent, it symbolises evil as the fruit of temptation given to Eve by the snake, then to Adam by Eve, but in the hands of Christ or the Virgin Mary it is a symbol of salutation. At Halloween, the Celtic New Year festival and All Saints Night in the Christian calendar, apples are used to test one's luck by 'bobbing' in a pail of water—trying to catch the fruit in your mouth without using your hands. In this custom the apples represent the underworld and the subconscious and are read as symbols of fortune; three attempts are allowed, and failure means a life of poverty for the coming year. The ancient ceremony of Wassailing the orchards, thought to bring good crops in the coming year and to bless the farmer and his company with good health, is still enthusiastically celebrated to this day.

Early fruit varieties used for making cider may have been seedling descendants of the indigenous crab apple, but as these apples produced little juice it was mixed with honey and spring water to make Cyser, a strong fermented drink related to mead. The crab apple later became crossed with the new varieties of apples brought to Britain by the Romans, which improved the size of the fruit, the juice yield and sugar content, enabling cider makers to ferment entirely from fruit juice without the need of added sugars, and so giving rise to cider.

Modern fruit varieties used to make cider in the west of England can be traced back to the pioneering work of Viscount Scudamore of Holme

Viscount Scudamore of Holme Lacy who did so much to develop the local cider apple in the mid 18th century. The famous Redstreak apple was his creation

Lacy in Herefordshire in the 17th century. Scudamore was ambassador to the court of Louis XIII during Charles II's reign and returned from France with a collection of cider fruit from Normandy. These he used to improve English fruit stocks through cross pollination and development of seedlings.

Amongst these seedlings was the Herefordshire Redstrake or Redstreak, the apple that created the enduring legend that Herefordshire cider was unequalled in Britain. Within ten years over 5,000 Herefordshire Redstreak apple trees had been planted across the West Country. Yet, barely more than a century later the apple's reputation had declined and as early as 1796 it was being reported that 'The Redstreak apple is given up'. In part this may have been due to the imposition of Cider Tax in 1763, to raise income for the Seven Years War. This had allowed the Excise man right of entry to farms to search for dutiable goods, an act violently opposed by farmers across the West Country. William Pitt the Elder coined the phrase 'An Englishman's home is his castle' while arguing against the tax. Although the resistance was successful and the tax on cider was repealed in 1766, it was the last straw for many producers who ceased production—at least for sale.

Then three more problems emerged. Some cider drinkers in the West Country were discovered to be suffering from Devonshire Colic, a form of lead poisoning. Secondly, wine merchants and their middlemen were purchasing juice straight from the press at low prices, fermenting it, and then watering it down or otherwise adulterating it to produce a low quality product, then sold at a high profit in town cider houses. Thirdly, the government added to the cider makers' woes by hailing beer as a wholesome drink, hoping beer would replace the popularity of gin, which was blamed for reducing production in the nation's factories. This move was supported by the emerging big brewing dynasties of Whitbread, Guinness and Bass, who described gin as Mothers' Ruin and promoted their beer as a healthy alternative for the working classes. As a result, the market for cider was greatly reduced and farmers were turning their land to other sources of income.

But a revival in fortunes was at hand, for orchardist and later fruit breeder Thomas Andrew Knight, was to take up the challenge of improving cider orchards. Born in 1759 he had a life-long interest in orchards, having grown up with them as a child at Wormsley Grange, near Ludlow. His book *Treatise on Cider* was published in 1797 following his work to survey Herefordshire for a government that was seeking to raise taxes, this time to fund the Napoleonic Wars.

Knight found the once proud Herefordshire orchards to be suffering from deep neglect. In 1795 he suggested to the Royal Horticultural Society that the decline in the orchards was due to each fruit variety having a limited life, coupled with a lack of good management of the orchards. In his book Knight described every stage of cider production, following it up in 1811 with his *Pomona Herefordiensis*, a lavishly illustrated volume produced at the request of the Herefordshire Agricultural Society. Knight's *Pomona* describes all the locally grown cider fruit and perry pears. In 1786 he also began grafting and breeding fruit trees, at one time having 20,000 apple seedlings. Sadly, few of his cultivars are now available.

Inspired by Knight's efforts and enthusiasm, both public and farmers again became interested in cider. Cider orchards were restored and a small scale cider making revived. The invention of the Ingenio rotary cider mill by John Worlidge, based on the design of a Cuban sugar mill, improved the efficiency of cider production, enabling two or three hogsheads (each 58 gallons) to be made a day, as opposed to one or one and a half by horse mill. As the century progressed advances in engineering initially enabled gearing systems operated by horse power to be added to the hand mills and then for the mills to be powered by a steam engine.

By the 1880s cheap food imports from abroad had plunged British agriculture into another depression, orchards in the West Country were again neglected and cider making was in decline. Prime Minister Gladstone urged farmers to improved their orchards and grow local fruit to compete with the dessert apples being imported from the U.S.A. Herefordshire was one of the first counties to take up the challenge, farmers recognising that the new rail links offered improved access to the metropolitan districts and an extended market for their culinary fruit and cider. Herefordshire's Woolhope Naturalists' Field Club organised a survey of the county's orchards, aiming to identify the best local varieties. Members also brought new varieties into the county from Kent and Somerset to test how they performed.

The Rev. Charles Bulmer of Credenhill, Herefordshire, who was the Woolhope Club's resident cider expert, invited the esteemed pomologist, Dr. Robert Hogg, to attend the 1876 exhibition of fruit collected and grown by members of the club. Dr. Hogg was a founder member of the Pomological Society and a member of the Horticultural Society Fruit Committee who had an unrivalled knowledge of apples. Impressed by the variety and quality of the display, Dr. Hogg suggested that the club produce *The Herefordshire Pomona* to record the county's fruits, offering to be technical editor. Dr. Graves Bull of the Woolhope Club took on the task of general editor, his role including receiving the hundreds of varieties of apples delivered to his door for identification and recording. The finest examples of fruit on display at the Woolhope Club's apple exhibitions were painted by Miss Bull, sister of Dr. Bull, and Miss Ellis, a gold medallist of the Bloomsbury School of Art in London. The resulting plates were reproduced by G. Severeyns in Belgium using the chromolithograph technique. Experts commended the delicately coloured plates as wonderfully accurate, capturing the true colours and shapes of the fruits. Dr. Hogg came to Hereford for the club's shows to assist in identifying the fruits and these shows soon became a mecca for pomologists.

In 1886, Drs. Hogg and Bull covered the subject of cider fruit in more detail in their volume *The Apple and Pear as Vintage Fruits*, becoming the first to use the term vintage for cider and perry varieties that produced consistently good fruit. Although 'vintage' is now used to define fruit of one year pressed as a single variety or blend, their book remains an essential textbook for cider makers in the Three Counties and beyond.

The propagation and management of cider and perry orchards was of great concern at the start of the 20th century. New developments transformed cider from a drink made on the farm for mostly local consumption to a commercial enterprise based around big mills producing cider for the masses in cities and towns. Farmers invested in power operated mills, hoping there would be an increase in cider sales and many small cider companies came into being, including Godwins, Evans and Bulmers in Hereford, Ridlers in Clehonger, Henry Weston's in Much Marcle and the Severn Vale Cider Company in Wickwar. Much of this revival of fortunes can be attributed to the tireless campaigning of the MP for Hereford, C.W. Radcliffe Cooke and the popularity of his book *Cider and Perry* published in 1889, which called for the revival of English cider as 'possibly the most wholesome of all fermented liquors'. The son of Robert Cooke of Hellens, Much Marcle, Herefordshire, Radcliffe Cooke was known in the House as the MP for cider, due to his strenuous advocacy of cider interests.

The new cider mills bought their fruit from local farmers, but many orchards were again suffering from old age and neglect, yields were low and fruit production was in decline. In 1903, Radcliffe Cooke, in association with the Board of Agriculture, the Bath and West Society and the county councils of Devon, Gloucester, Hereford, Somerset, Worcester and Monmouth, succeeded in establishing the National Fruit and Cider Institute at Long Ashton, near Bristol, later to become known as the Long Ashton Research Station. The Institute was formed to investigate and demonstrate the cultivation of all kinds of fruit and vegetables, but with special reference to the manufacture of cider and perry, to improve the existing varieties of cider and perry fruits and to create and introduce new varieties, passing on the results of this investigation and research to the cider industry. Early research at Long Ashton included the classification of rootstocks used for the grafting of fruit varieties, a project completed at East Malling Research Station in Kent, which now provides the virus free rootstocks that are employed world wide. Long Ashton also contributed to major developments in pest and disease control, the pruning of fruit trees, fermentation and preservation of cider and perry, including pasteurisation and bottling techniques, and identification of vintage fruit varieties.

Whilst apple trees can be grown from seed, the resulting seedling will be a different variety from the parent and may be unsuitable for use as cider fruit. Thus specific varieties of apples and pears are best propagated by grafting or budding onto a maiden rootstock. Both techniques require skill to make maximum contact of the cambial regions, between the bark and the heart wood of the wound, to ensure success. A biodegradable latex tie, which disintegrates in light, is used to secure the wound together. The graft or bud takes five to six weeks to establish, producing a maiden tree by the following autumn. Growers may also graft fruitwood onto existing trees in the orchard, but this risks the spread of viruses from one tree to another. Standard trees use M25 or MM111 rootstock, which produces a tree 10 to 15 feet high. The rootstock is tolerant of a wide range of soil types and is suitable for use in a grassed orchard or lawn. Standard trees are grafted in two stages, the first graft onto the maiden rootstock is made with a strong, straight growing variety, such as Bulmers Norman, which produces a 6 foot trunk that can be pruned to eliminate side branches. In year three of the tree's life, the vintage fruit variety is budded or grafted onto the trunk. Grafting takes place in winter whilst the tree is dormant, budding in summer.

Young trees should not be planted in the same place as old, as this could spread diseases such as honey fungus which killed the old trees and would be fatal to the young sapling. The soil around an old tree's roots could also have been drained of nutrients, giving a poor start to the new arrival. Where young trees are being planted to replace those lost in established orchards, it is advisable to use fresh soil or compost in the planting hole. To give the young tree the best start the soil should be tested and the ground should be well prepared to remedy any nutrient or pH deficiencies. A strong stake should be driven into the hole on the windward side before the tree is planted and the young tree supported by a flexible tie. This helps to establish the roots of the tree and prevent wind damage caused by rocking. Young trees also need protection from grazing stock and rabbits with a suitable wire guard. With care to avoid disease during early fast growth, and regular pruning to help establish good tree shape and allow light to the branches, a young standard tree should be cropping within four to five years, in maturity producing between 200 and 400 pounds of fruit depending on variety, and will live to between 20 and 50 years.

Trees obtained for planting are likely to be of known varieties, and books illustrating and describing characteristics of many of these have been published over the past few years. However, *The Herefordshire Pomona* remains a standard work for those seeking information about little-known and rare examples from the past. This endeavour, to seek out and save for posterity apple and pear varieties under threat of extinction, has been gathering pace over the latter part of the 20th century and has inspired the formation of local groups. For instance, Ray Boddington from Hereford, on a shopping trip to Hay-on-Wye, spotted, at a local greengrocer in that border town, some apples on sale labelled Stirling Castle. In his sitting room, with the *Pomona* by his side Ray remembers that, 'on asking to buy some to familiarise myself with the taste and features of the variety, the shopkeeper got very excited and insisted I meet the lady who had supplied them'. He was on the phone to her in seconds and they soon arranged to meet.

The grower of the apples was Sheila Leitch, who was interested in identifying varieties of fruit in the Welsh Marches, and their meeting led eventually to the formation of the Marcher Apple Network. The Network tries to ensure that as many as possible of the old apple and pear varieties are rescued from extinction, and stimulates public interest in them. This latter aim is achieved, in part, by providing exhibitions of fruit and identification sessions at local events, which also results in interesting apple discoveries and more members for the Network. Many hours are spent around Sheila's table each autumn, trying to identify fruits before they are past their best. In season, little boxes of apples arrive in the post at her house, piling up in the cellar until the group can get around the table to identify them. Sometimes, unexpected visitors also arrive in the post, as recounted in the Summer 2000 edition of the Network's Newsletter:

> The first of this season's packages of apples for identification has just arrived in the post. After opening the padded bag, I read the details from one of our printed forms and learnt that the early dessert apples were from a very old tree in Newport, Pembrokeshire. As I went to extract the wrapped samples from the bottom of the bag, I was greeted by a lusty half inch long specimen of a codling moth grub, with pinkish body and dark head, speeding out from its confinement in the bag. More of these I do not need! The six small apples were all affected by this pest, and I think the tree would benefit, next year, from a pheromone trap.

Apple identification is not an easy task. The Marcher Apple Network asks for at least three typical tree-ripened fruits in good condition to be provided, information on whether the fruit is thought to be dessert, culinary or cider, the usual month of ripening, along with the location of the tree, its approximate age and any history known about the orchard.

Fruit is normally examined for its shape, size and colour, and it is noted whether the skin is flushed or striped with colour and whether russet is present. The length of the stalk and the depth of the cavity in which it lies are features to be measured, and consideration is given to the depth of the basin at the apex of the apple, in which lies the 'eye'. This is the part of the flower remaining after the fruit has been formed and the sepals and other parts are all important aids to identification. A vertical and a transverse section of the fruit reveal core, seeds and flesh colour and a sliver of the fruit is tasted to assess the flavour.

By 2002, when the Marcher Apple Network had grown from the initial handful of founder members to approaching 300, there was enough expertise and enthusiasm apparent amongst the newer members for a sub-group concerned with cider apples and perry pears to be formed. The emphasis will be on identification and the creation of a register of known varieties in the area, with which unknowns can be cross-referenced, leading to more of the old varieties becoming available, from grafted material from a 'mother' orchard. Young trees will be obtainable for planting up orchards with the varieties which were extensively planted at the turn of the 20th century and again in the years after the First World War. Lists of Bulmers' plantings in the 1930s have already enabled two lost Gloucestershire 'styre' varieties to be located in a

Glasbury cider orchard, grafted and 'saved'. The Network now has a web site address—www.marcherapple.net—from which further information about its activities is available.

Cider apples are classified as bittersweet, bittersharp, sharps and sweets depending on the amount of tannin and acid present in the flavour. Culinary and dessert fruit, referred to as 'pot' fruit by cider makers, can also be used to make cider, either mixed with cider varieties or on their own. However, cider made purely with pot fruit may lack the keeping qualities and bite of cider made from cider apple varieties.

Not all fruit presented for identification will be found in the reference books, some may be seedlings of no identifiable variety or be a very local variety only grown in a specific area that has not been formally identified, having only been known by a local name. In addition, some popular varieties have been renamed in local areas, these synonyms further adding to the difficulty of identification. Fruit is also affected by seasonal factors, such as the amount of sun, rain and the quality of the local soil, which can change the colour, flavour, size and general appearance of the fruit.

Local distinctiveness of apple varieties suffered greatly from the introduction of bush orchards in the 1930s. Farmers welcomed them as they are easy to manage and produce a higher yield of fruit per acre. However, they have led to fewer varieties of fruit being grown as only the proven, high cropping varieties are made available as bush trees to growers. Standard orchards declined and many were grubbed up under subsidy from Europe during the 1970s and '80s to create more arable land, resulting in the loss of many local varieties of fruit. Those that remained were hidden in private orchards and along hedgerows, or in neglected orchards mainly used by farmers for grazing animals, where the land was not suitable for arable use due to steep slopes or other local topographical features. This reflected the plight of standard orchards at the end of the previous century, when the Woolhope Naturalists' Club had produced the *Pomona*.

The old standard orchard at Moorhampton Farm nestles in the Golden Valley, which runs north to south in Herefordshire close to the border with Wales. Ivor and his son Denis Gwatkins have farmed here since 1982, rearing cattle, sheep and poultry, growing culinary and cider fruit and making award winning cider and perry. Perry is pressed from small, tannic perry pears that ferment into a still, dry, clear and fragrant drink, much prized by the locals and connoisseurs. Cider and perry making at Moorhampton Farm is little changed from the time of Ivor's grandfather, preserving the wisdom and skill of generations of Gwatkins.

Along the bottom edge of the orchard the River Dore gurgles along on its way through the valley, passing close to the Neville Arms at Abbey

Dore, where the Gwatkins' ciders and perries are on tap. The old orchard at Moorhampton Farm is carefully managed without the use of pesticides or artificial fertilizers, providing a haven for local wildlife. It produces fruit for cider making as well as providing grazing for Ivor's rams and ewes in the spring and summer months. Across the road from the old orchard, modern bush and half standard orchards provide cider and dessert fruit for sale to Bulmers in Hereford and at local farmers' markets.

The Gwatkins' orchard is planted with standard apple trees interspersed with perry pears growing up to 30 feet tall. Cider varieties include Dabinett (full bittersweet), Michelin (medium bittersweet), Foxwhelp (bittersharp) and Yarlington Mill (medium bittersweet), all varieties which originated in Somerset, and that proved popular for planting in orchards from early in the 20th century to the present day. Also in the orchard is the rare local variety, Ten Commandments, so named as when cut across the middle, the apple displays ten red spots around the core. The apple trees are interspersed with mature specimens of Blakeney Red, Malvern Hills and Thorn perry pears. Some of the trees lean towards the south due to the prevailing winds, but the site is protected from late frosts by facing south-west, preserving the fragile fruit blossom in the spring. The trees are widely spaced, allowing for grazing of stock under the branches, with 6 feet tall standard trunks which prevent the animals nibbling the young fruit buds.

Ivor and Denis Gwatkins tipping apples into bags to take to the mill

In winter the trees are dormant and their bare branches are coloured by grey-green moss and lichens. Windfall apples, left on the ground after harvesting, provide sweet nourishment for over-wintering insects, including Red Admiral butterflies. For Denis, this is the time for pruning the trees and thinning out last year's growth to ensure plenty of light reaches the leaves and fruit, improving the crop. Decaying branches and leaves provide winter cover for hibernating insects, beneficial predators and small mammals so are left on the grass until summer. Winter is also the time to replace trees which have died or stopped cropping through old age, or have been blown down by the year's storms, though standard trees will often continue to produce fruit even if fallen.

Wherever possible, Denis tries to replant lost trees with varieties similar to those already in the orchard, to keep the balance of fruit for the cider making, so he has established a small nursery of traditional cider fruit trees to provide replacements. However, recent plantings have also included Stoke Red and Ellis Bitter, thereby increasing the selection of cider fruit available in the orchard.

As spring warns up the ground and wakens the roots of the trees, wild birds stake out their territories with song and make nests in the hedgerow along the side of the Dore. The fruit bearing branches begin to burst into bud and hedgehogs awake from their winter slumbers and search for emerging insects. By April, the early flowering perry trees are a mass of white blossoms, attracting early insects to drink nectar from their blooms and pollinate the flowers.

In late April the bees have arrived on their forays for nectar from the local hives. When placed in an orchard, hives are always put on the south

Denis Gwatkins tipping milled apple pulp into his grandfather's old travelling screw press

side as the warmth of the early morning sun activates the bees. Hedgerows and tussocky banks provide an ideal habitat for wild bees, including the well loved bumblebee, who is an excellent and hard working friend of the fruit grower, pollinating up to ten blossoms a minute.

At Moorhampton Farm in mid-May the ewes with lambs at foot are let into the orchard to graze. The manure from the animals helps to add nitrogen and other nutrients to the soil, which feeds the trees, essential for the success of the blossom and fruit set the following year.

By late May the petals from the fruit blossoms have fallen in showers of white petals and the fruit has begun to set on the trees. Denis may thin out some of the weaker fruit buds if it looks likely to be a heavy crop in the autumn, to prevent the trees overtaxing themselves, which could risk them turning bi-annual—whereby a heavy crop is produced one year, and a poor crop the following one. Birds, including thrushes, blackbirds, woodpeckers, hedge sparrows and finches, help to keep down unwanted pests in the orchard by foraging for food for their broods that have hatched in the hedgerow.

In late August the trees are laden with fruit turning pink and gold in the sunshine, hanging in clusters from the boughs. The sheep have been moved to pasture, to stop them prematurely dislodging the fruit from the branches and eating fallen fruit. As autumn days grow longer and wetter, beneficial fungi sprout from the grass and in the moist soil around the tree trunks, along with the fruits of the symbiotic fungi that help to keep the trees healthy.

Depending on the ripening of the crop, harvesting and pressing of the fruit will take place from late September until early December. Up until recently the Gwatkins were still collecting fruit from the standard orchard using the traditional method of shaking the tree with a long ash pole to which a large hook, forged from steel, had been attached to enable the trees' boughs to be gripped securely. The fruit would then be gathered up by hand into bags, to be picked up by tractor and trailer and taken to the mill and press beside the farmhouse. Within the last year, the Gwatkins modernised their operation. Cider sales are growing due to Denis's success in marketing his cider in glass bottles for shops and shows. This has enabled the purchase of a small secondhand tree shaker to go on the tractor and a small petrol driven hand operated machine to pick up the apples. If you shake a tree from side to side you damage the roots, so the shaker clamps around the trunk of the tree and gently rocks the tree in a way that mimics the natural effect of a strong wind passing through the branches, causing the ripe apples to fall to the ground. The apple collector uses rubber paddles to pick up the fruit from the grass under the trees, leaving leaves and twigs behind and depositing the fruit in a basket on the back of the machine for tipping into bags. Ivor is delighted with these purchases, which were made at a local auction. 'Machinery has made the harvesting much easier. We can pick up four to five tons of fruit a day, before we needed 40 people to do that work'. Some fruit also comes from Ivor's brother-in-law Brian's farm in Gloucestershire, plus 'any bags people bring to us that they don't want'.

When the fruit arrives at the mill it is allowed to mature in the bags until the time is right to mill and press it. Dessert apples usually go to market in September and the contract apples for Bulmers are picked in early October for delivery to the Plough Lane Mills in Hereford.

Standing in Gwatkins yard is the old stone cider mill now fallen into disuse. When it was new, it would have replaced the large wooden mallets, or beetles, that were used in a trough to crush the apples until the 1600s. In the early 17th century stone mills were being produced in the Forest of Dean from hardwearing, acid resistant stone. Stonemasons shaped the round millstone and runners in the quarry, with the new owner meeting the cost of transport to their farm. The price of a mill was usually set at a guinea per foot in diameter, and ranged in size from 4 feet, which could be pushed round by hand, to 12 feet worked by two, sometimes three horses. The most popular size was 8 feet in diameter, which could be worked by one horse. Mill troughs were made in two, three or four sections to make them easier to transport to the farm, where a local stonemason would match up the mill and fit it together. The wood for supporting the mill wheel, edging the trough and making parts of the horse harness would be supplied locally, with the fittings being made by the local blacksmith. Some mills would be built outside in the farmyard, others were built in a cider house attached to the farm buildings, or even in a cider cellar dug under the farmhouse.

Typical use for an old stone cider mill today—as a base for a garden display, this one at Luston in Herefordshire

Ivor's father sold cider at Tirley Mill, near Abergavenny when he was a lad, Ivor helping by leading the horse that drove the stone mill round. As they didn't keep horses on their own farm it meant either borrowing, taking fruit to a neighbour to be milled, or hiring a travelling press. The beam press which Ivor's father used to made cider at Abergavenny travelled with them to Moorhampton Farm, mounted as it is on wheels, and was used by Denis to make his first ciders and perries.

Wherever you go in Herefordshire and north Gloucestershire, where the Gwatkins farmed for a while, local farmers remember Ivor for his skill and reputation as a cider maker, often citing a time when he collected fruit at the farm, helped to get their old press or mill going again, gave tips to improve the quality of a particular vintage, or correctly identified a particular local cider apple or perry pear. As a young man Ivor helped local blacksmiths convert many of the Edwardian horse mills and scratters to mechanical power. 'Mr. Francis, the blacksmith at Garway village would have been the last one I worked with to be converting the old horse machines to tractors. I remember going with him to Lyne Down Farm in Much Marcle to help convert a mill there'. That old scratter, attached to a vintage tractor, is still used to crush apples at Lyne Down Farm today.

Brian Jones of Eardisley, north-west Herefordshire, has had a lifelong connection with cider and cider making, telling his tales with characteristic firmness and conviction. He remembers accompanying his father in the 1940s when he was working with the owner to convert an old Edwardian travelling mill into a housed installation. The mechanical mills sounded the death knell for the traditional stone mill wheel drawn round by a horse which, by the 1940s were becoming a rarity on farms, many having been broken up or lying discarded in the hedgerows. During the Second World War many soldiers and troops were billeted at Eardisley and Shobdon. It was difficult to obtain beer due to rationing so local cider became very popular, encouraging local farmers, who still had mills, to keep making cider and helping to preserve the tradition through the war years. After the war, when beer supplies were restored, the popularity of cider declined, cider making on the farms stopped and most of the fruit was sent on contract to the bigger cider mills as a cash crop, thus keeping the orchards viable as an additional source of income for the farmer at a time of year when there was little work to do on the land.

Brian started making cider by accident. A lady with a small cider orchard in Eardisley, planted just after the Second World War, had her fruit contracted to Bulmers. Every contract grower for Bulmers has a fruit permit based on estimated yields which gives them a two hour slot to deliver their fruit to the mill, depending on the quantity, ripening time and fruit variety declared by the grower. The forms were familiar and welcomed, but the year Bulmers installed a computer to issue the forms and permits to growers was a disaster for many farms. The new computerised forms came in envelopes that looked like bills, so many growers, fearing it was an official letter, trouble or a demand for money, destroyed the envelopes. This meant that Bulmers did not receive the grower's fruit delivery estimates, so accordingly growers were not sent their timed and dated delivery permits. This particular lady had already arranged and paid for the fruit to be picked and delivered to Bulmers, but since she had not returned her fruit estimate form, Bulmers would not accept her fruit at the mill as she did not have a permit.

Brian knew the fruit was of good quality, as he had been one of the pickers that year, so he offered to help out. He arranged to have the fruit pressed at the local mill his father had mechanised in the 1940s. After a bit of maintenance it was soon running again, and Brian pressed 200 gallons of juice which he made into cider. Brian found he enjoyed the cider making, and as the cider sold well the next year he advertised for fruit and continued making cider at the old mill for another four or five years until the mill became difficult to use, due to access problems. By this time Brian was containerizing his cider to sell at agricultural shows and making more each year. He'd seen a French travelling mill and press on a trip around Normandy and decided to buy one, but sourcing the machine and bringing it over from France turned out to be difficult. At first the machine's owner was not at all keen to tell Brian where to get a second hand one, but after Brian managed to find some rare parts in a scrap yard, that were needed for the Frenchman's vintage English tractor, he was persuaded to source a machine for Brian.

This page and opposite: Brian Jones at work with his travelling cider mill

Brian's travelling mill and press remained unique in the United Kingdom until the 1990s when Vigo, a firm based in Devon, offered a similar unit for sale. The travelling press can be towed into an orchard, where it is run from a tractor. A fruit lift carries apples up to the mill, controlled by a lever that stops the fruit from entering the hopper at the same time as the apple pulp is being delivered to the press below. Another lever controls the quantity of the apple pulp onto the press bed. Brian reworked the mild steel elements of the machine in stainless steel, enabling the machine to get a food and health certificate from Worcester Trading Standards. The efficiency of the machine fully justified Brian's expense and work, and it is still performing well and in regular use. Brian makes his cider from a mixture of vintage varieties, grown in his own orchard and collected locally. He is adamant that the quality of fruit is crucial in making a good cider and that the container the juice is fermented in should hold at least 40 gallons. He has found, from his experiments with short pressings, that small containers do not allow for enough natural conditioning of the cider, leading to a loss of flavour and quality, and prefers to use 330 gallon black plastic vats supplied from the fruit concentrate factories. He remembers one wine buff, on tasting his cider, remarking that it had a 'hint of orange'. Brian knew this was due to the previous contents of the vat, but he managed to convince the connoisseur it was the variety of apple he had used—Cox's Orange Pippins.

In 1980, in Minsterworth, Gloucestershire, Mr. Sid Trigg and Mr. Sam Wheeler were making cider on Sam's smallholding from apples called Ribston Pippins, Arlingham Schoolboys, Skyrmes Kernels and Underleaves, adding a few perry pears, to 'make it good - just like champagne'. Meanwhile, Ray Hartland, at Flat Farm, was also making his cider and perry using fruit from an orchard that was established in 1795. His

farm diary documents the start of cider making at the farm, helped by his father-in-law who was a cider maker. Ray bought a double screw press with a stone base and restored it to working order, along with a mechanical scratter that ran off the farm tractor. The diary records that as well as fruit from his orchard, Ray used to buy fruit from other orchards in nearby villages. Most of the work took place on the night shift at Flat Farm, when Ray had lots of willing helpers to mill fruit and press the cider. As there was no electricity, the darkness created tales of funny disasters, such as the old fella turning the screw press with a long pole (to get the leverage) who overbalanced, fell in the fresh apple pulp from the scratter, ending up all sticky and having to be hosed down. Ray was infamous for relating these stories to visitors and many have been preserved in local folklore and newspaper features. His cider was sold at market and at the farm gate, given in exchange, or bartered for favours and goods where money did not need to change hands, or would have been unwelcome. The use of cider as currency is commonplace in rural areas when cash is short, as cider is a welcome luxury in hard times.

Ray's son Dereck Hartland remembers that 'Grandad had a special barrel of cider in the place called The Dug Out. He hid the key, but one of the farm men found it and drank all the cider. When Grandad tapped the barrel there was nothing in it'.

In the late 1970s Flat Farm 'struck electric' and Ray bought an electric scratter, and in the 1980s added a hydraulic press. In 1994 the family moved to Tirley Villa and the old tractor, stone press and cider making equipment came with them. Ray set up a new cider house and continued making cider until he died in 1996. The old stone press now stands as a memorial to Ray beside the cider house, attached to it is a brass plaque in his memory, bought by his friends.

Dereck Hartland then took over the cider making. The family had planted a new orchard at Coldstocks, just past Tirley, a couple of years before Ray's death which is now coming into fruit. The orchard has 65 apple trees including Yarlington Mill, Dabinett and Michelin, plus 30 perry pears including Moorcroft, Thorn,

TIRLEY VILLA,
TIRLEY,
GLOUCESTERSHIRE
TEL : (01452) 780480

Hartland's Cider Label

Judge Amphelet, Barlands and Buts. Dereck still collects 'Big uns and little uns' from other orchards, but like his father he does not go far afield, most of his fruit coming from an orchard opposite the Canning Arms in Hartpury and from Eldersfield. The fruit is gathered by hand from the old orchards and pressed at Tirley Villa with the juice being fermented in black plastic vats next to the pressing house. Dereck's philosophy is simple: 'Good cider is made slowly; you could still be picking up apples in January some years. You haven't got to rush these things'.

When the cider is ready it is racked off into wooden barrels to mature, which are kept in the cider house, ready to supply callers at the farm gate. Most of Dereck's production goes to beer and cider festivals or is sold to locals. The shed is spotlessly clean, hung with memorabilia of cider making at Flat Farm, and awards won by Dereck for his draught cider in local competitions.

Cider has been made by the Johnson family at Broome Farm, Peterstow near Ross-on-Wye, Herefordshire for over 70 years. The farm-house is over 300 years old and built over a cellar dug into the hillside, the mill stone housed in a small barn opposite. Kenelm Johnson remem-bers helping his father crush apples in the mill when he was seven or eight years old, and when they no longer had horses for the work, they pushed the mill themselves. A barrel of cider was made every year from the old orchard close to the farmhouse for the family and farm workers. During the Second World War the cider mill was taken out and sold to a neighbouring farm for use as a garden decoration; the barn was turned into an animal house and the cellar into a potato store. The fruit from Broome Farm was milled and pressed at a neighbour's farm. The mill stone has since returned to the family and is situated at Kenelm's new home in Peterstow village.

Since the 1930s most of the fruit at Broome Farm has been sold to Bulmers, but in 1989 there was a glut of fruit in Herefordshire and the Johnsons were left with a quantity of cider fruit which was not required by Bulmers, so they used it to make cider in wooden barrels bought from a sheep-shearer. Kenelm Johnson remarks: 'at that time we were also doing cream teas and found that the cider was popular as a "take home" with our visitors'.

For two years the Johnsons hired an electric mill and press, then had built a combined mill and press that runs off an old Fergie tractor. Mike Johnson has the job of operating the machine and making the cider: 'it was cheaper than buying an electric mill and press, but has turned out much noisier'! Mike likes to press together two-thirds bittersweet to one-third bittersharp fruit. He has 40 varieties of fruit to choose from in the orchards, plus a scattering of favourite varieties he planted himself, including 27 varieties of perry pear planted in the mid 1980s that still have to crop. Mike finds most single variety ciders unbalanced or sometimes bland with a few exceptions, notably Dabinett, Foxwhelp (after a malolactic fermentation) and Kingston Black. 'But on the whole blends are better. It doesn't work so well if you blend cider after it has fermented, it can go cloudy, lose its balance or taste, often it makes it worse if you blend two uninteresting ciders to try to get "a good one"'.

Mike ferments in a variety of vats but especially likes the 300 gallon plastic ones. 'Fermenting in larger quantities works best, but it is a lot of work to fill one—thank goodness for the radio! Fermenting in vats seems to even out the imperfections of individual fruits, resulting in a better quality cider. I have problems keeping to my pressing recipes as the bittersharp apples tend to ripen early and the vintage apples late, so sometimes I need to use Bramleys to get the acidity. All my cider is 100% juice, perhaps 95-98% after full fermentation, as you have to keep the barrels topped up with water to stop air getting in and oxidising the cider. I rack out into wooden casks once fermentation stops and allow the cider to condition before selling it'. Mike admits he was not very good initially at keeping records of his blends, 'I remembered which varieties I put in a vat and chalked it on the side, but I didn't always remember to chalk it on the barrel when I racked it off, so it was difficult for me to recreate successful blends. Now I am more organised and have a simple but effective method of storing all the valuable information'.

Mike Johnson and his dog, Fizzy, having a well earned rest—sampling the finished results in the cellar at Broome Farm

Back at Moorhampton Farm, Denis has the heavy job of making the cider. With his long ringlets, full red beard and melodious Herefordshire accent, Denis represents the classic image of a cider maker. His philosophy on making cider also reflects that of his ancestors; 'simple is best, the less you do to it the better it is. I make cider like they drank a hundred years ago, no more, no less'.

Joe, a Polish prisoner of war who stayed on in Herefordshire after the Second World War, used to help Denis make the cider, until he died in the autumn of 1999. Joe was a big man of few words, practical and reserved about himself, but fond of cracking a joke if social banter seemed to be flagging during the work. Ivor remembers 'Joe said he didn't have any family and lived on the land, he found work and lodging where he could, a hard life he had. When he died we found out he had a daughter, who helped Denis arrange the funeral and sort out Joe's few possessions. He ended up living in a modern bungalow in Pontrilas, but all his stuff was old and worn, the place didn't suit him at all, probably it was the central heating that killed him'!

Joe helped Denis to mill the apples using a scratter that had been converted to tractor power. The pulp was loaded by Denis onto grandfa-

ther Gwatkins' old two screw press with a plastic shovel, Joe's big hands expertly smoothing it out to the corners of a wooden box, which was supported across the press bed by two thin pieces of wood and lined with a Hair— a rough cloth woven from light polypropylene—which has replaced the old heavy cloths made from coconut fibres, sisal or horsehair that are difficult to clean and handle. The corners of the hair are folded in to the middle of the press to make a neat parcel, then the box moved up to support the next layer. Eight or so layers of pulp are wrapped in hairs to form a 'cheese' ready for pressing. A flat board is placed on top of the cheese to even out the pressure, Denis turned one of the iron four handled wheels on the top

An example of an old scratter mill, this one at Franklins in north Herefordshire

19

of the press and Joe the other, lowering the heavy oak beam down the screws on to the cheese, and making sure the beam is level. As the pressure from the beam reaches the cheese, sweetly scented golden brown juice gushes out from a spout in the press bed. After the first rush of juice, the press is gently tightened a bit more with a long ash pole, which is used as a lever to turn the now tight wheels by wedging the pole across the handles.

Fermentation of the juice takes place in the cellar reached via steps leading down from the front garden. The cellar is built underneath the farmhouse and flagged with stone cobbles, the door faces north so helping to keep the cider cool on hot

A completed 'cheese' of hair cloths filled with apple pulp and placed one on top of the other. This one was photographed at Bulmers in 1936, and is being manoeuvred into a mechanical press. Note the shute for the apple pulp from the mill in the top right hand corner

summer days. On entering, a double line of oak barrels greets you, stillaged in between the arches that support the building above, each barrel gently bubbling with fermenting juice that taints the air with its sharp tang. All Denis's cider and perry is fermented and conditioned in oak. The barrels are reused from year to year, being cleaned out and sterilised after each year's vintage and replaced by new casks when they get too old or damaged to keep the cider properly. The freshly pressed juice is taken to the fermenting barrel in plastic buckets, and is poured through a large square plastic funnel balanced in the bunghole of each barrel. Denis needs a ton and a half of cider apples to fill one butt, which using Grandad Gwatkins' old press would take at least a full day, depending on juice yield from the fruit. Fermentation of the juice takes place through the winter and is dependent on the amount of sugar and yeast naturally present in the juice and the ambient temperature of the cellar. In a warm winter some cider may be ready by Christmas, other years the vintage could still be fermenting in May. Bernard has now filled Joe's place as Denis's assistant during cider making. Ivor says: 'we miss Joe, but Bernard is better with the new machinery, we have an electric mill and small hydraulic press now, which speeds things up for Denis, though we've still kept father's old press too. Can't be too careful about modern machines'!

An old glass or pot is always on hand in the cellar for a quick sample or two from a barrel, to help you choose the vintage you prefer, before filling up your container. Denis's ciders and perries are made from 100% juice, without adding sugar or yeasts, fermenting out dry, still and strong, usually around 7-8% alcohol, each displaying the distinctive flavours of the fruit varieties that have been used to create them. Denis produces five single varieties of cider and four of perry, all with unique characteristics reflecting the prevailing climate, local soil and age of the trees, just like fine wines, together with a selection of vintage ciders blended on the press. The Gwatkins family likes to drink perry; a butt of Malvern Hills is especially reserved in the cellar for friends and family.

A Gwatkins traditional cider blend and bottle label of note was the Rats Tail traditional cider, specially bottled in 330ml brown glass, to attract the restaurant trade. The label features that famous critter, the cider rat. Rats and cider are often mentioned together and there is no doubt that rats and mice enjoy a tipple from the barrel if they can get it. While the cider is going through its first fermentation, the door to the Gwatkins cellar is left open to prevent a lethal build up of carbon dioxide, also allowing rats and mice access to the barrels. Little ratty footprints can be seen climbing up the dust on the sides, heading for the sweet, sticky head thrown out of the vent hole by the fermenting juice. Though it might seem that the rats have tipped into the barrel as there are footprints going up, but not going down, it is more likely they have fallen off the slippery curved sides drunk from the fumes, to happily stagger off to their homes and sleep off the effects. The rats and mice do little harm in the cellar during fermenting time, like the spiders' webs decorating the stillage they help to keep down unwanted insects that are also attracted to the sweet liquid, protecting the cider from bacterial infection and spoilage.

Other animals visiting fermenting vats may not be so lucky. Bill Wood tells of the farmer who lost his best sow during cider making time.

> Cider and keeping pigs went hand in hand then, the pigs would scrump the orchards, then be killed on the farm and the cured bacon wrapped in muslin hung in the back of the cool cider house.

The fermenting cider helped the flavour, not very hygienic but the bacon was good! This farmer searched everywhere for his sow, but she had gone who knows where, and was given up as stolen or dead in a ditch. That year's cider was an especially good vintage and the vat of cider was soon empty. On opening the vat (for cleaning) they found the prize porker's bones - she had fallen in whilst drinking the fermenting juice and drowned.

Bill swears that it was the pig's meat that had improved the cider. When fermentation was stuck it used to be common practice last century to add a piece of raw meat, or the remains of the Sunday joint—the protein feeds the yeast and restarts fermentation. Cider is highly corrosive due to its high acidity and the meat is completely dissolved by the time fermentation stops. If cider could dissolve the meat off a whole pig, smaller animals could be completely consumed. So who knows, in Grandfather's cider house an unlucky rat or two may have accidentally ended up in the odd vat after all.

2   TALES FROM THE COSTRELL

The costrells and horns used by farm workers in the fields were practical vessels. Costrells, small barrels holding from two to four pints, were used to carry each man's daily ration of cider. A costrell has a metal handle on one of the staves of the barrel to enable it to be carried by hand to the fields or hung on a horse's harness. On arrival in the fields costrells would be placed under a hedge to keep cool and out of the sun. They were often made as apprentice pieces by coopers or later in life as trade pieces to demonstrate their skills to potential employers.

John Howes at Westons in Much Marcle tells the story of George Duddy, the company cooper, who made a new costrell for every employee, which was checked for volume by the farm manager before use. George would tell the man to take the costrell to be filled with water for measuring, then bring it back for a 'final check'. When the man returned with the costrell he opened up the end and removed a block of wood from inside, increasing the volume of the costrell and the man's daily allowance of 7 pints of cider to 8.

Cider was poured from the tap hole in the costrell into small horns, which held a 'drop' of cider from a $^1/_4$ to $^1/_2$ pint. A section of cattle horn is gently heated over a fire to soften the fibres, enabling it to be stretched over a wooden former to shape it into a horn cup. The tapered base of the cup is filled with a disc of horn, wood or thick glass while the horn is still hot. As the horn cools and shrinks it forms a tight seal around the disc preventing the cup leaking. To identify their individual cups owners often engraved their drinking horns with their initials or pictures of rural life.

Larger horns were less frequently used in the Three Counties, but these horns could hold from a pint to a quart of cider. The tapered end of the horn is fitted with a bung or drinking spout and cap and the wider end of the horn may contain a separate drinking cup made of horn or metal. They commonly have leather strap fittings enabling them to be carried on a belt or harness. Pottery 'owl' jugs with a tapered neck and a cork bung were used as both cider containers and drinking vessels. The

neck of the jug has two handles, just wide enough to fit in your thumb and forefinger, with which to carry the jug or assist you to tip it up onto your upper arm to drain the contents. These handles give the jug the appearance of a wise owl and gave the jug its name. They led to the development of the glass flagon, which is popular for marketing cider today, and was origi-nally devised by Westons' Cider.

Some of the many costrells held in Gloucester Folk Museum. The two smaller ones are made of leather

In the early part of the century slipware pottery had become afford-able for the majority of people, leading to the adoption of the pottery mug as a container and drinking vessel for cider at home and in the inn. Early pottery mugs were craftsmen made and often decorated with

Examples of intricately carved and painted cider horn cups held in Gloucester Folk Museum. That on the left and the centre is the same cup from different angles—it has a number of figures carved around the outside. That on the right has a painting of a cow around part of the vessel

A traditional double-handled cider mug

incised patterns or coloured liquid clay. The glaze was lead based which gave the mugs a yellowish colour, although manganese and iron was also used to give a variety of browns. This must have posed some risk to the drinker as cider is now known to leach out lead and metallic compounds from glazes and pewter vessels. Slipware mugs—cast rather than thrown—were decorated with transfer prints, including (surprisingly, but perhaps ironically) Charles Wesley the founder of Methodism, football and rural scenes, neoclassical and chinois prints. The classic mug bears the hymn *God speed the plough*:

> Let the wealthy and great,
> Roll in splendour and state
> I envy them not I declare it.
> I eat my own lamb
> My own chickens and ham
> I shear my own fleece and I wear it.
> I have lawns, I have bowers,
> I have fruits, I have flowers,
> The lark is my morning alarmer
> So Jolly Boys now
> Here's God Speed the Plough
> Long life and success to the Farmer.

Mugs rapidly became the most popular drinking vessel of all, with particular prize being set on blue glazed mugs, and mugs with more than one handle, known as Tugs or Wassail cups, which could be passed around the company at the inn or cider house, always in a clockwise direction to ensure good spirits.

A tradition in Herefordshire inns was the Strangers Mug which held a concealed surprise. Most local farmhouse cider sold in cider houses was cloudy, which suits the opaque vessels it was served in, as this disguised the colour and cloudiness. The Strangers Mug was designed to benefit from the natural cloudiness of the cider and surprise unwary drinkers. Regulars at the cider house would offer to buy the newcomer a drink, asking the barman for the mug, as everyone in the house would usually have their own special pot behind the bar. The mug was filled with cloudy cider and passed round the company to welcome the new arrival, making

Some of the 18th-century cider glasses from the Bulmers Collection. Dated around 1750, with delicate engravings of cider fruit and, in the case on the right, having exquisite spiral stemwork

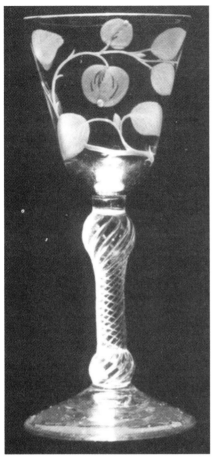

sure they got down to the last few inches in the bottom of the pot. Taking a mouthful of cider the stranger would be squirted with cider retained in a hollow frog set in the bottom or on the side of the pot, to the amusement of the company.

Of all the vessels used to dispense cider, the strangest and most spectacular was seen at the coronation of Queen Elizabeth II in 1953. On 26 June a ball was held at Hellens, Much Marcle, to commemorate the occasion. The highlight of the evening was the marble seahorse fountain in the forecourt of the house, flowing with sparkling cider for guests to capture in tumblers and drink the health of the new Queen. (Not surprisingly tickets to the event were limited).

Bill Wood of Leominster worked the land since he was a boy. Bill's uncle, Andrew Shayle, made cider at Mansel Lacy and Bill lived next door. Uncle Andrew used to call him in for a drink as a boy and say, 'only men drink cider, boys drink beer'—all the lorry drivers and locals used to call at Uncle Andrew's for cider. The Catholic Father liked a drop of beer, but he wasn't used to the local cider, as Bill recalls. 'My uncle gave him a pint and got him drunk'!

When I was a lad I grew up drinking Wickwar cider from Gloucestershire, it was 4d. a pint then, but four pints would still cost you a shilling (five new pence) - the same as for three. I could only drink three before I was drunk so I never got my fourth free pint. As a lad I remember having the job of carrying the water out to the field for the steam engine and the cider for the men doing the harvesting. There was always more cider than water. At 6 a.m. the engineer would be out in the field getting the engine going - it had to be ready by 8.00 am for the men starting work. The men would cut the crop by hand, thresh it with the steam, then bind the sheaves, then turn them out to dry. It was hard and dusty work - you needed some cider! The men would drink cider from a horn they passed round between them. They also chewed Twist - chewing tobacco. The nicotine from the twist would dribble down the outside of the horns, brown and sticky. It was awful, but you had to drink from it.

Farmer Fred Hanson had a workman called Percy Cooke who was a good worker and Fred was very happy with him, so he kept him on for years. Percy decided he would like to move on for some extra experience and asked Fred for a reference. Fred was very fair and gave a glowing report, including the fact that Percy was 'no good without cider'! Percy always took a gallon with him to the fields, hung on the corking handle of the horse's harness. The work was so hard you soon wore it off and did not get at all drunk. Percy was used to Fred's cider, but others could get caught out, it was stronger than was expected. Two lads came to help shear the sheep one year and got on the cider - it took them two days to shear just 80 sheep.

There were plenty of other cider makers in those days. The Rose and Crown Inn in Tenbury would make its own Crown cider, the Yeomans of Leominster (who now have the local coaches), the Langfords on Roman Road, the Duggins made cider at Kimbolton until they put tax on it, then they packed it up. Also old Bill Symonds at Stoke Lacy - what a character! He'd say 'it would be better if those girls drank my cider than took those prescriptions from the chemist'.

The landlord at the Bells in Almeley used to make a good drop of cider. One of his regulars used to get up at 6 a.m. and harness

Bill Symonds observing a cheese being made

The Bells in Almeley, in 2003

up the horse and cart to go to the pub - then he'd be off. If he left it any later his wife got up and stopped him going! He would get back about 8 p.m. - drunk - the horse would bring him home! When you visited the Bells the landlord would hand you a jug if you wanted cider and send you round the back to the shed where the barrel was kept. Of course, you'd be thirsty so would drink a pint there before you filled up the jug. On his day off he'd harness up his horse and take his friends for a day out. They would start from the Bells at 8 a.m. and make for the Rhydspence at Whitney-on-Wye as a first stop, then on down to the Boat on the banks of the River Wye, then the New Inn at Eardisley. At 4 p.m. they would be back at the Bells. The horse knew the way home!

When I worked on the lorries doing livestock handling, I used to go to Tom Evans's place at Forge Farm, Richards Castle, to pick up wool in the lorry. As soon as we stopped at the farm to load the wool the Boss would say 'start carrying the cider lad'. We usually bought two barrels off him to take back. Tom would offer you a 'drop of this' then a 'drop of that' to help you make up your mind. As well as cider he made country wine from fruit and ciders with other stuff in it, like herbs such as lavender and sage, or beetroot, which made the cider pink and strong. Before you knew it you'd be drunk! I called there at 10.30 one morning and only his wife was up and about. She put me up a bottle of the fruit wine and stuck a label on it, but it was crooked, so she apologised by saying she was the worse for drink.

When I worked at a farm in Almeley, where the farmer made very good cider, he had a big barrel of it in the shed that backed onto a neighbour's farm, with a tap in the front of the barrel. What he didn't realise was that his neighbour had drilled a hole through the back of the shed and the barrel and put in a peg. All he had to do was remove the peg and the cider ran into his mug.

Bill still makes his own ciders and perries, using fruit gathered around Leominster and Canon Pyon. He prefers to use rainwater for washing the fruit through his hydraulic press.

> I used to use pondwater in our old place until the pond was filled in - now I collect the water in a butt. Any impurities are removed in the fermentation of the cider. I've seen cider made by pulping the apples in a barrel with a pole, then the pulp is put into an old sack and put through a washing mangle - it works too!

Bill also sponsors the cider and perry class at Kington Agricultural Show each year, and enters his own cider and perry into the event.

> I don't always agree with the 'expert' judges though. One said my cider was not good enough to keep and marked it down. I said to him - it's not meant for keeping, you're meant to drink it so your barrels are empty for next year! I always have a couple of bottles in the back of the Land Rover for friends at the Show. My friend Eric wears a cap, you always know when he's had enough, he puts his cap on backwards! We say to him - 'turn your cap round Eric, here's another drop'!

Jim Franklin was born in Birmingham, then moved out to Leysters in Herefordshire when he was seven years old, just after World War Two. Twenty-five years ago he moved to The Cliffs on the banks of the Teme where he grows fruit for Bulmers and makes his own ciders and perries from local orchards.

The Franklins' farm

The Franklins' farmbuildings

Leysters was a typical Herefordshire village with a local school, church, parish hall and a pub serving 150 to 300 people. Women worked at seasonal jobs, hop picking and fruit picking, and there were still some Italian and Polish prisoners of war and land girls helping with the farm work. There were no tractors or farm contractors like now, everything was transported by horse and cart. The baker was first to get a shiny red van, the children would hitch a ride with him while helping deliver his orders.

Cider was part of the way things happened in the village and was taken for granted as part of village life. Every farm made it, up to five hundred gallons a year even on smaller farms. Workers would keep five or six small barrels, each holding 40 gallons, at home. The fruit would be picked up in mid to late October and taken to the local press where it would be milled and pressed and the juice would then be left to ferment in the barrels. As the postman did his rounds he would refresh himself at the cider barrels by the house he delivered to, he did not have to call at every house then, there was less mail - but he did anyway to get his cider rations!

Everyone knew that the cider had water added to it, usually reducing the alcohol content to about 3% volume, a healthy way to get drunk sensibly, or ease the pain of manual labour during hay making, ploughing and harvesting. If you look at the footpaths between the farms you notice they are never straight. The footpaths between farms and cottages were only straight if the occupants were Methodists! In the 1920s the depression in the Welsh valleys caused a migration into Herefordshire, but these Chapel people would not make cider, so they did not get many local people to help with the harvest. The farmer who made the best cider was helped first. They would all help each other, but cider was the priority.

In times past cider was used as payment for tithes to the Church and rent to landowners, as well as taken to market to be sold so the family could have clothes and winter essentials. All that remained was to grow the food. For smallholders with only seven to 30 acres of land it was essential currency.

Going into hospital was a major event - expensive too - it could ruin a family if someone got ill with something serious like scarlet fever - you did not have a choice, you had to pay the doctor's bill. Local remedies included 'sweating it out' with a pint of mulled cider with various herbs and folk remedies thrown in. One night of that and you were cured in the morning.

People knew their limit with cider at 3% volume. Some were naughty and used rum or whisky casks, or added sugar beets, or sugar, to the cider to make it stronger, which spoiled the cider and got people drunk. A farmer from Churchfield did not know that a neighbouring farm's cider was stronger, he got drunk and fell asleep on the way home. The next morning when he woke up there was 2 feet of snow on him, so he tried to get up. He gave the post-mistress an awful fright as all she saw was the ground rising up from nowhere!

Fermentation of apple juice into cider must have been a mysterious procedure before yeast was discovered by science. Almost magical. Local folklore grew up from observation by cider makers that certain practices improved the quality and keeping time of the cider in the barrel, like taking the cider off the lees [the dead yeasts and fruit particles that sink to the bottom during fermentation] once fermentation had finished. It was said the best time to take the cider off the lees was during a full moon, with a good frost and an east wind. Unscientific, but all factors that help yeast settle to the

Jim Franklin

bottom of the barrel, for the full moon affects large bodies of liquid, east winds is cold and frost stops fermentation. Barrels of cider were kept in outhouses with stone walls and slate roofs and near the duck pond which ensured high humidity and cool conditions in summer, preventing the cider from going sour. In hot weather water from the duck pond would be used to spray the barrels and keep the cider cool.

You never took cider to a football match - it was one of the rules. One day a stranger, who did not know the rules, brought a jug of cider along, there was no stopping the local team drinking it once it was there. The game went ahead, but due to the cider it was very rowdy. One player had his shorts ripped off.

In those days most cider was acetic and dry. It didn't matter then as all the farm workers chewed tobacco. After that acetic cider is beautiful! Farm labourers would be given six to eight pints of 3% cider, plus food, in return for helping with the hay making and bringing the hay from the fields by horse and cart. I remember my first harvest supper as a boy, when I was nine years old. The people of the village would help for the day as a way to get free cider. When evening came everyone gathered round the big pine table in the farmhouse kitchen. There were jugs of cider, served in old pottery mugs, cracked and black with mold and dirt, and free food. We were given fat bacon, one centimetre of lean with ten centimetres of fat and a soft rind, carved into slabs. To me it was revolting, this big tump of boiled fat bacon, but washed down with cider the men thought it was wonderful.

The first time I remember drinking cider I was eight coming on nine at Leysters. Instead of tapping the barrel at the bottom whilst on the stillage farmers would 'drill' the barrel. If you tapped the barrel near the bottom you risked the cider being cloudy and drawing off the lees. By drilling the barrel you drew the clear cider from the top. A small hole was drilled in the front of the barrel, near the top, and the cider would come shooting out under pressure. To stop it you plugged it with a goose quill. Air could not get in, so the cider stayed fresh. As the volume of cider went down, you drilled another hole further down and put in another quill - you might have four or five quills in a barrel which still remained bunged down. When you took out the quill you caught the cider in a jug - all the time the cider was settling you were taking it from the top. The cider would shoot out two feet from the barrel and as children we would play at removing the quill, catching the cider in our mouths. After a few games of this I had to go home, but it was more difficult than I expected - I could not find the pedals on my bike and had to push it home rather than ride that day!

The local culture that accepted cider as part of life came to an end between the two World Wars as machinery became more common. It started to fall apart after World War II, up until that war, horse transport was still common. With a horse you could shout 'stop' but with a tractor you couldn't and vehicles chipped away at the local cider culture. People who worked with horses had to learn a new awareness to work with the big machines - harvesters with unstoppable blades fast as bullets, 40 horsepower where one horsepower was good enough before - required greater concentration and skills from the operators. It was not possible to drink and work at the same time, you put yourself at risk of serious injury - one farmer lost a foot to a machine because he had not adapted to the new speed of work. Rural labour moved to the factories in towns and cities, as less workers were needed on the land. With the drop in farm workers needing refreshment, cider making on the farms stopped and the fruit was sold off to the large cider mills. The farmers and cider makers were all characters because they were close to nature, carving an existence out of the soil demanded that they adopt the natural behaviour of instinct, working with the seasons, weather and nature, humour and life was basic and harsh, demanding individuality and character to survive. With the coming of machines to the land everything moved on.

Mr. Charles, a sprightly octogenarian from Hucclecote, Gloucestershire, vividly remembers helping his family make cider as a boy.

The wall at the back of the shop on which the local lads sat to drink cider in Mr. Charles's story

My father kept a shop at Viney Hill, in the Forest of Dean. At the back of the shop was an orchard on about 2 acres of ground. It was mixed fruit, plums, walnuts and local cider fruit, Severn Bank, Worcester Pearmain, Blenheims - pigs were turned out into the orchard to scrump up the plums and rotten apples. They would get drunk on the fermenting fruit. Father also owned six cottages which he rented out, a mile or two away, which also had an orchard.

I was born in 1916 - when I was about 2 or 3 father decided to make cider. The children, there were six of us, helped to shake the apples off the trees with poles and pick up the fruit. In a bad season father would buy fruit in from local farms. Our cider was never sold, it was given away to friends and visitors. There was always somebody there drinking cider. We used to save the pears for perry for the family, everyone else (except the policemen) had ordinary cider. The policemen from Yorkley and Blakeney used to visit on alternate nights after cycling their beats for a 'drop'.

On a Sunday morning the local lads came round to sit on the wall at the back of the shop drinking cider. The children had the job of running to the shed to get the cider from the wooden casks. There was no money about, most of the men were on the 'dole' at 10 shillings (50p) a week, not a lot to live on. Mother was always very generous - we were owed hundreds of pounds 'on the tab' and in back rent for the cottages. People didn't have any money to pay even the 2 shillings a week rent on the cottages, so they lived almost rent free. But, people were always prepared to do things for a hunk of bread, some cheese and mug of cider. A man from Blakeney Hill who had lost an arm in World War One used to visit regularly and put a new washer in the tap - we had a new washer every week! Another used to visit 'looking for his sheep' and he'd get that drunk we had to take him home in the horse and cart.

When father's health got bad his brother-in-law came to live with us and helped with the general store and cider making, doing father's work. But when father died of his bronchitis at 52, mother got rid of the cider as she hated people coming to sit on the wall - 'that's it' she said and got rid of all the casks and stuff.

In Ross-on-Wye Margaret Wilce's grandfather, Andrew Symonds, made cider at Coughton, near Ross. He owned a building firm. The men always took a jug of cider 'on the job' to drink out of horns in their break.

When he retired Grandad opened up his little cottage to catch the workmen coming home - he called it his Pig and Whistle. The little toll house in Coughton that Grandad used between 1920-1930 was perfect for catching the men, the door opened straight onto the little lane. He would stand at the door and invite them in for a 'hornful'. He'd get them to drink cider with him and gossip about work - they never paid for the drinks, except with stories. His cider did not go to the head, it made your legs go wobbly.

My Dad got caught there more than once by Grandad. When he had enough he'd get back on his bike to go home, but the cider had gone to his legs! He'd get halfway down the lane and fall off - his bike would twist round, and he'd get back on again and ride the other way down the lane! He didn't realise he was going the wrong way because it was dark, so he couldn't see. He'd fall off again, or get to the main road before turning back - if he fell off again he'd be back the other way!

Jasper Ely with his ample white whiskers, twinkling eyes and rosy complexion, set off by his ever present tweed cap kept a smallholding at Priding Farm, Saul, next to the River Severn. A ramshackle collection of farm buildings set in a sea of acid mud washed up by the Severn Bore tides, housed a substantial stock of Gloucester Old Spot pigs, pedigree Gloucester cattle and an orchard tenanted by goats, donkeys, turkeys, geese and rare breed poultry. Yet the focus of the farm was Jasper's cider shed, once the stables of a former temperance hotel, the outside of which was covered with a collection of enamelled metal advertising signs, shouting out the qualities of Nectar Tea and Wills Woodbine cigarettes. Inside, the shed was long, high and narrow with wooden casks lining one wall containing the fermenting cider which assaulted your senses with its pungent smell, bravely battling with the smell of pig stys outside. Jasper kept the smallholding for 38 years, helped for 30 of those years by his right-hand man Pete Smithies. As Jasper grew older Pete gradually took on more work at the smallholding, including the cider making, until Jasper died of a heart-attack at 73. Pete still has the old cider making equipment from the farm, a Workman wooden mill that stood in the opening between the pig stys and a wooden press and trough operated by worm gears and a fly wheel, more than a century old. When Jasper died the Excise licence for the cider transferred to Pete, though the farm now has new owners. Pete has retired to a cottage nearby, though he still has the orchard and some land which he hopes one day to develop into a cider making museum.

Pete told me the stories connected with Jasper and cider drinking at Priding Farm and on The Island, the piece of land between Frampton and Saul which is cut off from the mainland by the Sharpness canal.

> Jasper was the Water Bailiff for the stretch of the Severn up to Wales but was famous for always being in the pub/cider house rather than on duty. In autumn when the salmon were breeding he had to take it in turns, with the other bailiffs on the Severn, to make sure the fish were not disturbed while breeding. If it rained the stream was so dark and muddy, and the water so deep, that the poachers couldn't work. So Jasper would go down the pub and drink with them instead. This got him hauled up before the management of the Water Board for not doing his job, but he defended himself by saying if the poachers were drinking with him in the pub, they weren't poaching - so the fish were safe - and he got off the charge.
>
> There was a big wall outside of Jasper's cider house, about 2 to 3 feet high to stop the Severn Bore tide flooding the cider shed. Charles Wright from Uley Brewery used to send us his spent grain

to feed our pigs. They didn't like it much, but the Gloucester cattle loved it. It was good business for Charles as his brewery logo is a Gloucester Old Spot - he used to tell folk that his grain fed the pigs - we used to go along with it as it did no harm.

One day Charles turned up at the farm with a group of journalists and photographers in tow - they wanted to get a picture of

Jasper Ely in his cider house

37

Charles feeding the pigs some grain. We were not expecting them, so the pigs had already been fed and watered, thus were not very interested in food. All they wanted to do was go to sleep. While we got one of the sows out we invited the chaps to have a drop from the cider house. It was only 9 or 10 a.m., but they all had a half. Then it was out to the pen to photograph the pig. Well, by the time they got into the yard in their smart suits and shiny shoes the cider was taking its effect. We put some cider in the bucket for the sow - usually she would be really keen, but she had drunk enough water that morning so was not interested. The photographers were trying all sorts of ways to get a good picture for the paper, laughing and giggling because of the cider, and getting their nice clothes and shoes covered in the smelly Severn mud that always coated the yard. It was funny to watch them! When they gave up it was back to the cider shed for another half. Quite a few had one too, particu- larly the non-drivers, so it was a jovial company that left the shed to get in their cars. Two or three of the men who were most keen on the cider forgot about the three foot wall outside of the cider shed that stopped it flooding in the Severn Bore tides. Over they went, flat on their faces in the mud - covered in it they were. We laughed and laughed, but they had to go home like that too!

We held pig roasts during the Severn Bore tide in the spring, people would come down to watch in the early morning and have pork rolls and cider for breakfast.

One of our regular cider drinkers, Bill, worked on the canals until he was laid off for not making it into work until 8 a.m. because of his drinking. He was a 'professional cider drinker' and I don't think he worked again after that. He would always turn up with something in his pocket, a tomato, an onion or a bulb of garlic, to exchange for his cider. That's how he was. He was famous locally for drinking 11 pints of cider then riding his bike backwards the length of Frampton on Severn village green.

Harold Clissold made cider at Hardwick, he used to hold a Sunday Session at his cider house every Sunday between 11 a.m. and 1 p.m. sharp. It was always 1 p.m. sharp as that is when his wife put his Sunday dinner on the table, so he shut up shop then. He did not really drink himself, just the odd tot to keep you company, but he enjoyed getting everyone else pissed. There would always be a good group there on a Sunday, but 1 p.m. sharp Harold would get everyone to drain their cups and out into the yard. I always remember the trick he used to play on them next. He would get you to look up into the sky at a nut tree next to the cider shed, then turn round three times - it always resulted in a big heap of blokes.

Harold's daughter took the license at the Red Lion in Arlingham where she sold her dad's cider at pub prices. It was known as Five Star as it was so good, amazing stuff. I went over to the Red Lion one day to see the greasy pole fight, a local tradition once a year. Two blokes sit on a bit of lino over a greased pole and try to knock each other off with pillows. I was drinking in the bar and Harold was helping behind it. He had to stock up so asked me to stand behind the bar in case anyone needed serving. I'd had about a pint of Five Star, with another half on the go - it is a good job no-one asked for more than a book of matches as I'm not sure I knew where I was. I couldn't even work out the price of the matches, the other bloke was also drinking Five Star and he couldn't either! Harold came out of the store with his bottles and saw us debating the matches, he said 'Pete, what have you been drinking?' I replied 'A pint of Five Star, plus this half here.' 'Drink that up' he says 'and get along home.' Well I trusted Harold and knew he would mean it for the best, so I did what he said. When I got in my wife was surprised to see me - it was still light! I went into the garden to water the cabbages and the ground came up to meet me, I couldn't tell you what happened. Five Star had the same effect on Bill, just two pints of it and he couldn't ride his bike. It was very strong stuff, perhaps it had other toxins in it as well as alcohol - who knows?

Brian Waters, in his book *Severn Tide* remembers a cider sale at Thornbury, on the banks of the Severn, in the heart of Gloucestershire cider apple orchards. The sale was held on the small lawn of an ivy clad farmhouse, surrounded by apple trees in full bloom in promise of next autumn's cider fruit crop. The barrels of cider were lined up on the lawn along with three or four benches, a trestle table and a score of blue and white pottery mugs. At a cider sale a purchaser does not know what he is buying until the cask has been broached and a sample tasted, so before the auctioneer starts the bidding on the barrel, his handyman fills up the mugs of the buyers as the auctioneer gives the company a flattering preamble of the cider and its maker. After the first sip the company is asked by the auctioneer to start bidding and off-handily he suggests his first price. Everyone drinks again and perhaps a full half minute passes before a voice makes an offer 40 per cent below that suggested by the auctioneer. The buyers are local cider merchants and publicans who will sell the casks in pints and quarts, accompanied by a scattering of old boys and cider makers eager and willing to try their competitors' cider and compare it to their own brews, but unable to afford to buy the casks. As these men have paid their dues by planting the trees and making the cider they are made welcome, as they have as much right to sample it as the next man. They sip again and with each sip the price advances, the auctioneer watching keenly for the next man to bid, whose smiling face shows he relishes the drink in his mug above the rest of the company.

The lot is sold and from time to time nuggets of Double Gloucester cheese, made from local Gloucester cows' milk, are handed round to cleanse the palate. Cask after cask is sold and the sale winds up with one cask, smaller than the others, containing a vintage blend of Foxwhelp or Kingston Black with another choice cider apple, forming a cider as rare as any to be tasted on Severnside. It fetches a magnificent price and with that the sale ends, each of the men a gallon or more of cider to the good for the afternoon's sampling.

It appears this was no more than an average day's drinking for a farm worker in the early to mid 1900s. 'A gallon of cider a day was considered fair and reasonable, though in some places cider was *ad lib* to the man who could carry it' writes A. Haggard in his book *Dialect and Local Usages of Herefordshire*. The amount some men could drink was phenomenal—a local waggoner who was cut down from a gallon to two quarts, owing to a shortage, was extremely annoyed and said 'I enna going to carry that tod out with me' and drank it on the spot.

Another waggoner—JR—when driven past a farm in Acton Beauchamp where he had worked as a young man, remembered 'I alus had me a quart of cider afore I drew out in the morning at 6 a.m., then my breakfast, that wur a bit of bacon and a quart of cider, and I'd fill my bottle up. [The 'bottle' was a costrell holding four or five pints]. My dinner, that wur a bit o' biff and a quart of cider, and I'd fill my bottle up. My tea, that wur summat and a quart of cider, and my supper wur a bit o' cheese and a quart of cider, then I mostly had me a quart hot before I went to bed'.

Farm cider as usually made did not keep very long and became increasingly sharp and acetic. As summer wore on it became so acid as to be virtually undrinkable, except by those accustomed to it. Then it became known by some as Belly Vengeance and others as Two Man Cider—it needed one man to drink it and another to hold him up. Three Man Cider was particularly acetic: it took one man to drink it, being held down by two of his friends as they poured it down his throat, while he squealed like a pig, thus earning it the name Pig Squeal in Herefordshire. Spilling or slopping your cider over the side of your mug was known as swillicking and to be avoided.

Kenelm Johnson at Broome Farm recalls Ernie Jones who worked on the farm as a lad for its previous owner, Mr. Percy Sexty. He would send Ernie off early in the morning to drive the cattle or sheep to Hereford market, a distance of some 14 miles. Percy would follow in the horse and cart just in time to see the stock sold and then retire to the Market Tavern where he would consume a considerable amount of alcohol, leaving Ernie to get him in the cart and drive home. If they both had too much to drink and were 'pert' the horse would make his own way, Percy and Ernie arriving home asleep in the back of the cart. As a valued employee, Ernie, when Percy was away, was entrusted with the keys to the cellar and was expected to ration out the cider to the other farmworkers, a job Ernie was none too keen on, often being bullied into giving out more cider than was allowed, and then having to face the wrath of Percy! After Percy retired, Ernie went to work for Hereford Council as a roadman, ditching and cutting grass verges, then in the late 1960s he retired and returned to work at Broome Farm, working part-time for the remainder of his working life.

In many rural areas cider would be sold at private houses that held a cider only license. Unlike a pub these cider houses did not stock beer, wine or spirits, only locally produced cider. Pete Smithies remembers Aubrey Allen's cider from Halmore, Gloucestershire, was sold at the Apple Tree in Purton. The cider house was run by an old lady and only open on Friday evenings, Saturday and Sunday. The bar was a room at the back of her cottage; you walked round the back, through the vegetable and flower gardens, lifted the latch and sat down to be served.

> She was very strict about hours - I arrived early one summer evening and she wouldn't serve us, told us to 'come back tomorrow'. She would only serve you half pints of cider unless she knew you could hold your drink - the cider was sold at 13p a pint - it would have been about £1.20 a pint for Strongbow then. Three young strangers couldn't believe it when they were served three pints and asked for 39p, they thought she meant 39p a pint and gave her £1.20. She came back to ask them if they were trying to fool her - that was enough for three pints each and you could only have two pints even if she knew you. One and a half pints was enough for most men. When the old lady died her relatives tried to keep the place going, but times had changed and people were getting used to better service, so it closed.

Yet such is the affection for the old cider houses, that some have survived into the 21st century in the three counties, almost unchanged and unspoilt by modern pressures.

Known locally as the Monkey House, the Old Bakehouse at Woodmancote, Worcestershire, is one such—unchanged for genera-tions, it preserves the atmosphere and culture of a rural cider house. The pub has been handed down through the same family for over a hundred years. In the summer drinkers sit out in the garden on makeshift benches, accompanied by dogs, chickens and an old retired pony. In the winter, or on rainy days, customers can enjoy their pints in the cosy atmosphere of the bakehouse which is furnished with farmhouse tables and basic wooden seats, and warmed by a fire lit in the oven. It is from a beam which spans the bakehouse that the place gets the nickname of the Monkey House—locals challenge each other to climb over the beam when drunk, without dislodging the onions that are stored on it or the nearby light shade.

The Three Tuns, also known as Lucy's, in Hay-on-Wye has been run by the same family for over 80 years. It is named after the landlady who grew up at the pub that her father and mother ran. When her father died the building was left to Lucy, whilst the licence remained with her mother. As her mother's arthritis became worse, Lucy took on more and more of the work, taking over the licence when her mother died.

The bar has not changed for decades, for regulars like it as it is. The bar consists of one room, entered from one door on the main road, or a side door along the road to the bridge over the Wye. The room is furnished with pew settles and stools around small round tables. A coal fire is lit in the autumn and winter in the Victorian cast iron backed fire-place. Thick curtains, scattered with a pattern of tiny flowers, hang at the small paned windows keeping the room cosy and warm. The walls and ceiling of the room are stained brown by tobacco smoke, which adds to the historic feel of the place. The bar is of plain, polished dark wood

The Three Tuns, locally known as Lucy's, in Hay

panelling with polycasks of Westons' cider stood on and behind it. Once you get used to the dim but relaxing lighting, you see that the walls are decorated with antique adverts for brands of cider, perry and babycham, including a 1950s cardboard Westons' girl, provided by the cider company's sales reps over the past 80 years. Lucy prizes her Westons' mirror, presented to her for years of unfailing service to the company and local community, which hangs above the fireplace. The presentation at Westons in 2000 was organised by her local drinkers as a surprise, and it was the first time Lucy had ever visited Westons' mills although she had passed them on many an occasion. She was delighted with the trip, as all the regulars came too in a hired minibus, and it turned into a 'right old knees up'.

Most of the drinkers arrive around 8 p.m., unless there is a special event happening in the town. The pub attracts people of all ages, types and backgrounds, who appreciate the cider sold by Lucy and the bar's unique atmosphere. By 9 p.m. the regulars are very jovial and friendly, with strangers always being made welcome and quizzed for news by the locals. After sitting a while, listening to the conversation and the sound of cider gurgling from the polycasks into glasses, you'll find yourself chatting happily about your life history and future dreams with people who you feel you have known all your life, but only just met that evening, whilst gently sliding down the settle as the local cider takes its effect on your mind and knees.

Perched on the top of the hills above Hay-on-Wye, the Bulls Head has been a stopping off point for walkers for more than a hundred years, and thanks to the imaginative restoration of the pub in 1997 you'll still find a good mix of walkers, farmers, families and local people from nearby Hay, along with visitors from further afield at the inn. Many are regular visitors, drawn here by the excellent home cooked meals and local ciders and perries on gravity dispense behind the bar. The locals here prefer cider to beer, but in cooler months there is usually a cask of Wye Valley Ale on tap for beer drinkers.

You approach the pub off the main lane, along the cobbled pavement alongside the garden, with spectacular views across the valley. Sauntering through the split stable door into the pub you are greeted by a stone flagged bar with wooden beams, settles and family sized polished dining tables, complemented by old high backed chairs. A gigantic old fireplace dominates one corner of the bar, providing comfort in the cold winter months when fragrant logs burn in the grate. The bar lies between the hatches at the back of the room where, peeking through, you can see the polycasks of cider and perry on the top shelf of the stillage, with casks of ale conditioning below on the bottom shelf.

The Bulls Head (in the centre of the picture),
at the foot of the Black Mountains at Craswell

A recent addition is a second room off to the right of the bar, up a short flight of wooden stairs. Converted from the old family sitting room of the pub, this room provides a more intimate atmosphere with smaller tables and high backed chairs, wooden beams and bare stone walls, heated by a small fireplace.

The pub also offers an extensive menu of mouth watering dishes from filling Huffers—gigantic sandwiches made with home baked bread, to full three course meals, made with local ingredients to soak up the cider. If you're a walker the lunch at the Bulls Head sets you up for the rest of the day's hiking, but if you are too full to move afterwards, you can camp in the field next door!

Situated just off the Gloucester to Cheltenham road, in the hamlet of Haydens Elm, The House in the Tree has been a cider house for over two centuries. It started life as a thatched cruck house, which is still preserved as the bar, along with the outbuildings towards the back of the garden, which were once used for stabling and keeping hens.

Entering the bar you are transported back to another age. As your eyes get used to the dim interior you find yourself in a small room of bare, black beams and bare brick, with a stone flagged floor that is complemented along one side by the ornately carved wooden bar. On wattle and daub wall panels are hung photographs showing scenes of local cider making and old village life, including a carved and dyed wooden plaque of cider drinkers. Wooden seats are fixed along the walls (some of the regulars bring their own cushions) with an assortment of old wooden tables on which to rest your pint. At the end of the room is a massive fireplace with an oak surround, set off by two high backed pews on either side, as well as stone topped seats in the fireplace itself. Just the place for relaxing on a winter's day with a cool glass of cider.

Extensions have added to the bar over the years, first a small lounge, then a sunny covered passage at the front of the pub, where the regular drinkers like to sit in summer and which provides cover from the elements in winter, plus somewhere to leave your wet wellies before entering the bar. The bar has been moved and replaced within living memory—once it stood at the far end of the room opposite the fireplace and was just plain panels. At that time the door to the cellar was in the bar room and there were only the seats by the fireplace to rest on.

The modern restaurant extension at the back of the pub was added in the late 1990s. It has already proved its worth in the local community, when the local Sunday School needed a new home. The vicar approached the landlady to see if they could use the extension for Sunday morning lessons, before the pub opened. The initiative has been popular with both the children, who delight in being taken to a pub for school, and the parents who join them for a Sunday lunch in the pub afterwards.

The House in the Tree at Haydens Elm

The pub keeps five ciders on draught, as well as 'tinned', the local term for cans. The regulars that drink the tin won't drink the draught, or *vice versa*. The 'tinners' say the cider from the cask is too dry. A lot of regulars here are cider characters.

Sunday mornings find the regulars arriving in ones and twos for their first pint of cider, accompanied by gossip and exchange of news. There is a burble of happy conversation and greetings to friends, accompanied by the whistling of one regular to his dog who waits patiently in the porch outside.

A Sunday morning regular, Ivor Cook, remembers that one of the earlier landlords used to make cider here as well as selling brews from local farms. The customers used to go down in the cellar helping themselves in a jug, but the trouble was that once you were down there it was difficult to find your way back to the bar. The brew was known as Hayden's Revenge, and even big strong men who were used to their cider had trouble finding the way home after drinking two pints.

Evlyn has been coming here since he moved to Gloucester to work, around 1940. He prefers cider to beer as it agrees with him better, except when he drinks too much! One such occasion was the night before the marriage of his son, when he was with his son and his mates at the House in the Tree. They were all aged about 27, but he tried to keep up with them and found he couldn't. Next day he was still suffering and couldn't drink or eat during the wedding, because of his hangover. Evlyn avows that the reason he got his hangover was because he wasn't eating when drinking the cider. He remembers going to a cider festival just outside Cinderford, Gloucestershire, which was held in a marquee. There were no tables or chairs, just a bar with 20 or so cider barrels. Evlyn asked the bloke behind the bar which was the best, and stuck to drinking the recommended barrel all night. 'There was a pig roast, so every pint I had, I had a little roll as well. I don't know how many rolls or how many pints I had, but I was sober at the end of the night. That was a night that was! If you keep eating you're all right'.

3 CHANGING LANDSCAPES

The amount of cider fruit needed to produce cider commercially has led to the development of bush orchards that are easier to manage and crop than standard trees, and produce more fruit per acre. Bulmers Cider in Hereford pioneered the development of many of the varieties of cider fruit in use today, and also the contracting of growers to produce fruit for the mills at a guaranteed price per ton. As a result, in the last 40 years bush orchards have spread across the slopes and valleys of Herefordshire, even stretching into Wales.

In 1903 the firm's founder, Percy Bulmer, said 'that if the cider making industry was to increase in Herefordshire, it would be necessary to have the raw materials, i.e. cider fruit, and in view of the demand for trees, I think that a greater supply should be produced by the Nurseryman. It would be necessary to grow trees on a larger scale than had hitherto been done in this country and in a commercial spirit'. Shortly afterwards Bulmers started to grow cider apple trees on a trial basis. It took close on 18 years to complete the trials, select the best varieties for cider making and produce the first trees for planting.

In the *Hereford Times* of 23 October 1937, Dr. H.V. Taylor, Horticultural Commissioner to the Ministry of Agriculture, addressed cider makers and apple growers at the Burghill Mental Hospital Farm Orchard. Planted under the National Fruit and Cider Institute Scheme in 1908, the Burghill trial compared the fruit yield of some of the recognised varieties of Herefordshire cider fruit with those of other counties that were unknown in the area, to identify the best varieties to plant for local commercial growers. The trial indicated that profits of between £7 7s. per acre, per annum, up to £14 per acre on the best cropping varieties were achievable, and provided much valuable cultivation information for growing new, high cropping, cider fruit varieties in the county.

In the course of his address to the assembled company Dr. Taylor referred to the change which had taken place in the cider industry. 'Thirty or 40 years ago', he said, 'the bulk of the cider made in this country was drunk by people in the countryside, whereas today a very large proportion was drunk by the man in the town. Both cider apple growers and manufacturers had to realise that the cider of the townsman was a very different product from the cider the countryman used to drink'. The modern type of cider was mainly made on a basis of sweet and bittersweet apples, in some cases with vintage varieties, and the grower of these apples was at the disadvantage that if he could not sell them to the manufacturer he could not dispose of them in the ordinary market as eating or cooking fruit.

At the beginning of the 20th century, the price paid for cider apples was so low that planting almost ceased entirely, and subsequently there was nothing like the crop of cider apples, especially of sweet and bitter-sweet varieties, that the cider manufacturers needed. A tax of 4s. 6d. per hundredweight (cwt.) was imposed on all imported apples in 1932, from which cider apples were exempted as it was felt to be in the national interest that manufacturers should buy imported apples and employ British labour to make cider, rather than purchasing the finished product from abroad. At the same time, the government joined hands with the manufacturers in an attempt to encourage a bigger supply of English cider apples. As a result the Association of Cider Manufacturers agreed to contract with growers to pay not less than £4 per ton for four years for all varieties of cider apples.

To encourage the planting of new orchards, Westons Cider planted an experimental bush cider apple orchard at The Bounds, Much Marcle, for Long Ashton Research Station containing practically all the well known varieties of cider fruit. This hosted demonstrations of spraying, grafting and pruning of bush orchards to demonstrate the advantages of bush orchard production of cider fruit. In addition, Fred Bulmer's scheme of encouraging growers to plant bush orchards through beneficial long term contracts was copied by other producers. As a result, growers planted well over 200,000 trees between 1923 and 1947.

The fruit buying scheme was severely tested in 1934, its second year, because there was an enormous crop of cider fruit and prices, if left to market forces, would have been low. Although they might have been able to buy the apples for half the price due to the glut, loyal members of the Association paid the minimum £4 per cwt. as agreed and the contract held for its full four years.

In the 1920s Bulmers bought Kings Acre Nurseries, just outside of Hereford, for developing seedling rootstocks. Kings Acre Nurseries, founded in 1785 by a Mr. Cranston to produce roses, by 1903 were producing 40-50,000 cider fruit trees, not only for Herefordshire, but also for export to South Africa, New Zealand, Canada and Australia.

The pomace from Ryelands Mill, including all the pips, would be spread between the rows of young trees growing in Kings Acre Nurseries. The pips in the pomace would sprout and the nurserymen would pick out the strong shoots to use as seedling rootstocks. A variety of apple tree that grew tall and straight would be grafted low down on the rootstock in its first year as a stem builder. After three years, when the maiden tree had produced a good trunk, the chosen variety of cider fruit was budded onto the stem. These improved varieties, chosen for their cider making qualities, were made available by Bulmers to their farmers and growers at discount prices.

Edward Ball, a cousin of Howard and Esmond Bulmer, having joined Bulmers in 1927 became director of research in 1933 and sought to combine the merits of the Foxwhelp, a variety superb in quality but low in cropping capacity, with the resistance to disease and the blossoming habit of the imported Medaille d'Or apple. The former was available in an orchard at Lower Breinton, the latter at Whettons Farm, near Pembridge. From hundreds of seedlings one was selected, now known as Ball's Bittersweet.

In a paper entitled *Cider Orchard Restoration in Herefordshire; 1923-1947*, published in 1947, Edward Ball made a forecast about planting needs for the next 25 to 30 years, on the premise that trees planted before the beginning of the firm's scheme in 1923 would disappear in about 40 years time. Farmers and growers were reluctant to buy the stakes and

Picking apples the traditional way

guards that went with the young trees and this resulted in many trees being damaged or chewed by cattle and other livestock grazing the orchards. Up to 1947 less than one-third of the trees needed for the future had been successfully planted.

In his report, Edward Ball estimated that more than 5,000 trees a year would have to be planted in 1947-1951 if supplies of cider apples were to be adequate for the period 1966-1981. To overcome the reluctance of the farmers and growers to protect the young trees from livestock, Bulmers upped the price of the trees, but included the stake and guard in the package. By 1960 Bulmers were selling between 5,000 and 10,000 trees a year and Edward's planting scheme was completed, if slightly late, by 1966.

Some farmers would try planting whole apples or selected pips in the ground, but this would not result in an identical copy of the parent tree. For that you need to graft or bud a recognised variety onto a seedling rootstock. These trees grown from pips have resulted in an enormous variety of cider apples found in farms and garden orchards, none of them named or recognised varieties. As a further complication to identification, Bulmers also produced stocks of seedling trees at Broxwood, a nursery established by Bulmers in 1898, that were allowed to grow to full standards in the hope of providing improved vintage varieties. These trees were planted along with recognised varieties in growers' orchards in the 1920s and '30s, being identified on the orchard plans as B1 or B2 trees. The meaning behind these tags and the names of the cross pollinators used to create the trees has been lost, so they remain a mystery to growers and orchardists alike. These trees can still be found in old standard orchards in Herefordshire and they present great difficulties for experts in apple identification as, although they are not true varieties, they may exhibit some of the characteristics of their parents.

During the Second World War cider production at Bulmers continued, the government exempting agricultural workers and cider makers from the draft. Cider was spared as a morale booster. In the mid 1950s a glut of fruit caused the price of apples to drop, falling to as little as £35 a ton, a sum that made it hardly worth growing cider apples without a guaranteed contract with a commercial cider maker.

In the late 1950s Bulmers were working with Long Ashton Research Station to identify a list of varieties that would be regular prolific croppers if grafted to bush rootstocks, which would reduce the planting distances between trees and enable the mechanical harvesting of orchards. Bush rootstocks had previously only been used on dessert and culinary fruit, so it was a vast project. Ray Williams joined Long Ashton Research Station in 1952 as a pomologist and took on the project:

At that time cider orchards in England were not flourishing. There was no attempt by farmers and growers to control bi-annualism, where trees would crop heavily one year then poorly the next. To make up for poor crops at home commercial cider makers imported fruit from Normandy and elsewhere in northern France. The management of orchards was poor, along with growers' understanding of the effect of weather, soil, altitude and local climate on the trees. Yields were low, as little as 1 ton per acre, if a grower managed 5-6 tons per acre on average he was doing very well. One grower was managing 10 tons an acre, which I felt was superb.

Long Ashton had compiled, from earlier research, a list of recommended varieties of vintage cider fruits which were available to growers from the early 1950s. In the selection process the cider making quality of the fruit was considered paramount, orchard characteristics were not considered important. Growers, like Bulmers, who had taken note of the list found they had poor results, trees were not cropping as they had hoped and they were having difficulty with fruit set. My first research project involved discovering the reasons for these problems and providing scientific solutions. I approached the John Innes Institute, the experts on pollination and fertilisation of dessert fruit. Together we identified that the majority of the popular varieties on the Long Ashton list were triploids, which have three chromosomes. Triploid pollen is sterile and will either not germinate on the stigma or will not fertilise the ovary of the flower, resulting in low fruit set. The answer was to ensure that diploid (two chromosome) varieties were included during the planning and planting of the orchard to assist pollination, providing enough compatible pollen to produce fruit, as long as the flowering periods of both varieties overlap.

Another problem encountered in the 1950s by growers was the poor growth and light cropping of many young trees and new grafts on mature tree stock. We discovered that the widespread practice of grafting new varieties known to be high croppers onto old local trees was encouraging the spread of viruses from the old wood to the new. Also, once established these grafts were being used as bud wood, or graft wood, onto another tree, further spreading the virus. Growers were in effect building a chain of accumulated viruses from tree to tree.

A mother nursery was established at Long Ashton to provide virus free bud and graft wood of popular cider varieties on the Institute's preferred list, plus a few old standard varieties of regional importance for future research. By always going back to virus free mother trees the growers were able to overcome their problems, improving the quality of their trees and increasing the tonnage of their crops. In the late 1960s some of these varieties were developed as bush trees on virus free semi-dwarfing rootstocks obtained from East Malling Research Station, which promised to further increase growers fruit yields as more trees could be planted per acre and the trees came into crop at a younger age.

Robert Wellington, the first director of East Malling Research Station, had begun a collection of rootstocks in 1912. There were a number of rootstocks then available and it was recognised that those were the key to producing good quality fruit on a large scale, but little was known of their individual benefits and the varieties were often misidentified. The research was completed by Robert Wellington's successor (Sir) Robert Hatton, who during the 1920s made the selections that formed the basis of the East Malling series of standardised rootstock which are now used around the world.

The East Malling dwarfing stock M9 will give a full bearing tree, no more than 8-10 feet high, within five years of being planted, and allowing up to 1,300 trees per acre. This compares to the 12 years or it takes a standard tree to come into full cropping, at 48 trees per acre. It was quickly recognised by the growers that these dwarf trees were the key to the production of good quality fruit on a large scale as they are easily managed, give early returns on investment and make efficient use of manpower and space.

A group of men gathering fruit from tumps into sacks,
a scene that would have been seen in orchards over many a decade

Ray also researched the benefit of manuring orchard trees to increase fruit yield. The grower who produced 10 tons per acre on his standard orchards was employing the ideas of Bickham, published in the *Journal of Pomology* in 1928. Ray doubted the paper's claim that nitrogen application in summer produced a better crop of fruit in the following autumn, and his research indicated that the nitrogen application in fact benefited the tree the next spring, producing better blossom and higher fruit set. It was standard practice at that time to apply nitrogen or manure in the winter while the tree was dormant. However, summer application allows the tree to absorb, store and utilise the nutrients more efficiently. Ray continues:

> There were also cases of serendipity. Monoculture was taking hold in bush orchards, especially for dessert fruit where orchard varieties are selected to ripen at different times of the season for ease of cropping. One grower had brought over an early variety called Scarlet Pimpernel from the U.S.A. whose fruit was fully mature in August, giving four weeks' lead on English varieties. But, early cropping also means early blossom, in this case 10 to 14 days before other apple varieties were in flower. Although the trees were growing well and producing lots of blossom, they were not setting any fruit. John Innes and East Malling had both looked at the trees and failed to find a solution referring the grower to me. Every year the grower kept phoning me for an answer to his problem, until one year inspiration struck. I realised that his trees were in flower at the same time as the ornamental crab apples growing outside the lab, so I suggested the grower try planting some early flowering crab apples between the existing trees to increase pollination. I did not hear from the grower for a few years so assumed he had given up and grubbed out the orchard. Three to four years later I found out that the idea was a success and the grower was reporting good early crops. Since then the practice of using ornamental crab apples (*Malus*) as pollinators has been adopted by other growers, including orchardists in the USA.

By the late 1960s/early 1970s commercial cider makers realised that there would soon be a shortage of fruit in the UK and France. Old orchards planted at the start of the century were reaching the end of their life due to neglect and farmers were grubbing them out with the assistance of government schemes that gave them money to replace the unprofitable fruit trees with arable food crops. No new orchards were being planted and trees lost to storms or disease were not being replaced. The large cider makers became worried about the massive loss of acreage and decided something had to be done. In the early 1970s Bulmers were one of the first companies to introduce intensive orchards using the bush orchard techniques developed at Long Ashton. The cumulative total of trees sold by Bulmers in 1970 was about 300,000—260,000 standard and 40,000 bush, proportions soon to be reversed by the company's enthusiastic promotion of high yield bush orchards.

Chris Fairs joined Bulmers' orcharding team in 1971, after previously being involved in agricultural work in Herefordshire. He is the Orcharding Department's Growers' Adviser, overseeing all aspects of orchard management and fruit production for the company, from its suppliers' orchards.

> When I started work for Bulmers there was a cider apple shortage and we were working with Ray Williams at Long Ashton Research Station to identify varieties that would give regular, prolific crops, when propagated on semi-dwarfing rootstocks, such as MM106 and MM111. These would improve precocity, allow an increased tree planting density, and still permit the mechanical harvesting of fruit.
>
> Bulmers was acquiring land to plant with orchards, starting in 1968 with Monnington Court, and rising to manage more than 2,000 acres by the mid-1970s. At this time, land prices began rising sharply, and Bulmers took the decision to offer 20-year apple supply contracts to local farmers. A low-interest loan, made available to cover establishment costs, was a further inducement to plant. Faced with a 330% increase in the price (from £300-£1,000 an acre) of good agricultural land, this change, to encourage even more contract-grown fruit, still gave the company an assured supply of fruit into the future. Family farmers in Herefordshire took a while to support this new venture. A few enterprising farmers did sign contracts, and were pleased enough with results to tell their relatives, who, in turn, also signed up. In this way Bulmers built up its overall orchard acreage, and still, today, many of our contract-growers are related. By the end of the 1970s, Bulmers had amassed some 3,800 orchard acres (of which 1,800 acres were being grown on contract), and had succeeded in meeting its target for local, fresh apple supply.

In the late 1970s to early 1980s demand and fruit prices were static. Only the growers under contract to the company were guaranteed an income from their orchards, because there was an excess of cheap apple concentrate on the international market that was pushing prices down.

One of the growers at that time was Keith Knight of Crumpton Oaks, Storridge, near Malvern. His home and cider mill is directly opposite the house on the other side of the valley where Elgar wrote his *Enigma Variations* whilst gazing over the Malvern Hills. The cellar doorframe of

A young orchard at Knights' cider, with the Malvern Hills in the background

the cruck-built farmhouse is made of strong oak beams provided with runners that are the right width for manoeuvring wooden casks into and out of the cellar, suggesting that cider has been made here for more than 300 years. Keith moved to Crumpton Oaks in 1969 when the farm included 140 acres of land.

> The farm had been neglected by its owners - a mining company who wanted to quarry stone from the hills. When planning permission was refused by the council, the farm came up at auction but failed to sell. The farm was in 'quite a state', just the house and three acres of blackcurrants. We didn't have much capital to buy stock or machinery, so we decided to grow fruit. In 1972 we got talking to Bulmers who were offering to plant trees on a 20-year contract with the grower. In 1973 we planted 25 acres on such a contract. It took a long time for the orchard to establish. We did not know as much about maintenance as we do now, so it took us eight to nine years to break even, a great stretch on our finances that were further hit by a fall in the price of apples due to rampant inflation in the 1980s, which meant the price was falling behind the cost of growing the fruit. I therefore called a meeting of 26 growers who were contracted to Bulmers, which resulted in the forming of the Herefordshire Cider Fruit Growers Association to negotiate better fruit prices with the company. I and Hugh Snell [who had orchards at Lower Lulham, between Bridge Sollars and Madley in Herefordshire] were the original negotiators. Within a few months the Association had grown to 66 farms representing 1,400 acres. At first things were a little acrimonious, but both parties recognised it

was good to talk and since then the Association has been recognised and respected. This led to the adoption of a minimum price per ton for growers on a 20-year contract, along with a free advice service providing technical help and training. Association members help fund research and development through a levy of 25p a ton on fruit which is paid into a common pot used to fund research and development for the industry.

Sales of cider, related to raw material supply, remained in balance until the early 1990s, when the continuing, successful promotion of Bulmers' brands increased the demand for cider apples, especially as the price of foreign concentrate was very unpredictable. Chris Fairs picks up the story.

In the early 1990s, Bulmers saw support for the agricultural community, through the offering of contracts to new growers and the expanding of contract acreage with existing suppliers, as the desirable way forward. This came at an ideal time for Herefordshire farmers, who had seen incomes from mixed, livestock, and arable units decline during the previous decade. They were all seeking ways of diversifying. The Bulmer nursery was expanded to meet the demand, which often came from the sons and daughters of farmers who had taken out a 20-year contract in the 1970s. These farms 'old' bush orchards were performing better than anticipated, and a 10-year extension of contract-term was issued to them. The contracts for new plantings, however, were set at 30 years, providing a guaranteed income for the next generation of the family, as well as the current one, and firmly establishing a 'family tradition' of growing fruit for Bulmers. The expansion in acreage has also made it possible for farmers to purchase their own harvesting machinery.

Many of the original bush orchards, planted in the 1940s and 1950s, were 'thinned out' at a later date, as the rootstocks proved too vigorous. Our 1970s plantations, on more reliable rootstocks, were planted at densities of approximately 200 trees per acre. By the 1990s we had found we could sensibly increase this to 250-300 trees to the acre, thereby improving both early yields and revenue for our growers. The company's offering of a five-year, interest-free loan, was, for those fortunate farmers in the European Union's designated '5b Marches' parishes, supplemented by grants which contributed towards the cost of establishing their orchards, on the grounds that these helped secure and enhance rural employment.

Bulmers also bought two new farms. We now have 180 acres at Kinnersley; a small trial, organic, bush orchard at Staunton on Wye, on rented land, and more than 400 acres at Penrhos Farm,

Llantilio Crossenny in Wales. 'Fresh' land is used for nursery tree production, and is rented from local farmers, as required. Bulmer-managed orchards now comprise some 2,400 acres, with an additional 5,500 acres grown under contract. These include orchards in Devon, Somerset and Dorset. At its peak of production the Bulmer nursery was providing 200,000 bush cider apple trees per year to cope with demand.

Bulmers' varieties have been chosen to crop in mid to late season and produce a consistent crop with a minimum of bi-annualism. Early apples were found to have less density and weight, therefore to produce less juice and were more prone to rotting before they could be milled and pressed. Apples that ripen too late present problems as winter conditions increase the amount of leaves and mud which makes harvesting difficult. Development of the ideal bush orchard is slow and laborious—Bulmers have been active in developing varieties with good disease resistance to minimise the cost of herbicides and pest sprays, encouraging beneficial predators to the orchard.

The planning, planting and upkeep of a modern bush orchard requires a scientific approach. The site must be assessed for its suitability, notably as to its previous use, altitude, rainfall, prevailing wind direction, soil depth and condition. Ideally core samples of soil are taken from across the site, at depths of 0-6 inches and 6-12 inches, and tested for parts per million of phosphate, potash and magnesium, plus soil pH. It

Planting trees and grafting an orchard—in medieval days

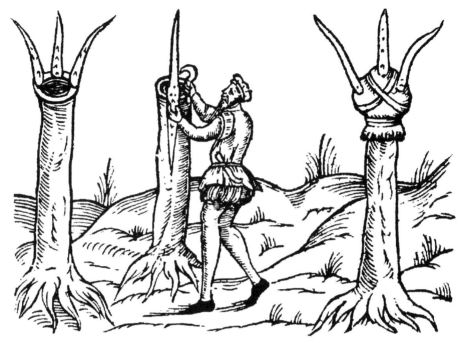

Medieval grafting techniques

is important that the soil contains enough nutrients for the establishment of the young trees, so ploughing and cultivation of the ground with
added fertiliser or farmyard manure to correct any imbalance should be
carried out prior to planting. The orchard must be provided with a wind-
break hedge and rabbit proof enclosure to prevent damage from
prevailing winds and vermin. As mechanical harvesting is a key part of
modern bush orcharding, flat or gently sloping ground is preferred.
Cider apples flower later than culinary varieties, so the risk of frost
damage on flat sites is less. Poor drainage can hamper harvesting and
lead to the loss of trees through canker and fungus root (*phytopthora*)
infection, which spreads upwards from the roots and kills the tree.
Therefore, on heavy soils or in areas of high rainfall drainage should be
provided under the tree roots.

Planting takes place while the trees are dormant, after leaf drop, and
is dependent on soil conditions. December planting is preferred, but
sometimes it can be as late as early April before conditions are suitable.
The ground should be prepared to a fine tilth, then a team of three can
plant the trees in a quincunx pattern—one tree in the centre and one on
each corner of a large square. The orchard is first marked out with the
support stakes. A hole is then drilled with an augur in which the support
stake is inserted and supported, only then is the hole for the tree roots

dug by hand. The support stake is positioned so that the prevailing wind blows the tree away from the stake, to prevent wind damage. The stake and the tree are joined with a flexible tie; this prevents rocking which can lead to shallow roots or damage from fungus root in wetter soils. Mulch mats, or old matting, can be put around the base of the trunk to prevent competition from weeds or grass for water.

In the first summer after planting the young trees should be pruned to build a strong stem by reducing the lead branch by one third and pruning off any competitive shoots. Ideally, a young tree will have an evenly spaced spiral of branches with at least 10cm between the leader and the first shoot and each lateral branch. Any surplus branches to this are removed. If the time can be found, the sward between the rows should be mown five to eight times between March and August, depending on rainfall.

In the second winter the new season's feathers should be cut back to two to three buds and the lower, older laterals removed to create a smooth stem. The sward is mown as before. Most trees will carry some fruit in years two to four and this helps the training of the tree, increasing the angle of the branches, reducing excessive lateral growth and encouraging the tree to produce more fruit buds the following year. Further pruning in the third and fourth year should mean that by year five a balanced tiered system of branches is forming.

Harvesting cider fruit from traditional orchards relies on hand-picking the apples from the grass sward at fruit drop, with any fruit left on the tree being shaken off with a panking pole or lug, a long ash pole

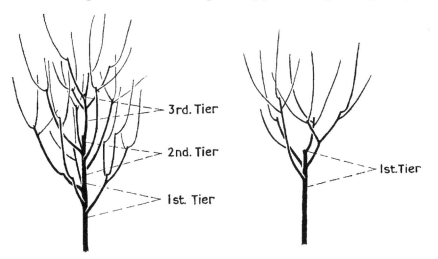

A more recent pruning guide—as shown in a Ministry of Agriculture, Fisheries and Food bulletin on Cider Apple Production in 1962

with a curved hook which securely grips the branches so they can be shaken. Apples were left in sacks to mature in the orchards or piled up in low heaps in the farmyard until ready for milling. There is still a place for the hand-picker in standard orchards on traditional, sloped sites where it is difficult to get access for machinery. As has been said on many a farm over the years—'You never see a good picker's face - you recognise their bums'!

Early attempts at apple picking machines used a horse drawn roller which picked up the apples on steel spikes, then knocked them off the spikes with a comb of metal rods so they fell into a basket. In the late 1950s/early 1960s these harvesters were refined by the addition of a motor, and a reduction in the size of the roller enabled one picker to manoeuvre the machine. The design was not a success as the spikes damaged the fruit, reducing its keeping ability, and they failed to pick up smaller fruit from the orchard sward, which then needed to be collected by hand. An example of a motorised Morris's Hedgehog machine from 1960 can be seen in the collection of Hereford Cider Museum.

With the growth of intensive bush orchards in the 1970s and the lack of hand pickers, there was a renewed interest in mechanical harvesting. One of the first machines trialed was the Cacueval pedestrian operated harvester. Powered by a motor and steered over the sward by one man, the harvester used rubber paddles to pick up the fruit, covered at the front with a flexible hood. The apples travel on the paddles to a conveyor which takes them over a cleaning plate, which allows dirt and leaves to

A tree 'shaker' in action at Knights, dislodging fruit

60

fall to the orchard floor, and the clean fruit is deposited in a basket. However the machine quickly became blocked with mud and orchard debris. The design was improved, but you still cannot use the machine in muddy conditions, and it works best on a flat dry sward with plenty of clearance for the operator and machine. It is possible to collect one or two tons per hour with the pedestrian machine, the limiting factors being the emptying of the baskets by the operator.

Tractor operated machines that used the same paddle and hood arrangement as the pedestrian harvester were soon available. But they too had the same drawbacks of blocking up with mud and leaves, in addition to failing to pick up fruit in ruts caused by grazing animals in standard orchards, or by the tractor on green sward. A combination of a forward rotating paddle reel and suction fan was tried in an attempt to solve the debris problem.

The long term solution was provided by George Tuthill, who designed and manufactured a harvester using two webbed belts, rotating in opposite directions, which picked up the fruit and transported it between the two belts to the cleaner unit and conveyor without bruising or damage to the apples. Dirt is eliminated by a set of rubber flaps attached to the apple inlet that lets apples through but not leaves or twigs. The harvester can only pick up apples directly in its path, so the tractor is also provided with paddles or brushes, side mounted on the tractor, to move apples from under the tree canopy into the path of the harvester.

Self-propelled harvesters are also available for large orchards, which have the advantage of being specifically designed for the harvesting operation, eliminating the risk of tree damage by collision with machinery, having a lower profile and better traction on orchard sward. With all the machines, harvesting requires a firm, dry sward and a front washing facility to ensure cleanliness.

Unlike manual pickers the machines cannot tell the difference between sound or rotten fruit, which can spoil the resulting juice for fermentation. Therefore, apples are shaken from the trees prior to wind-drop to eliminate rot, using a pneumatic arm side mounted on a tractor. Damage to the tree roots and branches is kept to a minimum by the use of two, unbalanced inertia wheels rotating on one axis, but in different directions, which can quickly and effectively shake whole trees. Clamps with two large pillow pads, each covered with two large rubber flats, ensures the shaker does not damage the bark of the tree. As a large proportion of the crop falls under the tree, some farms use a blower machine to move the fruit from under the branches to the centre of the sward for harvesting. In dry conditions a harvester can collect 100 tons a day from a mature bush orchard; in very wet weather as little as 40 tons a day. The autumn of 1998 started very dry—and ended particularly wet, with severe flooding. Apples still on the sward in the Bulmers orchards at Monnington-on-Wye were carried down river and round the bend to Harry Cotterell's land. When the floods receded there were apples perched on the top of hedges and littering his meadows, so he picked them up and brought them into the mill at Plough Lane!

Cedric Olive was born at Greenland Road in Hereford, next door to Bulmers Ryeland Street mill.

> I went to Lord Scudamore School and remember coming out of class in the autumn and seeing all the horses and carts taking apples to the mill at the Ryelands Street site. The children would sneak up to the back of the carts to scrump the apples, eating them on the way home. When trucks and tractors started to bring fruit in sacks to the mills after the war, children would stand on the back bumper and hitch a free ride home, hanging on the back of the lorry or trailer.
>
> Sidings for the trains that delivered apples and carried cider away from the mills ran to what is now the front of the Cider Museum and up by Barton Yard, now the site of Sainsburys. The whole area was a massive marshalling yard. In those days the trains were steam, magnificent engines, they used to pull alongside the mill into the coal yard for refuelling. It was a dead end so there was a turntable built into the ground to turn the trains around. The engine would drive slowly onto the turntable then big machinery

A GWR goods train in Bulmers' Barton Sidings, loading the first consignment of cider to go to the USA after the ending of Prohibition in 1934

underneath would revolve the engine until it faced back the other way. It was magical to watch those monsters being turned around in the yard. The sidings also ran to the back of the Moorfield site. During World War II they were full of trains which were loaded with bits of aeroplanes, shells and other military scrap and surplus from the war effort.

I started work at the Ryelands Street mill in September 1951, in the laboratory taking samples of the apple pomace from the mill for quality control, and worked for Bulmers all my life until December 1999 when I retired: 48 years, 84 days, for the same company. As mill manager and cider maker I was 'everyone's best friend'. Orcharding would give me an estimate of how much fruit to expect before the start of the picking season, then as fruit ripened would refine their original estimate to something near accurate. I'd make plans to accommodate the fruit coming into the presses and get the permits issued to the contractors. When the fruit arrived at the mill the vehicle and trailer is weighed, then the driver is told which silo to tip the apples into, then the vehicle and trailer is weighed again - the difference is the amount of fruit they are paid for by the fruit office. Apples used to arrive in all sorts of vehicles, from the boots of cars to tractors and 20 ton lorries - and still do. However, not all the vehicles were always up to the job - one farmer who delivered his fruit in an old dilapidated tractor and trailer caused an emergency, when his trailer coupling broke as he tipped the apples into the silo and his trailer ended up in the canal as well! We had to hire a crane to get it out and destroy all the apples in case of contamination with oil.

Another time a contractor delivering apples caused a disaster that shut down the whole mill for 48 hours. I was called to the mill room because one of the engineers could smell diesel, but could not work out where it was coming from. A spare can of diesel had been put into a trailer of apples by mistake, then tipped with the fruit into the silos. It had been washed into the mill with the apples and crushed, releasing diesel into the apple pulp. Everything right through to the juice and pomace was contaminated with diesel oil. Our insurance company estimated over £340,000 worth of damage to stock and equipment. Cleaning it all up with special detergents took 48 hours, but the mill still smelt of diesel so we could not start production. Eventually a small pool of oil was found lurking underneath the mill that had crushed the can and production resumed, but all the apples, juice and pomace that had gone through the mill that day had to be specially disposed of. We couldn't get a local tip to take the spoilt stock, so it was shipped by road to Shrewsbury for decontamination and disposal.

Over the years we have had to tighten up on the quality of fruit being delivered. Mechanical harvesting of bush orchards created more leaves, sticks and stones mixed in with the fruit, which would have been left on the ground by hand pickers. Also wet weather means muddy fruit and if the apples have laid too long on the ground - rotting fruit. We also have the problem that twigs, stones and mulch outside the factory in the orchards is classed as agricultural waste, but once it comes into the factory it is industrial waste which we have to pay to dispose of properly, according to strict regulations. We prefer not to pay for sticks and stones, so growers who deliver contaminated or dirty fruit are penalised on the price per ton paid. It is a particular problem in the first one or two mechanical harvests in new bush orchards - the machines cannot pick up the difference between loose stones and apples, so there are always a quantity of stones in the fruit until the new green sward has been cleared of loose pebbles. When the fruit is washed into the mill the fruit elevators sieve off the sticks and stones, leaves etc. and the mud is washed off.

Storage space and cider production revolved around the fruit supply. The mill opens in September, with the early fruit starting to trickle in - around 100 tons a day - until the last week in November when we are processing 1,200 tons of fruit a day. At first we run only half of the mill to press the early varieties. During the pressing season we are still adjusting our plan to accommodate everyone's production requirements, asking the fruit office if they expect a farm to be low on fruit, or have an unexpected glut, controlling the varieties coming into the mill (bittersweets/bittersharps/culinary) to control the quality of the blended juice, stopping this and starting that according to day to day circumstances and the unforeseen disasters with equipment or fruit supplies.

When the bush orchards planted in the late 1970s/early 1980s

Cedric Olive, 50 years on the cider making team at Bulmers

were just starting to crop, the orcharding department found it difficult to estimate the expected fruit crop for the mill. They were 100% out that year - we had 400 tons of fruit tipped on Barton Siding, 300 tons on the Baynam Garage site (before the garage was there) plus full silos and canals. We just couldn't press the fruit fast enough and it was rotting in storage - it was a nightmare. Everyone gave a lot of advice, but very little help, including one of the company directors. He turned up at a particularly bad moment to see the problem for himself, innocently remarking that we had a lot of apples this year. I replied 'there's too many B*** apples, can't you see?' and he went away. Perhaps in hindsight it wasn't a very clever remark to make to a director, but he never mentioned it!

Deliveries of fruit to the mills used to stop over night for ten hours, but from autumn 2000 deliveries started arriving during the night, with fruit arriving 24 hours a day during the pressing season, now the new bush orchards are in full production. In 1999 we processed 83,000 tons of fruit, in 2001 we processed a record 100,000 tons!

Robin Haig and his father, Major R.B. Haig, have been growing apples for Bulmers, under contract, for 30 years or so. Their orchards total about 90 acres, with about 70 acres of cider and 20 of dessert. Robin takes up the story of Hill Farm.

My father bought this farm in 1969, after he retired from the army, and planted it up with dessert apples. It was only in the mid-70s that he planted the first cider orchard, under a Bulmers' contract. More recently - in the last six or eight years - we've pulled up quite a few of our dessert orchards and replanted with cider varieties, or grafted the dessert trees over to cider - it's a very quick and simple process, actually. We decided that cider apples were more profitable to grow than dessert, but of course just as the orchards are starting to have decent crops we find that the cider market isn't as rosy as we hoped - just our luck. Still, we live in hope!

We have quite a range of varieties - Dabinett, Ball's Bittersweet, Harry Master's Jersey, Ashton Bitter, Foxwhelp, Major, Michelin, Yarlington Mill, Ashton Brown Jersey, Stoke Red and Kingston Black. The last four varieties were planted specifically because they are renowned for making good cider, the best known of course being Kingston Black. This is a notoriously difficult variety to grow and we have spent huge amounts of time and money spraying them against all sorts of diseases, going round painstakingly cutting out diseased shoots and coaxing them into giving us a crop.

Cider apples are a lot easier to grow than dessert apples; they don't need nearly as much spraying or pruning. It doesn't matter if a cider apple looks horrible just so long as it makes good cider! When we still had mainly dessert apples we used to employ three people full time, plus up to 60 seasonal pickers. But more recently we have just employed one man, plus 20 to 30 for picking the dessert apples. We get a contractor to harvest the cider apples, and the season lasts from early October, when the Foxwhelps ripen, up until November when the late varieties such as Yarlington Mill are ready to harvest.

Bulmers hold an orcharding competition every two years, and we have won the top prize, the Golden Apple Trophy, no fewer than five times. Most of the credit for this goes to my father, who is very painstaking and conscientious in the way he looks after the orchards. The competition measures how well the orchards are managed in terms of pruning, disease control, keeping down weeds, mowing and so forth, and also whether they are managed in an environmentally friendly manner. This is something which we are quite keen on.

Kenelm and Michael Johnson of Peterstow have been growing fruit for Bulmers since 1934. They are medium sized growers with 40 acres of orchard under contract, plus their own home orchard and bush trees for the production of Broome Farm cider. Mike Johnson discussed the problems of contract growing.

Most of our fruit is contracted to Bulmers. We have bush orchards from over 20 years to four years old cropping now, plus an old orchard of standard trees. Not all our planting has been successful, we have problems with the land being dry in summer which restricts the tree growth, and in the early years were prone to attack by mildew, scab, canker and aphids. Forty acres is difficult to manage on my own, labour being very expensive, but hopefully as tonnage increases I will be able to employ more help. I do most of the jobs myself, such as mowing, spraying and pruning. Chris Fairs points me in the right direction with constructive advice, and this must be used in conjunction with a local knowledge of the land and weather conditions. I dislike using chemicals, but would find it difficult not to resort to them at times. Being organic sounds very appealing, but is too risky when it's your main 'bread earner' and have to rely on a regular crop. You can't afford to lose it to disease or pests, and you must also have a consistent quality to supply your contract.

My main concern is about ending contracts with growers. The new contracts are offered for 30 years from date of planting. These appear to be secure, however the original contract order which ran out after 20 years are on a new 10 year contract which will not be renewed. The first five years are all capital outlay and repaying the loan for the trees, before you start to make any sort of profit. The sheep farming side of the business was meant to keep us afloat but it no longer pays, the last of my sheep were sold last autumn - it's such a shame. Many of the trees require a 'good' prune - they are losing their leaders and becoming difficult to crop, but there doesn't seem to be enough hours in the day, energy or money to employ help. I restored the old orchards with some of the varieties that my grandad had planted in the 1930s - dual purpose varieties such as Newton Wonder, Annie Elizabeth and some cider varieties. The last orchard planted, of Harry Master's Jersey, I received a Millennium grant from the EEC. The family planted five Thorn perry trees as our own Millennium project, in a ring behind our house - one each for my wife, three children and myself. We each dug a hole and planted them on 1 January 2000. Thorn was my wife's maiden name so they have a family connection.

Jim Franklin, at the Cliffs, Little Hereford, has just 4.8 hectares of land under orchard contracted to Bulmers. Jim says:

The trees are harvested in five days in mid October. Bulmers pay a higher price for contracted growers than would be the case on the open market. Having a 'contract orchard' of approximately 15 hectares would give a family a living if it was under contract for 21 years.

To make ends meet, Jim Franklin started producing his own cider and perry:

The imbalance of managing the orchard and the fall in the price of fruit in the mid 1980s was the spur for us, it became clear that our small orchard was unprofitable. We planted an extra 1.8 hectares of Dabinett, Michelin, Kingston Black and Villbery, not always the best four varieties. At first we made cider with 60% Dabinett and 40% Michelin, which provides a reasonable 'country' cider, then we started to collect small amounts of fruit from local farmers, picked in old orchards that were uneconomic to cultivate and deliver to Hereford. The fruit in these orchards is just little pockets that we purchase weekly as we are ready to press. Normally the fruit is unsprayed, unattended and bi-annual so a cross section of orchards are needed to get the volume we require to make cider. Many orchards contain interesting varieties, but we cannot guarantee to pick the same fruit each year, because of the bi-annual nature of the trees. Really it is saving waste from the countryside.
    We closed down the cider and perry production in 2001 and I have gone back to apple growing, still under contract to Bulmers.

Cider maker Brian Jones of Roughmoor near Eardisley, Herefordshire, is also enthusiastic about using old varieties to make good cider.

> I saw that many of the old orchards in North Herefordshire, even those planted just after the Second World War, were coming to the end of their lives and I wanted to ensure that there were local varieties of fruit preserved for the future. During my 20 years of cider making I had managed to identify many local trees that produced good cider fruit. Although I could not identify the varieties, I had them grafted onto rootstock by Bulmers nurseries and have planted my own 'Museum' orchard near Pembridge.
>
> I feel strongly that fruit trees should always be bought and planted in the district they were reared - trees from nurseries and garden centres that have travelled from one county to the next will never seem to grow as well as a local tree.

Some of the trees in Brian's orchard are unique, all are difficult to find as the parent trees are scattered across the north of the county and some have since died or been grubbed up before proper identification was made. The orchard ensures that Brian, and others who are interested in making cider from rare varieties, or in preserving orchard fruits, have access to these true local varieties now and in the future.

In Gloucestershire, the Restoring our Landscape grant scheme launched by the County Council in 1992 resulted in the planting of over 3,000 fruit trees. In 2000 Gloucestershire County Council launched the Charles Martell Collection which provides access for the public to 77 local apple varieties, including dessert and cider apples. The collection is being established in a mother tree orchard, which will provide the public with rare varieties to help create new orchards or simply plant individual trees. It is named after Charles Martell, a farmer near Dymock on the Herefordshire/Gloucestershire border who is an expert in fruit identification. Charles now spends most of his spare time identifying apple and pear varieties to add to his collections. He has dedicated his farm to preserving local distinctiveness. Rare breed Gloucester cattle graze the orchard and produce milk for the Gloucester cheeses made on his farm and sold around the world. Along the way he has also collected many tales about the apples and their history from local people. His enthusiasm shines through during an afternoon walk around his collection.

> To find the old varieties you have to go and ask the old boys what is in their orchards. Many trees are named after the place from where they came, or after local people who developed the varieties.

They form a link to local history and tradition that is held by the old boys.

One such variety is the Hagloe Crab, named after Hagloe in south-west Gloucestershire. In the 17th century it was very famous and was still being used for cider until the 1950s. It was recognised and loved, then people lost contact with the tree and it was forgotten, it was not being pressed so the cider side of the heritage also goes. Ray Williams told me that it used to be at this farm in Tibberton, so I went there and there was one tree, bent over with a shoot coming out of the top. I collected the apples and came home, then looked in Hogg and Bull's book, *The Apple and Pear as Vintage Fruit*. There was a drawing of it so I knew that was it. Ray Williams also verified it. It was such a good cider variety in Gloucestershire, such good quality, people would exchange it barrel for barrel for 'spirituous liquor' but then it went out of favour. Why? Why did so many of these great varieties that people raved about suddenly become lost?

My theory is that it was a virus. Each time you graft a variety you pick up a bit more, I think that would have affected the flavour, but now like the restoration of old masters, you can restore these varieties by heat treatment. You have one graft which you put onto rootstock and place into a hot cabinet which provides high humidity and ideal growing conditions for the grafting. So it really grows fast, and while it is growing fast you snip off the top shoot and do the same again grafting onto a seedling. You do this several times and you get ahead of the virus, as it has not come up into the tip. Then you test it to confirm it is virus free. When you buy fruit trees today you get virus free stock, yet with the old varieties no-one has thought to do it, yet what you are getting is that variety when it was first started, so if you did it with Hagloe Crab and made cider you would be tasting cider as it was 300 years ago, isn't that fascinating?

Another local apple, the Chaxhill Red, is a cider apple from Chaxhill village on the River Severn. The fruit was sent by boat down the Severn to the miners in Wales and when it got there they would change the name to Welsh Cox's. It is a very pretty apple so that's how they sold them for eating. When they first named the apple in the late 1800s they got the oldest man on the Chaxhill estate to stand up and say a ditty after the harvest supper:

> We've had our fill of meat and bread,
> I name this apple Chaxhill Red.

The old man who helped me find this variety, who is now dead, remembered that old man. That's what I really like about the work, it's the contact with the past. When Ray Williams was researching for Long Ashton in the 1950s he met people who remembered other people coming round years ago in the 1900s and 1870s - now I'm going round and they remembered Ray Williams. Ray Williams had people remembering Dr. Durham and Dr. Durham would have had people remembering William Hogg. That is nice, that contact with the past.

A selection of five apples collected by Charles Martell has also been included in the National Fruit Collection at Brogdale in Kent (the Brogdale Horticultural Trust took over the running of the National Fruit Trials at Faversham, Kent, from the Ministry of Agriculture in 1990). Brogdale's collection contains the greatest variety of temperate fruit cultivars anywhere in the world and is open to the public. Brogdale also undertakes trials work for supermarkets, government departments and fruit growers in the cultivation, storage and development of fruit varieties. A cider festival is held there every September.

In the late 1980s Hereford and Worcester Council ran a fruit tree planting scheme adopted by both authorities, when the counties once more went their separate ways, as part of their commitment to local distinctiveness and landscape preservation. In Herefordshire, old orchards are an important landscape feature, a valuable wildlife habitat and the basis of many local traditions. Herefordshire Council's Parks & Countryside Service have developed several special initiatives to preserve this local distinctiveness, as James Bisset, Principal Countryside Officer, explains:

> Our Environmental Improvement Grant scheme can offer cash support towards the planting, gapping-up and restorative pruning of traditional standard orchards containing cider, dessert or culinary apples, perry pears or a mix with other traditional fruit types. Any landowner can apply with an application for five trees or more. With support from the Countryside Agency we can currently offer an improved rate of grant aid for projects situated within the parts of the Malvern Hills and Wye Valley Area of Outstanding Natural Beauty that are in Herefordshire, reflecting the extra importance placed on the local landscape character by this national designation. There is only a limited amount of money available each year and competition is fierce.

Over the last two years this grant scheme has supported the planting of over 1,000 new fruit trees and the pruning of 500 more. Hedgerows are often an important feature of orchards and fields and the scheme has additionally grant aided the management of some 10 kilometres of hedgerow. Other landscape enhancement projects have also received support. James Bisset adds:

Many people don't want to undertake the planting of a whole orchard or just want a traditional variety apple tree for their garden so we have developed the council's Fruit Tree Kit scheme. Each year we commission the budding of around 600 apple trees, all locally grown or raised varieties that we then sell to residents of the county. Because we order large quantities at wholesale prices we pass the saving directly on to the buyer. The scheme can only continue by being self-financing with the council contributing by donating the officer time to manage it. Working with the Marcher Apple Network we ensure all the varieties are 'special' and not normally available from retail nurseries. Although mainly dessert and culinary, many of the varieties we include were also traditionally used to make farmhouse cider. This scheme helps preserve these important old varieties for future generations to cherish and enjoy.

The Worcester Traditional Orchards Forum brings together a range of organisations in Worcestershire interested in orchard management and preservation. Worcestershire was once depicted as a 'forest of fruit trees' with many local varieties of cider apples, as well as culinary and dessert apples, plums, cherries and nuts. The forum is seeking to conserve traditional orchards in Worcestershire, associated fruit growing skills and provide a market for locally grown fruit. They can give advice on grant opportunities for planting new orchards or restoring existing ones and provide fruit tree kits, grown by Avonbank Nursery in Pershore, for planting in local gardens or for restoring orchards using local varieties. The forum is co-ordinated by the Countryside Projects Officer for Worcestershire County Council.

Peter Weeks, a farmer from Ombersley, near Worcester, writes in the summer 2001 issue of the forum's *Orchard News* about his perspectives of the last 50 years of orchard decline in Worcestershire:

> As children growing up in the early 1970s, my sister and I spent a lot of time in a couple of old orchards on our family farm. Our lack of respect for boundaries meant other orchards received attention too! Primarily, we were looking for birds' nests in the holes and cavities of these veteran trees. We clambered amongst the blossom-laden branches to see how the jackdaws, little owls, tits, tree sparrows, and stock doves were getting on with raising their families.
>
> Later in the year we would help our father pick fruit (no commercial use was made of the orchards any more) as he talked about different varieties and how long they should keep. Years later finds me working on the farm with my father. Nearby orchards have been grubbed out to enable easier fieldwork. Perhaps because our orchards were near the farmhouse they were just left alone. But

every time another tree blew down, it was a bit easier to mow the field for hay and no tears were shed.

Then one day I thought about how the landscape had changed in my relatively short life. How the spring blossom had gone, the nesting sites for the birds, the mistletoe, the fun and joy of picking fruit, and the stock lying in the trees' shade on a hot day. And each year the number of trees decreased.

For all these reasons I determined to try and recreate a traditional orchard. At the back of my mind was a slight commercial potential of old varieties, but that would be years away, and could not be relied on. It did, however, help persuade my father that I was not completely mad, and just recreating a hindrance to modern machinery use!

In December 1995 I planted my first trees, with grant aid from the county council. With a few more each year since, I now have 55 trees of 28 varieties. It has been a thrill to learn about old Worcestershire varieties, and then find out if I can obtain them. Sometimes is has involved customised grafting, and you can't rush that. I've learnt the hard way, but I can now make a cattle and sheep-proof guard, deter squirrels with spinning CDs on strings, and prune the trees into the tall standards I want. The first flowers are exciting, and the temptation to leave fruits on young trees, when they must be removed to let the tree grow, is great!

I know that the trees will not be old enough for me to be climbing them in my 80s, but some of them may be there for someone else to have that pleasure.

The Marcher Apple Network are in regular contact with the Trust at Brogdale and also get visits from other groups and individuals keen on preserving apples in their own areas. The Network has established three orchards of rare local varieties at Crickhowell, Westerhope, and Donnington Hall near Putley, containing almost 300 trees altogether, planted with the assistance of members, patrons and Herefordshire Council.

Bulmers has a collection of old, traditional varieties of cider apples at Hampton Bishop, near Hereford. This provides a gene bank for future orchards and preserves local varieties. Bud wood from this collection has assisted in the re-establishment of standard orchards by county councils, and through Stewardship Scheme grants in retaining the diversity of local landscapes. Chris Fairs at Bulmers recognises that standard orchards are a valuable landscape and beneficial environmental feature:

As very old trees decline and fall, they provide a rich habitat for wildlife and encourage beneficial predators. Because these trees are rarely, if ever, sprayed, the orchard supports a diversity of wildlife, as well as providing shelter for farm animals in winter, and grazing in summer. Some dead trees are usually replaced, keeping the orchard productive.

Bulmers encourages all its growers to undertake farm development surveys and make orchard conservation plans with the assistance of specialists, such as the Farming and Wildlife Advisory Group. These plans could include leaving, un-mown, the area around the edge of orchards, restoring and 'gapping up' hedgerows, replacing lost trees in traditional standard orchards, and the maintenance of natural ponds and wetlands, all of which provide additional wildlife habitat.

Organic orchards are one of the most difficult to manage. The Rules and Regulations of the Soil Association, which monitors use of the word 'organic' on any products that they approve, must be met and the agreement of the Soil Association to European Legislation on grazing of non-organic stock in organic orchards in 2001 has stalled Bulmers' new organic sponsorship scheme for standard orchards. Farmers are having to choose between keeping their grazing land or going organic, as it is likely the EU regulations that currently allow only 120 days per year grazing for non-organic livestock in an 'organic' orchard will reduce to a total ban by 2006. This means that as many traditional orchards are dual purpose, providing a valuable over-wintering resource for stock close to the farmhouse, fewer farmers are likely to take up the organic scheme.

Bulmers is trialling an organic bush orchard at their nursery in Staunton-on-Wye. The orchard has been planted in two sections, one half of which will be grown without any spray and the second half will use products approved by the Soil Association. The orchards contain a huge range of varieties chosen for their disease resistance, including local, French and Belgian fruit. In particular scab may be a problem in organic management, due to the recent wet summers. It will be five plus years before the results of the trials are known and organic bush orchards are developed to be commercially viable options for cider fruit growers.

Ivor and Susie Dunkerton, their two sons and Ivor's mother, moved to Herefordshire in 1980, to the farm at Hays Head, Luntley, near Pembridge:

> We wanted to make a living from the smallholding by keeping a few farm animals. We tried sheep, pigs, cows and goats - the goats we chose were difficult, not used to open paddocks they huddled in corners instead of grazing. To produce a real income we needed to create an end product. We started making cider to survive.

Ivor and Susie Dunkerton

We had memories of old fashioned cider and were pleased to find that ours turned out clear and golden. We started by pressing local varieties like Hope, Hangdown and Loyal Drain that we bought from a dairy farmer, but later he ploughed the lot up. We have always bought in fruit, some from as far away as Monmouth.

When Ivor's mother died we used our inheritance to buy the field next door - an additional 10 acres making 30 acres of land in all. This enabled us to start planting our own orchards of bush trees in 1989. We felt some responsibility to plant old varieties but found later that, in our ignorance, we had not provided trees to pollinate the flowers for fruit production. We could not find out what the pollinators should be - Ray Williams suggested Foxwhelp and Knotted Kernel which have worked for the Court Royal, but the Bloody Turks were full of blossom in 2002 but we only harvested one apple! Also Hays Head is Grade 2 land which is too rich for some varieties. We were cider makers not orchardists, but orchard management is rapidly becoming less of a mystery to us.

We decided finally to go organic when early connections were being made between cattle feed and BSE. The feed mill supplying mix for our suckler cows would not reveal the protein source. We had also developed distrust of conventional farming as we could see it was destroying the countryside - numbers of curlews, hares and trout in the streams were suffering. We were already buying

Shoveling apples from the washing tank onto the lift to the mill at Dunkertons

our cider fruit from orchards which had not been sprayed with any artificial pesticides, fungicides or fertilisers; with the co-operation of our suppliers these orchards were registered as organic with the Soil Association after a monitoring period of three years.

We will continue to concentrate on our own orcharding as the demand (and price offered) for organic fruit has risen. We always pay a premium for our fruit, £30 a ton more than for non-organic, but in the past have noted the risk of losing supplies to competitors. Our newest orchards require more careful work and planning to make sure we do not make the same mistakes as before. We will continue to manage them organically - we have seen this pay off with an increase in the population of mice, voles, little owls and tawny owls hunting in the orchards, as well as blue tits feeding off the winter moth caterpillars.

Keith Knight feels that the premium price being paid by consumers for organic cider may be broken by the involvement of the big cider makers:

I may be proved wrong, but the current trend for organic cider, like all other organic products, will result in the current premium price being driven down by overproduction and market competition.

In the *Hereford Times*, on 1 December 1894, Mr. Henry Weston gave one piece of advice to any farmer thinking of going into fruit production, which agrees with the experiences of Ivor Dunkerton and Keith Knight one hundred years later:

> If anyone is desirous of going in for fruit farming and cider making, let him first of all be well grounded with information, choose the best trees suitable to the district and then go into the work, not in a half hearted, happy-go-lucky style, in an earnest, practical and, above all, a thorough manner.

4 MASSIVE MILLS

At the start of the 20th century large cider works were established in the Hereford area. Fruit for the mills was purchased from local farmers and pressed in bulk, then fermented, blended and sent out in bottles to towns and cities via rail and road.

Godwins Jubilee Cider Works was established at Holmer on the north of Hereford by Henry Godwin in 1898. A retired builder and manufacturer of English Encaustic Tiles in partnership with William Hewitt, the Godwin and Hewitt tile works stood next door to the cider works. Mr. Godwin's third son, John Henry Godwin, joined his father in the cider business to help run the mill.

The cider mill was powered by steam and was capable of pressing 20 hogsheads a day. Fruit was milled using coarse scratters, then ground under rollers, a two stage process that crushed the fruit much finer and faster than the old stone mills, as well as increasing the yield of juice per ton of fruit. The resulting must dropped from a hopper onto a trolley running on rails, was wrapped in manilla cloths and lifted onto the press by three men. After the first pressing the cheese was returned to the trolley and sent along the rails for a second pressing on another press. Juice from the first pressing was reserved for premium ciders, juice from the second pressing for second quality.

The racked juice, with the addition of charcoal as a filter, was left in casks to 'keeve' for two or three days. During this time the juice would throw a thick brown head of suspended solids, comprising floating particles of fruit while wild yeasts would fall to the bottom of the cask. This French technique is little used today as it increases the potential of spoilage in the cider, due to delayed or stopped fermentation. Fermented juice was eventually racked into clean casks, first being filtered through simple linen jelly bags, two being used, one inside the other, to prevent contamination of the juice by the lees in the barrel and to further clarify it during maturation.

Interior of Godwin's works, Holmer, Hereford,
with a stone mill in the foreground

Interior of Godwin's works, Holmer, Hereford, showing a line of presses

Shoveling apples at William Evans' apple canals, c.1954. That the crop was a bumper one can be seen in the use of sacks of apples to build up the height of the wall. The lady concerned, Pat, was known both as being unusually strong and for her swearing

Each variety of fruit was pressed separately, fermented then blended. Cider apples used included Strawberry Norman, New Foxwhelp (an improved variety), Cherry Norman, Kingston Black, Handsome Norman, Skyrmes Kernel and Jovial Crab (listed in Godwins' records as growing in the Holmer district of Hereford), as well as Barland, Oldfields, Moorcroft and other perry fruits. A cooper was employed on site to make the casks, and bottling was done by hand with bottles closed with corks.

Godwins' underground cellar was kept at a constant temperature, using heating in the winter months and ventilation shafts, covered in canvas flats, in the summer. The cellar held 60,000 bottles of cider and perry in quarts, pints and splits ($^1/_3$ pint). Bottle necks were encapsulated with foil—gold for the choicest cider and perries, and silver for the second quality. Godwins' cider won medals at local agricultural shows and at the Royal Agricultural Show.

Henry Godwin died in 1910 at the grand old age of 82—it was said in his obituary that he 'knew how to make money better than he knew how to keep it'. His bust, by Mr. T.A. King, can be seen in Hereford Cider Museum, along with the hopper, cheese trolleys, racks and presses from

Henry Percival Bulmer, founder of HP Bulmer Ltd in 1887

Fred Bulmer

the cider works, later converted to electricity.

Similar ventures were started by Ridlers of Clehonger (1870); W.M. Evans, Widemarsh Common (1850); Henry Weston of Much Marcle (1880); not to forget Percy Bulmer of Credenhill (1887).

Percy Bulmer started making perry and cider from the fruit of Credenhill Glebe Orchard using a stone mill belonging to a neighbouring farmer, Mr. Richard Whiting at Magna Castra. Percy left Credenhill in 1888 to set up in Maylord Street, Hereford, where the Maylord Orchard shopping precinct now stands. In August 1889, after successfully making 4,000 gallons of cider which realised £157, Percy moved to Ryelands Street, named after the home of the owner, a Mr. Lane of Leominster. Percy bought a field of $10^1/_2$ acres on the east side of the street, where he built a single storey brick building with a tiled roof to house the mill. The construction was funded by a gift from Percy's father, Rev. Charles Bulmer of Credenhill, who raised the money against his life assurance policy. The finances did not run to a steam engine or hydraulic presses, so the two brothers (Fred had joined Percy in the company in 1898) turned the wheel of the mill and screwed the presses down by hand.

*The old cellars at Ryelands in which Pomagne sparkling cider
was produced in the champagne method*

Fermentation took place in 100 gallon casks and filtering was accomplished with linen jelly bags. No draught cider was sold, it was all presented for sale in bottles.

In 1894 Percy set out to visit Épernay in France and was shown how champagne was made by the Desmont family, who passed him onto M. Thomas, Head of the Municipal Wine Company in Rheims. Over the next few months Percy learnt from the French the most important techniques for making good cider and champagne, and brought back from his trip the latest books and literature on the subject. In 1906 the firm started making champagne cider, marketed as Cider De Luxe until 1916 when it was renamed Pomagne.

The cellars for the champagne cider were excavated from the gravel beds beneath the Ryelands mill. As there was a demand for quality building materials due to the expansion of the city, Percy and Fred managed to sell the gravel at a profit, enabling them to construct and equip the cellars at no cost to the firm.

The technique Percy brought back from France required the whole of the champagne process to be done by hand. Only the juice obtained at the first pressing was used to create Pomagne. The juice was sterilised with sulphur dioxide to kill off any natural wild yeasts that could impair the flavour and aroma of the cider, then specially selected yeasts and

The first cider mill built by Percy in Ryelands Street, Hereford.
Today it is part of the cider museum building

sugars were added. Once the first fermentation had finished, in March to May of the following year, the cider was filtered and blended to produce the right balance of alcohol, tannin, acidity and sugar—a skilled job as the cider would vary greatly in quality from year to year, depending on rainfall, soil fertility, sunshine and age of the trees bearing the fruit. The blended cider was then primed with sugar and more yeast to start off the second, effervescence forming fermentation. Once primed, the cider was immediately bottled and corked and staple (*agraph*, or stirrup clip) put over the cork to hold it firm during fermentation. (The top of the corks, pre-soaked in sterilised water, would take on the familiar mushroom shape.) Then the bottles were immediately lowered into the cool cellar in baskets as any delay, even as little as a few hours, could spoil the cider. The bottles were stacked horizontally in wooden laths, forming floor to ceiling walls of bottles, the cellar holding 30,000 bottles of fermenting champagne cider. Secondary fermentation took at least a year at a constant temperature of 68°F.

Once fermentation had stopped the bottles were stacked *en point*, upended on their corks, so that the sediment would fall into the necks of the bottles. Not all the sediment would be dislodged from the side of the bottle by this method, so after a while the bottles would be stacked in pupitres (wooden racks) which held the bottles cork down at an angle of 30°. The base of each bottle was marked with a white stroke of paint, then the bottle turned a quarter turn every day by hand until all the sediment had settled in a layer on the cork. The clarity of each bottle of cider was examined by candlelight and if completely free of sediment of haze the bottle was then restacked *en point*.

The next step was to remove the yeast and sediment from the neck of the bottle, a process known as disgorgement. The neck of the bottle was inserted two and a half inches into a tank of freezing brine, which froze the yeast deposit and imprisoned it between the cork and a plug of ice. The bottle was set upright and the cork was drawn in a special lever corkscrew cabinet, the pressure in the bottle shooting out the plug of ice and sediment like a bullet from a gun.

The bottles were then topped up with a small quantity of syrup and brought to full level with purified dry cider, recorked, dressed with foil and labelled, the neck band giving the year of vintage, usually two years previously. To prevent breakages each bottle was wrapped in tissue paper and given a straw jacket before being placed in a wooden box, a dozen bottles to each crate.

Pomagne cider continued to be made and marketed by Bulmers as Champagne cider until Bollinger took them to court in 1974 seeking to preserve the use of the word 'champagne'. Although Bulmers won the case, Bulmers stopped making Pomagne by the expensive champagne process in 1975, changing to a process of bulk fermentation in which a 6,000 gallon tank was used, secondary fermentation producing a similar, natural effervescence. (It was in 1979 that the then EEC ruled that 'Champagne' was a designated area of origin, preventing anyone outside the Champagne district describing products made by the 'method champenois' being called champagne. This ruling affected Showerings of Somerset and their popular brand of sparkling perry known as Babycham.)

Artificial carbonation of liquids was developed in the 19th century by the mineral water industry. From 1896 up to 1913 Bulmers had supplied their still Woodpecker brand draught cider in bulk to brewers in pipes of 110 gallons or hogsheads of 58 gallons for them to bottle themselves, under their own label—often the cider was bottled so badly that Bulmers did not want their company's name on the label. In 1919 Bulmers began to carbonate their cider themselves. The liquor was filtered and sweetened, then compressed carbon dioxide forced into it during bottling. In 1926 Bulmers started to sell Woodpecker cider in 2 quart flagons, sealed by internal screw stopper and rubber rings.

In 1911 Bulmers were granted the Royal Warrant, which they have proudly held ever since. Bulmers cider was becoming popular in the towns and cities, although the drinking of cider was declining in rural areas with the introduction of mechanical farm machinery. Bulmers cider was served at state occasions and a cider cup—Pomagne and brandy—introduced by the king, increased its popularity with the gentry and aristocracy. Several brewers started to set up cider factories of their own in south-west England so that they could make maximum profits out of the new fashion, which squeezed out many of the small farm based enterprises.

In the Severn Vale, a consortium of fruit farmers fought back against the shrinking market for cider fruit by setting up their own cider mill in buildings originally constructed for Arnold, Perrett and Company, brewers at Wickwar, Gloucestershire. The building is 60 feet high and set 60 feet into the ground, incorporating cellars carved from granite, and benefiting from naturally pure water which had been found on site during the work to construct the nearby mile long tunnel for the Bristol and Gloucester Railway. The new cider mill, established in 1924 and named the Wickwar Cider Company, purchased fruit from investing farms and others in the local district. The head cider maker was Herbert Watts, who had been the master cider maker at Long Ashton Research Station. The company benefited from arrangements with the Cheltenham Original Brewing Company, who had bought Arnold, Perrett and Company in 1924, to sell cider in all the brewery's tied houses, giving them a guaranteed market for their produce.

Back in Hereford, enforced changes were underway at Bulmers. In 1918, Fred and Percy's father, the Rev. Charles Bulmer, died and so had Percy's son, Geoffrey (1885-1918), who had been involved in the company in a role of employee welfare. Percy was also terminally ill. The brothers reluctantly decided to turn their business partnership into a limited company with £70,000 of £1 shares, with three-quarters of the shares being held by Percy and Fred as governing directors, and trusted employees and family holding the balance.

The papers were signed on 27 June 1918 and 18 months later Percy died leaving Fred the sole director. Percy's sons joined the company once they had finished college—Howard in 1919, becoming head of sales then chairman from 1941 to 1965 after Fred's death; Esmond in 1921, initially under Dr. Durham in the scientific department and then as works manager; and Edward who took on marketing and advertising, but was killed in 1944. Edward had three sons—James Esmond, chairman from 1982 to 2000; David, a director; and Jonathan, who did not join the company. Bertram Bulmer (1902-1988), son of Fred, became chairman after the retirement his cousin Howard. Bertram's son, Giles, also served as a director and retired in 1997.

By the end of 1919 Bulmers had 200 employees. During the General Strike in the summer of 1926, all the employees, now numbering 300, continued to work full time. Bulmers has never experienced serious unrest in the workforce, in fact there has always been a prevailing spirit of goodwill throughout the company. One employee, Arthur Evans, looking back on 48 years service (1921-1969) recalled Howard and Bertram Bulmer shovelling a record 125 tons of apples into the canal that carried apples to the mill on one shift. 'This was, and still is, the great thing about the family; they were always ready to get stuck into a job and to help out on the shop floor whenever necessary'.

One of the reasons for this remarkable record in employee relations may be due to the efforts of Fred Bulmer who initiated a great number of schemes to benefit his employees that still exist today. In his early years Fred was a radical and raged at the injustice of poverty, with little respect for most of the politicians he met. In 1898 he was treasurer of the local Liberal Association, though he did not, by any means, approve of all Liberals. He was on the county council as a Liberal from 1898 to 1904

Bulmers replaced most of their wooden vats in 1924, with most of the rest being decommissioned in 1999. Six are retained, however, and still used

and from 1907 to 1913, Alderman from 1913 to 1919 and on the city council from 1905 to 1911 (Mayor 1908-1909), and from 1925 to 1931 (Mayor 1925-1926). Despite his radical leanings, he was never drawn into supporting Labour. His political leanings caused some family tension for his brother Percy was a Conservative by temperament.

Fred's political interests lay in housing, education, health, law and order and women's rights. In 1901 dismayed at the slum conditions in the city, he founded Hereford Dwellings Limited and the first 12 cottages for the poor were built in Moor Street. This was followed in 1908 with the founding of Hereford Co-operative Housing and the building of the Garden City, modest family houses with gardens in the Penn Grove area of the City, the first real working class houses.

Fred's concern for the working man encouraged the creation of a pension fund for Bulmers' employees in 1898, with the investment of £100 per annum by the company. This was extended in 1920 with the modest sum of £1,000 being given to trustees to manage from which to provide for pensions and gratuities to men over 50 who had served the company well. Employees also benefited from Fred's bounty in other ways: a sports ground was established off the Brecon Road in 1935, and works socials and outings were arranged.

In 1931, in a speech reported in the local press, Fred described himself to his workers as 'A man who used to wear clogs and a shirt without any collar, and to sleep on the floor, who became a bloody capitalist ... There has to be capital, but the capitalist must be judged by the use he makes of it and the amount which he spends on himself'.

At the start of 1938 Fred retired from active participation in the company, though he remained chairman until five months before his death in 1941. He marked his retirement by donating 10,000 old £1 shares in Bulmers to set up a Welfare Trust to provide, in the first place, family allowances to each permanent employee of the firm who had more than two children and was in need of help. Provision was also made for non-contributory sickness benefit and for holidays with pay.

In 1938, Bulmers purchased the 17.5 acres of land on the Moorfields side of Whitecross Road. The expansion of the business between 1926 and 1935 meant that space was running out on the Ryelands Street site. In 1924 the company installed reinforced glass lined tanks of 100,000 gallons capacity (compared to 60,000 gallons for the largest wooden vat) to augment storage. Twenty-two were erected on the Ryelands site between 1929 and 1935. Fred wrote 'it looks to me as if the days of the picturesque oak vat are over', but it was not until 1999 that the majority of oak vats at Ryelands were decommissioned and six vats are still preserved and in use at the Moorfields site today.

Wartime shortages saw a canteen opened in 1941 to ensure every employee got one nutritious meal a day. Raw materials and bottles were in short supply, leading to the company launching a consumer awareness campaign—'you can replace the stopper, we can't'—to encourage the return of both flagons and stoppers for reuse. The company resorted to buying in bomb boxes to make into crates (the box planks were cut to size and the ends used as firewood) and sourcing secondhand bottles. There was also a shortage of cider fruit as imports were prohibited, so culinary and dessert fruit was used and the production of some brands was suspended. The war also delayed the construction of new storage facilities, which were not completed until after 1945.

Cedric Olive, who grew up next to the Ryelands mill, remembers the Moorfields site as a boy:

> Moorfields was a storage depot at first, with the wooden crates and flagon bottles stacked up in the area near the Canny Brook. As children we would play there, building dens out of the crates. One time we accidentally set fire to some crates, but we acted quickly to throw the burning crates into the Canny Brook to put out the fire before it spread, then ran! Inspector Bob James from Hereford Police

Unloading fruit from a cart
in front of Bulmers' newly erected cidermill on the left, c.1908

Station came round our houses that evening to caution us; he was very fair and it did not happen again.

In those days what is now the packaging plant and warehouse was an orchard, whilst the field at the top of Mostyn Street was used to store the spent pomace at pressing time - the tumps of pomace were piled as high as a house. The company cart horses used to pull the wagons round the factory were stabled at Moorfields where the mill is now; we used to get in at night and sit on the horses' backs. During the war years a dam was built at Moorfields on the Canny Brook for use in fire fighting, somehow the dam got full of fish and we used to go there to catch them. The Canny Brook now runs under the packaging hall in a culvert, not to be seen again until it leaves the factory boundary. Along Plough Lane the Almshouses and pub were there, but on the right, where the Bulmers' office block is now, was a gravel pit. On the left were allotments, all the way up to where Whitecross School is now (which was fields then).

When I started work at Ryeland Street in 1951 the mill was still producing cider like it had in the old days. The technical director then was Edward (Teddy) Ball (cousin to Howard Bulmer). He was followed by Raymond Cooke. Some of the factory workers were real characters - two of them, Tommy Evesham and Tom Kettle, still wore clogs and sack aprons at work. When they had to wear wellingtons for cleaning out the vats they didn't have any socks, so they wrapped rags round their feet.

Fruit arrived at the mills by horse and cart. At a steady pace it would have taken a farmer all day to deliver his apples to the mill and return home if he lived 5-10 miles outside the city. Bulmers had a farrier, Mac Trumper, who tended to the horses and when they were replaced by lorries and tractors he continued to make decorative ironwork at his home forge, but also worked for the Company in the orcharding department.

Fruit sacks were lent to the farmers by Bulmers in which to deliver their fruit and they were charged if the sacks were not returned. When the apples had been tipped into the silos the sacks would be put through a washer, like a giant washing machine, then hung on a rack which travelled through a tunnel dryer so that they would quickly dry for re-use. If it was wet and muddy at the mills, the workman's overalls were also sent through the sack washer and dryer.

Ryeland Street Mill had two press houses, the 'old' mill and the 'new' mill. The old mill worked on a cascade system on three levels, with the fruit being lifted to the top floor by a bucket elevator to be pulped using a Stowe mill which had a solid drum with blades attached, which forced the fruit up against the wall of the drum to shred it into a pulp to be processed through the two lower floors. The new mill used a tram system which ran on rails where you had building stations and pressing stations all on one level. The fruit was milled using a Stowe mill into a hopper above the building station, the cheese was built onto the tram then transferred to the pressing station. After the first pressing the cheese was stripped and the pomace transferred to the second building station and pressed for a second time, then taken out of the mill as waste pomace. The motive power was provided by electricity whilst the presses were operated by water driven hydraulics. The Stowe mills have a coarse pulp suitable for these types of presses. It was very hard working as the sisal hairs were very heavy when wet with juice and it took four men to strip them off the press, one on each corner. In the very early days of cider making on the farms, barley straw was used to build the cheeses, or cloths made from horsehair for stability and to drain the juice.

The Moorfields mill was built and commissioned in 1949/50. New Baron mills soon replaced the Stowe mills and are still in use today. These mills work on the same principal as a food liquidizer, giving a much finer pulp which suited the modern presses. The presses used here were of the most modern type then available: Rosedown, Bucher Guyer and Tange. The presses had a building position and a pressing position which rotated on a central

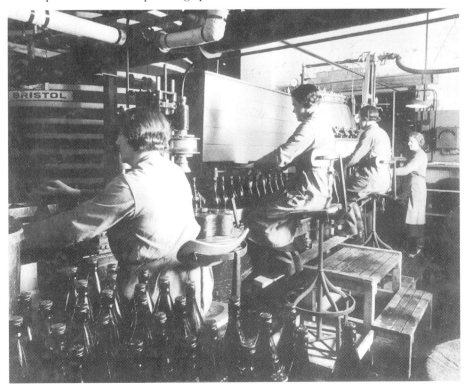

Filling flagons and fitting stoppers at Bulmers in the mid 1930s

column; when one cheese was being built the other was being pressed. There were 14 presses in the mill, eight on first time and six on second time, each press capable of pressing six tons per hour. Two men worked a press, building and unloading cheeses while another team would strip the spent pomace for transfer to the second time presses where a measured quantity of water would be mixed in with the pomace to help extract the remaining juice (50 litres per tonne), then build it into a fresh cheese ready for the second pressing. The press cloths used in the Moorfields mill were much lighter than the old sisal cloths, being woven from polyester. The empty cloths were hung over a portable structure like a clothes horse to be re-used. Working on the first time presses was not as physical as the second time as the pulp would spread itself being very wet and full of juice, but working on the second time was hard work and the men were soon tired out.

Tommy Snowzell, who was in charge of the filter room at the Ryeland Street factory for 40 years, was responsible for the preparation of all the finished ciders. He had a terrific memory and could remember all the recipes for the blends, never writing anything down. He could tell you what was in any of the 166 wooden vats, plus the glass-lined tanks holding up to 100,000 gallons each. You could ask Tommy anything about blend adjustments or recipes and you would get an instant answer (never wrong). Also he could instantly tell you how much was left in any of the vats. If you said to him there was 6 feet 1 inch in, say, vat Breinton, he'd come straight back with the answer 'that's 51,000 gallons', and he could do that in his head for all the vats. It was a unique talent that he had.

In the early days at Ryelands Street vast vats were emptied and cleaned mainly using a bucket and hose. Twenty-four hours before cleaning a fan with a long tube of fabric attached would be placed in the vat, to expel lethal carbon dioxide and blow in oxygen. Men cleaning the vat wore a harness in case of emergency and had a workmate observing them from the outside, sat on the top of the vat to make sure they were not overcome by carbon dioxide. If the vat was to be left empty the men did a process of 'mopping and matching', drying off the water on the floor to prevent warping of the vats and algae build up, using a sulphur match to fill the vat with sulphur dioxide gas as a preservative before closing up the lid and so keep the vat sweet and free of yeast infections.

The Moorfield site started to be fully developed just after the end of the war. It was not possible to get permission to construct a new building due to wartime shortages, so instead the company bought a redundant seaplane hangar from Greenock on the Clyde, had it dismantled and 'shipped' to Hereford, then re-erected lengthwise between Plough Lane and Mostyn Street. The hangar was re-roofed with aluminium rather than the existing steel as the girders were not strong enough to take the weight of insulation materials and steel together. The insulation was needed to stop bottles of cider from freezing in the winter or overheating in the summer.

Once the government had lifted the sanctions against new buildings, work began on constructing a new mill and press house on the Moorfields site, completed by the end of 1958. Accompanying this development was the installation of larger and more modern apple silos. One silo was designed to receive apples from freight trains. Apples were shipped from Normandy to Newport, Swansea and Weymouth, then transferred into tipper trucks normally used for coke. The trucks had to be thoroughly cleaned to ensure no coke remained which would mix with the apples and spoil the fruit on pressing. If tipper trucks were not available at the port, apples had to be shovelled out by hand into the silos, an expensive and exhausting job for the mill team.

The Moorfield silos were trough shaped, divided into three compartments and built into the ground to enable faster unloading of fruit from vehicles. To shorten the seasonal queues of lorries and carts on Whitecross Road and Ryelands Street a permit system was introduced for growers, speeding up the reception of apples at both Ryelands Street and Moorfields mills. (The original Ryelands Street mill remained in use till the early 1960s.) When the fruit in the silos was needed in the mill, water flumes on the sides of the troughs washed it through underground canals to one of two fruit elevators, which lifted the apples into the mill.

Once the fruit was in the mill a grader would remove any rubbish and rotten fruit. Some would fall through the holes in the fruit transporter and the occasional rotten fruit would be removed by hand. The fruit was then crushed in the Baron Mills, designed and built by an engineer, Mr. Baron of Gloucester. As fruit drops into the mill it is pushed off to the sides by centrifugal force where it is grated by blades on the inside of the drum, then spun out to be collected in the pulp hoppers. The pulp is much finer then that produced on a farmyard scratter mill and, therefore, releases more juice. Air operated valves in the cellars distribute the pulp to the hoppers above the presses. Three probes were hung in each hopper, one at the bottom, one half way up and one at full level, which lit corresponding lamps on the control board upstairs. As each hopper filled the lights would glow, and when three lamps were lit it was full. A team of men upstairs operated the air valves manually, opening and closing them to deliver the pulp to the presses—they had to be quick or the men on the press got covered in apple pulp.

The men on the presses could control the dropping of the pulp onto the hair cloths on the press with a button or lever on the doser. To fill a hair the doser was primed with pulp from the hopper then flipped over to drop the pulp onto the press, then the cloth was folded to enclose the pulp. Each cheese used 23 hairs ($1^{1}/_{2}$ tons of apples) extracting some 80% of the residual juice. Moorfields mill had 14 presses, eight first presses and six second presses. At first the mill had Swiss presses with three beds, allowing one cheese to be pressed whilst another was being built and another dismantled. The press beds revolved around a central post, but the company found that the rams on the press snapped like carrots under the strain, so they were replaced with the tried and tested two-bed presses. It took four men to operate one of these presses: two emptiers and two fillers. The new mill at Moorfields was able to process 1,000 tons of apples a day, producing 175,000 gallons of apple juice, with mill workers on three shifts working round the clock.

In 1954 the first steel storage tank was erected at Moorfields. The tank was round, like a small gasometer, 45 feet high and 56 feet in diameter, lined with an acid resistant material, capable of holding 550,000 gallons and named Jupiter. By 1960 there were seven tanks, each named after a planet: Jupiter, Mars, Venus, Saturn, Mercury, Pluto and Neptune. In 1969 the company built an eighth tank, called Apollo XI after the space rocket which landed man on the moon, which was lined with epoxy resin.

Looking out from the 'Strongbow' tank over the planet tanks at Bulmers

This lining was a great success and is now used on all the vats, including the ninth vat, Taurus, named after a constellation. In 1975, Strongbow, with a capacity of 1.6 million gallons, was added to the collection of planet tanks—and also entered the *Guiness Book of Records* as the largest alcohol container in the world.

Further development on the site required delicate negotiations with the city council. The site had originally been zoned for residential use and there was a section of the council, often a majority, that were not agreeable to the re-zoning of the area for industrial use. Nevertheless, in 1952 Bulmers bought Cannon Moor Farm, bringing their total land-holding on the Moorfields site up to about 24 acres. Despite providing trees beside Plough Lane to replace under-used allotments, and new footpaths and footbridges at the company's expense, continuing obstruction from the city council made Bertram Bulmer request a meeting with the councils of Leominster and Ross to discuss company expansion. The prospect of Hereford losing jobs and wealth changed the minds of the opposing councillors and the city council signed an agreement with the company in 1957, agreeing to re-zone the area for industrial use, except for the existing homes in Mostyn Street.

In 1948 Bulmers had bought 2.4 acres of land from P. Bolt and Son, between the warehouse hangar and the tyre works on Whitecross Road. The increase in car ownership by employees led to this area being developed as a car park in 1962. In 1959 the company acquired Red Barn Farm, extending the Moorfields site to a total of 65 acres.

The next major building required was a new bottling hall. The company had acquired Godwins Cider in 1948, along with the premium perry brand, Golden Godwin, which they wished to market in baby sized bottles as a rival to Showerings' Babycham. The new bottling hall was erected at the end of Plough Lane in 1957 and by 1964 most of the bottling operations had been transferred there from Ryelands Street.

In 1945 the Cheltenham Brewery, which sold cider made by the Gloucestershire Cider Company (the successor name to the Wickwar Cider Company) through its tied houses, merged with the Hereford and Tredegar Brewery Ltd to become the Cheltenham and Hereford Brewery. In 1958 a merger with Stroud Brewery Company resulted in a change of name to West Country Brewing Holdings Ltd. with 1,275 tied houses. In 1963, West Country Brewery was taken over by Whitbreads. This was a nervous time for Bulmers as it appeared that the Gloucestershire Cider Company would have the majority market share through its increased number of outlets in the Whitbreads' chain. However, Whitbreads agreed to sell the Gloucestershire Cider Company to Bulmers in 1958, so giving Bulmers the equivalent opportunity.

Terry Watts had joined the Gloucestershire Cider Company in 1949, when he was 16. He was the third generation of Watts to work at the company and his father, Reginald Watts, was cider maker, general manager and company director. The firm's G.L. brand was well established locally and in the pubs of the Cheltenham Brewing Company. The company's reputation was of making good, but strong ciders, local slang naming them Stun 'em and Tanglefoot. One of Terry's first jobs was sorting out complaints and letters from customers. Four workmen from Newent wrote to complain that the cider was too strong. They liked to go to the pub at lunchtime where each bought a round of cider, making four pints each. However, they found that four pints of G.L. was too much to be able to work properly in the afternoon, and asked for the strength to be reduced so they could continue buying their rounds. G.L. still remains on the Bulmers portfolio, though it is now known locally as 'Guaranteed Legover'.

When Bulmers took over the Gloucestershire Cider Company, it became clear that they did not wish for the Wickwar company to be run by the Watts family, but rather to split them up across the Bulmers' interests. Bertram Bulmer indicated that he had a job for Terry in Hereford, but that if he had 'other plans I will understand'. It was clear from Bertram's voice that it was 'move to Hereford or get another job', so Terry moved in 1959 to become bottling foreman at the expanding factory. Eventually the Wickwar cider factory was sold off and the cellars are now used by Howells of Bristol as a Bond Room for the maturing of vintage spirits for private clients, including Hereford Cider Museum's King Offa Cider Brandy. Terry Watts graduated to the position of Production Director of Bulmers in 1977, and eventually retired in 1996.

The bottling operation at Ryelands Street in 1959 was still mostly manual. 150 women worked there, turning, disgorging, decorating and packing Pomagne cider—even the gold foil capsules were smoothed by hand. The bottles used were mainly second hand champagne bottles and were a job to clean—women scraped off the labels and cleaned the inside of the bottles with long brushes. The gold foil was dreadful to get off. Flagons and cork stoppers were also reused for Woodpecker Cider—the stoppers were expensive to replace at 1d. each. They were made of ebonite and before sterilization took place, the rubber sealing rings had to be visually checked and in many cases replaced. In the early days at Ryelands Street the filling of flagons was done by hand as was the insertion of the cork stopper. The stopper was hand tightened then given an extra twist with a flexible drive that tightened it into the neck. At Moorfields, the stoppers were introduced to the bottle mechanically and tightened. The two lines at Moorfields could package 800 dozen flagons per hour of Woodpecker and 2,000 dozen per hour baby bottles of Golden Godwin sparkling perry. Cider was pumped to the bottling plant from the Ryelands Street site along bitumen lined pipes.

A kegging plant was installed at Moorfields in 1975. The kegging line was first used for Strongbow, then later for all Bulmers draught ciders, except Bulmers traditional which was filled at Ryelands Street into wooden casks or polycasks and was cask-conditioned with an injection of pure culture yeast. From 1932, new hand made casks had been produced at the Coopers shop on the Ryelands Street site for the Company's use. Since 1956 only repairing had been done, mainly on casks below 30 gallons. Yet when the kegging line started R.B. Carpenter and his staff were still repairing 9,000 casks a year.

During pressing time up to 130 casual staff would be brought into the mills at Ryelands and Moorfields. There was a small nucleus of local casuals who would return year after year to work at the mill, but the majority were recruited from the agriculturally depressed areas of Roscommon and County Cork, some of the men coming back every season for up to 16 years. Later on the company recruited from the South Wales mining villages, whose workers were being laid off by the Coal Board. Valley workers were accustomed to being militant and had $1^1/_2$ hours each on the bus (laid on by the company) to work up their grievances. They didn't get on too well with the Irish workers either! One of these disputes ended up in a one hour strike, the only industrial dispute ever suffered at Bulmers. However, as the men were paid by how many gallons of juice were produced on their press, they worked extra hard the rest of the day, which resulted in record volumes on the presses!

The casual workers from abroad would be put up in staff accommodation at Redhill Hostel, Bullingham Hostel and 22 Whitecross Road, a large family house attached to the Moorfields site, set in its own gardens, down the lane between Moorfields and 24 Whitecross Road. They were also fed on-shift by the company in the mess room. Cedric Olive remembers:

> Goodness, could they eat! They would really feed themselves up when they were here, as if they never got fed at home, and also enjoyed drinking bottles of Hereford milk with their meals. Saturday nights the men would all go into town drinking, often the Sunday morning shift would be down to half the men, the rest would trickle in by 10.30 am, looking dreadful! Once or twice I had to go to get an extra man from Whitecross Road to make up a team. The mess in the dormitory was unbelievable, groaning men and half eaten take-aways everywhere - not a pretty sight.

The evening shifts fared little better, often the men would be drinking at the Horse and Groom in Eign Street, next to the Moorfields mill before their shift. They would arrive drunk and the foreman would have to keep them out.

There was one Irishman who would never work the Saturday shift. I found out why after a bit, he was something of an entrepreneur. He would be down the local jumble sales buying clothes for pennies, that he would pack up and post back to Ireland, where they would be washed and pressed and sold on for pounds. A 20p suit in Hereford would fetch him £1-£2 in Ireland.

Margaret Thompson joined Bulmers in 1966 to work in the wages office, which was then at Ryelands Street:

At 9 a.m. and 2 p.m. a line was drawn in the book, if your name appeared under it you would be called to see the supervisor to explain why you were late.

The working day was from 9 a.m. to 5.30 p.m. sharp, it was quite strict. You would work at your desk until 5.25 p.m. when you could start clearing up and putting the files away safe for the night. At 10 a.m. and 3 p.m. you heard the tea trolley rattling out of the canteen doors, with its two urns on top. You got a ten minute break and could choose between tea and Cidona, a non-alcoholic drink made by Bulmers from apple juice sweetened with sugar and saccharine and produced from 1955 as a Temperance drink to rival Cydrax, Pomol and Pomril produced by other cider makers. The wages staff were quite privileged as we seemed to be the only employees who met both the office staff and the workforce. This made us quite popular with both. Everyone who worked for the firm, from the man sweeping the mill floor to the directors, were understood to be essential cogs in the wheel and given credit for the success of the Company.

I can still remember several of the workers that used to come over from Ireland to help with the cider pressing. The work here was probably the only proper job the Irish workers had all year. They would come for their wages after the first week, take a little spending money out of the packet and ask us to save the rest for when they went home. We would keep it safe for them until the last week and give it back to them. They were always generous and wanted to give you a little for saving it for them, of course we never accepted - it must have seemed to them like an absolute fortune they were taking home to their families. Later on, after Bloody Sunday made it insensitive to employ Irish workers, men were bussed in from the Welsh valleys. They were not as conscientious as the Irish, when they got their pay packets on a Thursday afternoon at 4.45 p.m., they would be off down the pub to drink it. Often there would be no workers on the Friday morning shift until they had run out of money and sobered up. Having spent all their wages they would be back for a sub on their next week's pay packet.

During busy times the office staff were offered the opportunity of work on the evening shift, between 5.30 p.m. and 9.30 p.m. The workers on this shift were mostly women who came to work after their husbands' arrived home, to earn extra money for their families. The tannoy would go and announce that the office staff would be welcome to join the shift that evening as factory extras. Only the wages office seemed keen to go on the factory floor, perhaps because we were already familiar with the staff.

We were always playing pranks while working on the packing lines. One evening when we were asked to make cardboard boxes, we spent most of the time chatting and messing around. Half an hour before shift end, I made up a few boxes and stacked them up around the perimeter of the work area. The supervisor came by and complimented us on our hard work - it appeared we had filled the bay with boxes, but the middle was empty!

Most of those working at the mills throughout the year could not afford to buy alcohol, so their drinking was done at work. Cedric remembers:

On a cold, frosty morning we would get some raw Pomagne in a stainless steel bucket and plunge it into a barrel of hot water. After a couple of cups of this warm brew you were glowing for the rest of the day.

The wooden vats at Ryelands Street all had an airlock on the top with a small quantity of cider in the tube. The men would go up there and suck the cider straight out of the vat through the airlock, we used to call it 'being on the monkey'. Some boys would be up to this as early as 10 a.m. in the morning.

Fred Bennett, head cider maker at Ryelands Mill in the 1940s, had a bad smoker's cough. You could always tell where he was in the mill by listening for his coughing. The men used to use this to their advantage, so they could get out of the way before he caught them on the monkey. One afternoon, some outside contractors were working in the mill on the electrics. They should not have been in the vat house, but had got up on the top of the vats for a drink from the airlocks. Fred went into the vat house to check on a brew for a blend, coughing away as usual, the electrical contractors were nowhere to be seen, they had dropped over the sides of the vats - holding on by their fingers, 27 feet up! When Fred left they pulled themselves up again and got back to work.

The men on the cask washer line used to drain the dregs into a bucket before washing the casks and then drink the dregs from the bucket during the day. Rum barrels that came in for cleaning were particularly prized, the rum would be drained and mixed with the cider for a potent brew.

In 1960 Bulmers took over the goodwill of W.M. Evans and Co, Widemarsh Common, from the brewers Webbs of Aberbeeg. Evans had been cider makers in Hereford since 1850 when its premises were in Widemarsh Street. In 1884 the company was sold to Mr. W.F. Chave who moved the operation to the larger Widemarsh Common site. Evans remained in the Chave family until 1946 when it was sold to Webbs.

Evans' popular brand of cider was Golden Pippin and the company had, until 1925, a mill in Devon as well as Hereford. It had also acquired the interests of cider makers Ridlers of Clehonger before being sold to Webbs. The purchase of the goodwill in the company gave Bulmers an extra 558,000 gallons of cider storage in tanks lined with ebon—the trade name for the material used to line concrete tanks—at the Widemarsh vat cellar, as well as the right to sell Bulmer brands in all of the Webbs' licensed premises.

The major commercial interest of Bulmers in W.M. Evans was the production of pectin, used for setting jams and jellies and in the production of confectionery, from pomace. Since 1917 Evans had been pioneers of pectin production in the U.K. and had one of the largest pectin plants in Europe, capable of producing 25,000 tons of liquid pectin a year by 1960. Until 1938 Bulmers had sold their pomace to Evans for reprocessing, but then the company found that the pomace could be sold in Germany for twice as much, so Bertram Bulmer set up an experimental pectin production site at the Ryelands Mill. The process was very rudimentary, simply soaking the pomace in barrels and stirring it by hand to release the pectin. During the Second World War Bulmers got a permit from the government to construct a pectin plant, due to the rising cost of Canadian pectin imports. When Bulmers took over Evans it transferred the pectin operation to the Ryelands Street site. In 1962 a new stainless steel evaporator was installed at Ryelands Street, capable of concentrating one million gallons of juice in the pressing season and used for pectin production during the rest of the year. In addition to apples, the skins of citrus fruit (limes and lemons) were imported from Mexico and Spain to increase the output of pectin. In 1967 a new citrus pectin plant was installed on the Ryelands site, capable of producing 400 tons of powdered pectin per year. Bulmers now accounted for one seventh of the world production of pectin, which provided a useful contribution to Bulmers' pre-tax profits.

A couple of years earlier had witnessed a change in management style at the company. In 1965, for the first time, a director was recruited from outside the family circle. Peter Prior joined Bulmers as financial director, becoming managing director in 1966 when Bertram Bulmer succeeded Howard Bulmer as chairman. In the same year the company was restructured into a group consisting of HP Bulmer Ltd, two property companies, the Gloucestershire Cider Company, a wine and spirit agency—Findlater Mackie and Todd, plus a citrus peel processing plant in Ghana.

In August 1967, Peter Prior abolished clocking in, saying that Bulmers 'believe that everyone employed by the Company is equally important to the success of the operation and should be accorded the same measure of trust'. In 1968 the Woodpecker Social Club was established in response to a survey of employees and merged with the existing Sports and Social Club off the Brecon Road. The Woodpecker Club opened on the corner of Ryelands Street and Whitecross Road on 4 July 1969 with 600 members; by 1971 there were 900, all employees of the firm.

The company was floated on the London Stock Exchange on 7 December 1970, with the family retaining 65% of the shares. Employees were offered first chance to purchase up to 10% of the shares on offer, and 200 took up the opportunity. Bertram Bulmer retired as chairman in 1973 to be followed as chairman by Peter Prior until 1982.

By 1975 company employees in production and distribution were represented by the Transport and General Workers Union. In 1978 a new office block was erected at Plough Lane to house 300 administrative staff, plus a canteen seating 250. Bulmers had 60% of the UK cider market and were the second largest pectin producers in the world. The company also embarked on an ambitious plan to modernise and refit the Moorfields cider mills and production plant, concentrating its investment in cider production.

In 1988 Bulmers purchased Symonds from brewers Greenall Whitley. Symonds was one of Herefordshire's longest established cider firms, having been founded in 1727 by the Symonds family, and it was in family ownership until sold to Greenall Whitley in 1984. Symonds' flagship brand was Scrumpy Jack, a strong Herefordshire style cider originated by Bill Symonds. Far from being a traditional cider mill, by 1984 the Stoke Lacy works milled and fermented cider using the latest modern technology, including stainless steel vats, advanced filtration and specially cultured yeast. The Scrumpy Jack brand was adopted as a premium cider brand in the Bulmer portfolio of drinks. Greenall Whitley's head cider maker was Jeff Williams. Jeff had joined Long Ashton Research Station in 1955 as a trainee cider maker, becoming acknowledged by the industry as an expert on cider making and cider fruit. He joined Symonds in 1984 and served as head cider maker at Stoke Lacy until his death in 1996, at the age of 56. Shortly afterwards Bulmers discontinued the cask conditioned version of Scrumpy Jack and concentrated production on the carbonated versions in can, keg, bottle and PET.

By 1993 dried pomace from the Moorfields mills accounted for just 10% of the raw materials needed by the pectin plant at Ryelands. A second pectin plant had been acquired in Brazil which produced pectin from local orange peel. As pectin production seemed to be becoming peripheral to the core cider business, Bulmers sold its interests in both pectin plants to a private company—Citrus Colloids Ltd, with many of the Bulmers staff continuing their service with C.C.L.

In 1998 the Citrus Colloids business at Ryelands Street was sold to an international pectin company, Hercules Incorporated of Delaware, U.S.A., the biggest pectin producer in the world. The Ryelands Street pectin plant was closed down by the new owners as unviable due to its high production and transport costs—100 local people lost their jobs, many of whom had been long serving Bulmers' employees. Hercules worked alongside Bulmers to find alternative employment, or offer retirement packages, for the redundant workers, and to enable the demolition of the factory, which stood on land 50%, owned by Bulmers and 50% by Hercules.

Pomace was still dried at the Moorfields site and fresh pomace was also sold at £5 a ton (collected) to local farmers as a supplementary feed for cattle. Pomace complements other feeds and provides a low cost basic feed with good levels of protein, fibre and energy. It is only available during November and December, but can be made into silage with the addition of chopped maize as a supplementary feed for use right through the winter.

In 1996 one of the pomace dryers at Moorfields exploded. Cedric Olive was mill manager at the time.

> You need to be careful when you start up the dryers at the start of the season or after a shutdown, as the chimneys get full of soot, which is cleaned out each time, but there always seems to be a lot left in a corner that can cause problems if you are not careful. As soon as the new parts were fitted the engineers fired up the dryer. It was a calm day with a fine rain falling, but there was a light breeze blowing up around the chimneys that could not be felt or seen in the rain, as it was blowing around 60 feet above the ground. As soon as the induction fan kicked in a ton of soot shot up the chimney and was distributed by the breeze all over Greenland Road. Everything in the street was covered with soot dust.

As mill manager I went over immediately to apologise on behalf of the Company and offer to clean up the street at our cost. One woman was very distressed, she had been in the road as the accident happened and was covered head to toe in black dust. I reassured her that we would take care of the mess, and her cleaning bill. The dust was running down her face and it was difficult not to laugh for she was so upset. 'That's all right for me' she said, 'but what about my dog?' The little fellow was called to present himself for inspection, he was as black as his mistress, but I couldn't help laughing when I heard she called him Sooty!

A promotional picture for White Lightning cider

In 1996 Bulmers bought Inch's Cider in Devon for its white cider brand, White Lightning, a strong (7.5%) clear, slightly appley, sparkling cider which was popular with supermarket consumers. Production of Inch's ciders in Devon was stopped in 1998, though Bulmers has retained the company's orchards and contract growers. This also meant the loss of Inch's cask conditioned ciders, which did not have the volume required for economic production at Hereford. White Lightning has been retained as a Bulmers' brand.

The development of the Moorfields site, begun in 1958, took until 1999 to complete. Computer run, temperature controlled conical fermenters were installed in 1994, followed by new storage vessels, canning and bottling lines, improved fruit handling, a new technical centre hosting the company's laboratory (both for orcharding and cider production), new product development and innovation centres, in all costing the company £35 million over six years. The head office of the company in Plough Lane also received a facelift. Once the Moorfields site upgrading was completed the company stopped fermenting cider at Symonds in Stoke Lacy and storing cider at the vats in Ryelands Street.

Cedric Olive says of the wooden vats:

It was a shame to see them taken out of Ryelands Street mill before it was demolished. They were unique but had to go. It's progress I suppose. They would have been very expensive and difficult to maintain as they had to be kept filled with liquid to preserve the wood and joints. You could have made a house of some them, if you had the money, as they were 27 feet high and 12 feet in diameter, held together by wooden pegs with brass bolts holding the head-board in place. Some of the vats were 100 years old, others had been bought in the 1930s to increase capacity.

The wood was 2 inch thick seasoned oak, dressed with linseed oil on the outside and discoloured by the cider inside. A lot of people came to look at the vats, but even so 600 tons of timber is a big investment, and the buyer had to provide the labour to dismantle the vats as well. A chap in north Wales bought all of the wood for making oak doors and floors. I had a piece of the vats planed up and polished and it came up a lovely patina. It was quite a challenge dismantling the vats, the workmen couldn't get scaf-folding up inside the vat house as there was no headroom between the top of the vat and the cellar ceiling. Instead a door was cut in the side of the vats and they were dismantled from inside out.

In 2002 Bulmers pressed a record crop of fruit influenced by new bush orchards coming into full yield, beating the previous record by a staggering 13,400 tonnes. The mill also set a new record, pressing 1,200 tons of fruit in 24 hours. In the new plant, mud that is washed off is recov-ered and replaced onto the orchards to stop erosion of orchard soil. Sticks and leaves are treated as agricultural waste and removed by a waste contractor, though in future the company hope to be able to compost them on company land. The fruit is washed a second time before being sent to the mills located under the fruit washers and from which a pulp falls into vats.

The pulp is pumped along stainless steel tubes to the presses. The press house is noisy due to the large machinery, and safety equipment and ear defenders must be worn. The presses are cleaned regularly with power washer jets.

The juice is sent to the evaporators for concentrating to one sixth of its original volume, the evaporators processing approximately 10 million hectolitres of juice a week—hence the clouds of steam often seen over the site. Spent pomace is sold for use as animal feed.

Fermentation of juice is controlled automatically from the comput-erised fermentation control centre. Information is sent back from the tanks via sensors to the computer. Selecting juice to be fermented, pitching yeast, monitoring fermentation, pumping to conditioning tanks and cleaning of tanks and pipes is all done remotely from the control centre. The fermentation plant has nine conical stainless steel fermenters, each holding 7,000 hectolitres. Concentrate is pumped over from the storage tank, pasteurised and sterile water added to it, along with liquid glucose and yeast that has been cultured in Bulmers' labs.

Carbon dioxide given off during fermentation is recovered for adding to sparkling ciders. Alcohol is extracted from the spent yeast to blend back into finished cider and the almost alcohol free yeast goes to feed pigs.

The cider is then conditioned, the length of time depending upon the brand being made. Malo-lactic fermentation is avoided. Also known as secondary fermentation, this fermentation is a bio-chemical reaction where various bacteria present in the cider convert malic acid into lactic acid and carbon dioxide. No alcohol is produced during this fermentation. Because lactic acid is less acidic than malic acid, ciders that undergo this process become softer and smoother with added complexity.

The conditioned cider is then pumped into holding tanks where it is analysed and the results entered into a computer to work out the right mix of ingredients required—sugar, saccharine, lactic and malic acid, caramel—to create a specific brand. Up to three different ciders may be used to create a blend. On its way to packaging the cider is pasteurised and tested by the labs. There is also a panel of experienced tasters who taste the ciders every week, giving the process a personal touch at the very end.

Looking out from the 'Strongbow' tank over the Bulmers site and that of Sun Valley poultry in Hereford

Rather than have warehouses full of cider, Bulmers now ferment and package on demand. The canning line processes 1,000 cans a minute, whilst the bottling line uses both glass bottles with crown caps, brought in by lorry, and PET bottles blown on site. PET, Polyethylene Terephthalate, is a plastic resin and a form of polyester that makes strong, transparent, lightweight, inexpensive containers, which can be recycled into a wide range of plastic products. PETs come into the factory as preforms—little pieces of plastic like test tubes. The preforms are heated, then air is blown into them to expand the plastic into a mould that gives shape to the bottle; over 300,000 bottles a day can be blown on site. The sterile bottles look like bubbles as they pass, upside down, onto the bottling lines. Screw tops are fixed to the bottles and labels automatically pasted on, then the bottles are shrink wrapped and sent to the warehouse.

Bulmers have a fleet of their own lorries, but also use contractors for cross country distribution from the Hereford warehouse. Companies like Tesco, Asda and wholesalers send their own lorries to pick up stock. The acquisition of The Beer Seller, a wholesale drinks distribution company in 2000, gave Bulmers a direct line into delivering its brands to pubs and clubs across the U.K.

Esmond Bulmer, grandson of Percy Bulmer, retired as chairman on 7 September 2000, but remained a non-executive director on the Board. In the company's Annual Report for 1999-2000 he was upbeat about the achievements of Bulmers:

> In the forty years I have been with the business, I have seen the Company grow from a small family business into a public company which is a leader in its field. Long drinks markets around the world are characterised by fierce competition and significant change, none more so in the U.K. These changes create opportunities for companies (like Bulmers) with a proven track record in brand building. The apple is the core of our business, our investment in orcharding continues and we are now looking at our future production needs on a global basis. Of one thing I am certain and that is, that environmental changes, actual and perceived, will increasingly concern politicians. We are giving a great deal of thought as to how best to ensure that we understand the issues surrounding sustainability and to respond appropriately wherever we operate. I believe that proper concern for those who work in the Company is the essential source of the motivation, which alone delivers long term success. We have many long serving employees who have given the Company exceptional service, and an increasing number of talented recruits in key areas whose contribution is another reason for my confidence in the future. At no time in the past have I felt as confident as I do today in the future of the Company and its ability to take advantage of the exciting opportunities springing up around us.

The 2001 Annual Report shows that Bulmers have 60% of the U.K. cider market, with Strongbow being the tenth most popular long drink in the country and the main alternative to beer. (It had risen to eighth position by the summer of 2002, and fifth by that December.) Export business is also flourishing, especially in southern Europe, with 46 countries around the world selling Strongbow. Bulmers was placed second in the *Sunday Times* list of the 50 best companies to work for in 2001.

In September 2002, Bulmers' share price collapsed due to an over ambitious plan to create a global market for the company's ciders. This came as a shock to both shareholders and to Hereford, as for over a century the family business has been one of the mainstays of the local economy. The share price which began at 13s. 6d in 1970, peaked at £6.25 in the mid '90s, then dropped as low as 75p as the company announced a record five profit warnings during 2002, with no dividends expected to be paid for a couple of years until the company's debts of £120m were cleared. A company worth some £250m a couple of years before, was suddenly worth just £60m.

Worst hit by the slump were the Bulmer family, who owned 51% of the shares in the company and rely on the twice yearly dividends for their income. There was the usual stock market speculation that the company was ripe for takeover, but the family remained steadfast in their commitment to the firm and its continued independence, guaranteed by their 51% stake. Also hard hit were the employees, who lost the sense of job security that had always been a part of the firm's ethos when 280 of the 1,000 employees were made redundant as the company fought to cut its running costs. Others made their own sacrifices—farmers owed £4m for their Autumn 2002 cider apple crop agreed to accept payment phased over six months to ease the company's cash flow problem.

Bulmers announced it was axing its international expansion plans and withdrawing immediately from interests in South Africa and China. In February 2003 it sold its Australian business, ironically set up by David Bulmer in the 1970s to help pay off debts. Bulmers interests in America and Europe were also under review. Bulmers still have 65% of the UK cider market and all Bulmers main brands—Strongbow, Woodpecker and Scrumpy Jack—have growing sales in the UK.

Mike Hughes, the Chief Executive whose expansion plans had so spectacularly failed, left the company, to be replaced by Miles Templeman, a former managing director of Whitbreads, with a brief to rescue the company from its debts and put it back to basics, concentrating on the core UK cider business. The company struggled to recover for another four months before the Board, supported by the Bulmer family, announced that they were proposing selling the company to Scottish and Newcastle Breweries, subject to approval by the EU competition commission as S&N already had massive brewing interests in in Europe. Approval was given in July 2003, marking the end of Bulmers as a family business in Hereford. S&N intend keeping the production of cider at Hereford, honouring existing growers' contracts and marketing and promoting Bulmers' major brands, but more than 250 staff in administration and sales lost their jobs as they were surplus to staff in S&N's equivalent departments.

5 WESTONS & KNIGHTS

Henry Weston came from Upton Bishop in Herefordshire to The Bounds in Much Marcle, in 1878, as a tenant farmer of the Homme House Estate. The 100-acre farm did not provide enough income in the first year to support young Henry and his wife Emily, so Henry, encouraged by C.W. Radcliffe Cooke who lived at nearby Hellens, used the fruit from the Bounds orchards and the horse-powered stone mill and hand press outside the farmhouse to press his first cider and perry.

The cider sold well through merchants, encouraging Henry to invest in a steam engine to drive a scratter mill with stone rollers that crushed the apples with less labour than the horse mill, and also provided motive power through a worm wheel to mechanical presses. It was a very dangerous machine which Henry soon hoped to replace, but it stayed in operation until the early 1900s.

Cider was supplied to the merchants in wooden barrels, and sold in cider houses as Weston's Rough. Yet Henry was sure that he could improve on his products, selling direct to the public rather than through merchants who often preferred to buy cheap, inferior ciders. In an interview given to the *Hereford Times* in 1894 Henry said:

> I should not like to say that cider is adulterated when it passed through other hands, but a great many farmers just make cider in the rough, then send it to the merchants. If farmers would take the necessary precautions and make cider and perry themselves throughout, selling direct to the consumer, the latter would have more faith in it and a better trade would be the result.

Henry's vision was of a cider made from single varieties of fruit, milled and fermented in clean conditions, then blended to produce a clean-tasting, pure product, free of infection and off flavours. To achieve this he only sourced his fruit from neighbouring farms, carefully sorting each variety of apple or perry pear into piles in his fruit yard, and removing rotten fruit by hand before it entered the mill.

The area around Much Marcle is claimed by pomologists to be the best area in Herefordshire for growing cider fruit. An entry in adjacent Dymock's parish register notes the area's superior cider making reputation:

> Dymock and Kempley - two of the most noted parishes in England for making of the most and best rare *Vinum Dimocuum* or that transcendent liquid called Red-Strake Sider not much inferior to the best of French wines.

Henry marketed his blended ciders as The Wine of the West so perhaps he was aware of the special properties of the area.

Using the steam powered mill, about four tons of fruit could be milled an hour, the pulp from which was pressed twice on two chain driven power presses. The juice flowed into slate lined tanks before being pumped uphill to the wooden fermenting vats. Fermentation was by ambient temperature, relying on the wild yeasts present on the fruit skins, so could take up to three months. Once the cider had stopped fermenting it was rough filtered through linen bags into the conditioning vats in a cellar carved out of the local stone, which kept the cider extremely cool. The cider was then blended before being filtered again through an Invicta filtering machine and filled into steam-cleaned wooden casks. This ensured the cider in the cask remained clear and of the highest quality.

Will Smith, a friend of Henry, joined the company as its first salesman, promoting Westons' ciders and perries in Birmingham. With Will's assistance the new Westons' blends soon took off and orders started to roll in from cider houses and private individuals as far away as Scotland.

In 1885 a railway station opened at Dymock, only two miles from the Westons' mill, with direct lines into Newent, Ledbury and Gloucester. The station was kept busy with horse-drawn wagons bringing Weston's cider from the mills at Much Marcle for delivery by rail, almost 75% of the company's products being sent to customers this way. Teams of horses and their drivers parked outside the Crown Inn at Dymock while both men and horses refreshed themselves.

So popular had Westons' ciders become that C.W. Radcliffe Cooke had Westons appointed as cider and perry supplies to the House of Commons; a price list of 1916 shows that the public could purchase from Westons 'Cider or Perry in a cask or bottle, as supplied to the House of Commons'. With production at the mill growing, Henry envisaged replacing the steam milling equipment with the latest hydraulic system. An order was put in with Hereford firm Naylors, who manufactured the machinery, but the First World War intervened. Henry died in 1917 and failed to see his dream fulfilled.

Emily had borne Henry nine children—five girls and four boys. Hubert, Leonard and Stafford succeeded their father to become the company's new directors. Hubert took on the farm, including the famous Bounds herd of pedigree Hereford cattle, Stafford took on the cider mill, including the blending of the ciders and perries, and Leonard developed the company's transport and distribution networks. The company bought its first lorry in 1919, a 3-ton Guy which was driven by Harry Probert and used for bulk deliveries to Birmingham and Bristol.

In 1920 the steam mill was replaced by the Naylor mill and hydraulic presses, powered by a paraffin internal combustion engine that also ran a generator providing electric light. The Westons' mill was the talk of the country and visitors came from near and far to see it. In 1922 Westons purchased The Bounds farm and two smaller adjoining farms—Nuttall Farm and Caerswall Farm—from the Homme House Estate. This gave the brothers 450 acres of land, with 20 acres under orchard, later extended to 50 acres of fruit in 1938 following a successful trial of bush orchards.

Westons' ciders were supplied to the public either in wooden casks, or corked and wired bottles with foil capsules. In casks of 10, 12, 18, 20, 28, 30 or 36 gallons were Supreme Brand (first quality), Bounds Brand and Farm Brand, described on Westons' promotional material as rough or

Fruit on its way to the mill at Westons in the 1950s

medium rough cider, also Marcle Brand perry, especially recommended for customers with rheumatism. In champagne quarts or pints were sold: Sparkling Marcle Cider, Gold Seal or Red Seal (old dry matures), Marcle Specialite Perry, Green Seal or Black Seal and Apple Brand—full bodied ciders—were bottled in quarts, pints, half pints or nips—a third of a pint.

Leonard Weston was introduced by a friend to new bottles with elaborate screw tops being used to package beer. He saw the potential of the easy to open and fill flagon for cider and persuaded his brothers to adopt the packaging for quarts and pint bottles. Westons were one of the first cider makers in the country to use the new flagons, which proved a great success with both the licensed trade and the public. The popularity of the flagon led to an increase in the workforce to between 60 and70 permanent staff, plus 30 to 40 casual workers during pressing time. A regular sight at agricultural shows was a Westons' promotional lorry with its body constructed in the shape of a flagon.

The old Guy lorry, bought by Leonard in 1919, had by 1925 developed into a fleet of vehicles. To service them a public garage was built on the Marcle crossroads and Harry Probert, the driver of the first Westons' lorry, was put in charge of the garage, which was until recently still run by his descendants. In 1926 Leonard organised the first local bus service to take children and shoppers from Much Marcle to Ledbury and other towns, and to provide transport for the mill workers, 15 per cent of whom lived in Newent, Ross, Dymock and Kempley due to housing shortages in Much Marcle.

In 1929 Hubert died, but the brothers continued to manage the firm, Stafford looking after the farm and cattle and Leonard the garage, with both taking a combined interest in the cider and perry making. In 1932 Hubert's young son, Norman, joined the firm to work in the cider mills and was quickly dubbed The Foreman by his work colleagues, partly because of his inexperience and partly because of his stature.

In 1930 Westons opened their first (and only) cider house on the Harrow Road in London. Selling only Westons' products, it was furnished in Victorian style with barrels as tables, which had a shelf set into them where you could rest your pint. The cider house became a great success and was so renowned it was mentioned in London guide books. In 1970 the cider house had to make way for a road improvement scheme, so was closed and demolished, and distribution of Westons' products for the London area were moved to a warehouse in Clapham, south London. It has often been regretted by the firm that the Harrow Road cider house was the only licensed premises it ever owned and controlled. Yet due to plenty of publicity for Westons' cider, sales built up to include contracts to all the main breweries in Birmingham and the

Westons' cider house on the Harrow Road in London, opened in 1930 and closed in 1970

west midlands, including Hereford, Ross and Stroud, along with direct trade to privately owned houses and individuals in the West Country, Wales, Oxfordshire and London.

In 1952 Westons added quality control laboratories to the mill at Much Marcle. This enabled the company to measure the quality of its cider with scientific accuracy. In 1956 John Howes joined Westons from W.M. Evans in Hereford, as chemist with responsibility for the quality control of all Westons cider and perry production. John's job involved analysing and tasting samples from the vats to select which to blend into the various Westons' brands,

Norman Weston

John Howes working at Westons in 1957

depending on their individual characteristics and tastes, sweet or dry, stronger or weaker, farmhouse 'rough' or superior 'vintage' and carbonated ciders, also if necessary controlling the addition of sugars to create medium and sweet blends. The process of fermentation was also improved, using a stable yeast cultured from the lees in the best vats, to ensure clean and even fermentation without loss of the desirable flavours, characteristics and quality of the finished product.

Other than scientific developments in the lab, the making of cider at Westons had changed little since 1920. The cider mill is surrounded by orchards which, like the buildings, fruit yard, vat houses and bottling hall have been added as needed, creating a disorientating jumble of buildings at different levels due to the hill on which the Bounds stands. At the top of the slope is the fruit yard, then the fruit trough cut into the ground so that fruit can be pushed straight in. Farmers delivering fruit pile the apples (or pears) up in great tumps. The piles are then shovelled by hand, tractor or JCB into a channel where water from an artificial lake floats them into the main trough, via an underground canal. Between the fruit trough and the milling and pressing rooms are the fermenters, then the labs, then down seven steps the milling and pressing room.

One employee, who worked at the mill in the 1960s, vividly remembers working in the pressing room:

> The apples were floated in on water, then washed on a conveyor
> which elevated them to the floor above for milling. A man above

Building the cheese at Westons

Pressing at Westons

shovelled the pulp from the mill into a hopper above the press. You pulled a handle to draw the bottom of the chute back and the pulp fell onto the cloth. When you had enough for that cloth you rang a bell to stop the fella above shovelling, while you closed the chute again. You needed 20 layers of pulp on the press to make a full cheese. The pulp was pressed twice, no water was added the second time. When the first pressing was done the pomace was put on a belt which carried it up to the hopper above the second press. We processed about 50 tons a day then, yielding 170 gallons of juice per ton of pulp.

The juice from the presses then had to be pumped back up to the fermenting vats where it ferments for up to three months before being pumped through to the conditioning vats in the cellars below the fermenting, mill and press rooms.

Westons have 72 oak vats holding between 1,200 gallons and 42,000 gallons each. All the vats and fermenters have names, the earliest vats were called after the founding family, then composers, cider making counties and Leonard Weston's favourite football teams. For several years Leonard was chairman of Hereford United Football Club and was proud when he was made president of the Southern League Football Association. Leonard named one vat Hereford and the one next to it Wembley. A worker joked, shortly afterwards, that this was the closest Hereford United would ever get to Wembley! Vat 52 was christened

113

Shortly after the commissioning of the Naylor Mills, generator and electric light at Westons in 1920

Queen Elizabeth to mark the 1952 coronation. The three biggest vats, Pip, Squeak and Wilfred, were rescued from a west midlands brewery. Cleaning the vats was once a risky business—a worker remembers:

> I got to clean the wooden vats with a broom and hose. It was pretty primitive, the vats were not tested for carbon dioxide, you guessed if it was safe to go into the vat. Once I nearly went unconscious because the gas wasn't properly vented out - I felt dizzy and sleepy and had to get out quick. There was no safety harness or rope, just a ladder, dangerous when you think about it now, but we didn't think about it then.

Through the cellars housing the conditioning vats is the bottling hall, filter room and store room. Whilst another level down is the warehouse and Bounds farmhouse, annexed to which, in a converted first floor feed store, are the company's small offices. The original stone mill on which Henry Weston made his first cider still stands outside the farmhouse in the gardens. The farm stables and cow sheds are grouped together round the farmyard another level down and have now been made into offices, a museum, shop and restaurant.

In 1961 Norman Weston was appointed to the Board and made managing director. The marketing director at that time was Major William Jaine, who had joined the company as a sales representative after his retirement from the regular army in 1954. In 1971 Leonard and

Stafford died within a few months of each other, their places on the Board being filled by Mrs. Frances Weston, widow of Stafford, and Mrs. Doris Weston, widow of Leonard. In 1972 Norman's son, Henry Weston, joined the family firm, followed by his sister, Helen, who succeeded to the role of Managing Director on her father, Norman's, retirement. Henry and Helen's brother, Timothy, also joined the firm, whilst Michael Roff took over from Major Jaine as marketing director in 1980, the year of Westons' centenary. The current marketing director is Roger Jackson. Norman Weston still takes an active role in the company as its Chairman, driving his fork lift truck around the goods yard and warehouse and the staff still affectionately refer to him as The Foreman.

By 1985 Westons' range had developed. Bounds Brand (sweet, medium and dry) was still the premium cider. Country (medium dry) had been added to Farm Brand as a draught cider, along with Special Vintage, made from selected vintage cider apples and matured for over a year in oak vats. A special cider, Vat 53, was also on offer, but described as difficult to find in the three counties. Champagne style ciders had been discontinued along with Apple Brand. Perry was available as Black or Green Seal, matured in oak vats for at least two years. Draught ciders and perries were now presented in polycasks of five or eleven gallons, or in glass flagons and bottles. Westons had produced a keg cider, Stowford Press, for Camerons Brewery in Hartlepool, which was sold as a house cider. It was sent in a tanker of 3,000 gallons at a time to Hartlepool and kegged by the brewery. The name was thought up by a PR whiz kid who was visiting the Cotswolds, combined the names of two villages, Stow on the Wold and Burford, then added 'Press'. When the Camerons Brewery was sold, Westons bought the name and continued to make the brand, putting in a kegging line at The Bounds.

The demand for Westons' ciders and perries, along with projected growth for the firm in the future, meant that the company needed to produce more cider, more economically and faster. So, in 1998, under the direction of Helen Weston, the company invested £500,000, over two years. The mill and presses were replaced, and automatic fruit handling introduced. Three stainless steel holding tanks for finished cider were installed, being named by Norman Weston's grandchildren: Eeyore, Piglet and Tigger! Westons have retained the fermentation and conditioning of cider in wooden vats, as well as sourcing home grown fruit from their own orchards and over 200 neighbouring farms, which they believe gives their ciders and perries their special character and appeal. A new bottling line was also installed. Having moved from wooden crates to cardboard boxes to please the supermarkets, Westons now ship their products in pad and shrink wrap which creates less waste.

Improvements have also been made to visitor facilities on site. The cow shed, redundant since the disposal of the Bounds herd of pedigree Hereford cattle, has been converted into the Scrumpy House Restaurant, which opened in the winter of 1998. In 2000 the old stables adjoining the farmyard were developed into a museum containing exhibits of rural and cider making equipment, including one of the original Naylor Hydraulic presses used by Westons for over 80 years, plus a collection of over 700 cider and perry bottles from around the U.K. In 2002 Westons landscaped the gardens at Bounds and developed an education room for schools, plus a new shop area offering tasting and sales of Westons products.

The fifth generation of Westons, Guy Lawrence, son of Helen, joined the firm in 1999 and is keen to keep the family tradition of making quality ciders and perries alive for the future. Like his grandfather, Norman, before him, he is learning all aspects of the business from orcharding to final product, to ensure the Westons' tradition is in good hands.

Keith Knight, of Knights Cider Company in Storridge on the edge of the Malvern Hills, did not start making cider until 1979.

Building a cheese at Knights, 1989

We were growing contract fruit for Bulmers at Crumpton Oaks, but were having no great results so decided to look at making cider ourselves, but not from contract fruit - we started planting our own orchards. I went along to Long Ashton Research Station to study how to make cider under the late Jeff Williams - he talked in easy to understand terms and with an enthusiasm that inspired me to make fine cider. At the time we had also tried pick-your-own fruit and had built a farm shop, which is still on the same site now, so I applied for a license to sell cider from the shop.

In the first year I made 18,000 gallons using a Beare press with a pres-

Scratter at Knights, 1988

sure of 250 tons that had come from Showerings; it had been lying in long grass and nettles at Julian Temperly's farm in Somerset. [Julian is a master cider and cider brandy maker at Burrow Hill in Somerset.] That first year I was very inexperienced. I put the juice to ferment in six 3,000 gallon glass-lined steel vats, having been told that when fermentation stopped you bunged up the vat to keep out the air, so I turned out six oak pegs. When I thought the fermentation had finished I got up on to the top of the tank and drove in the pegs, wrapping them in hessian for a tight fit. A few days later I visited Jeff Williams and told him I had bunged down the vats - he suggested I leave them lightly bunged, not firm down. On the way home I called on another cider maker, Vernon Bland, from whom I had bought the vats, who in his rather droll manner told me to get home quickly and make sure the bungs were released. I got onto the first tank in the barn with a lump hammer to try and release a bung. It took some knocking out, but suddenly it shot out like a rocket, just missed my chin and hit the roof of the barn. Then the tank erupted, a geyser of cider foam hit the roof and like a fool I tried to hold it in as it continued to foam for ten minutes, while I contemplated how much cider I was losing from the vat. I was completely soaked and had the same problem with the other five bungs.

Over the years we have purchased two small adjoining farms and expanded our orchards to 200 acres, mostly Dabinett with Michelin pollinators. All the new plantings were grown in our own nursery. We also have 80 'trial' trees for future research as part of the National Association of Cider Makers' trials, one of four blocks of Williams Copas named after the pomologists Ray Williams and Liz Copas. We make up our fruit through buying from local farmers, to boost the quantity of cider and provide more varieties.

Around 1992 we stopped using the old bed press which took five men to operate and switched to a French Spechime continuous screw press which only needs two men to operate it. It satisfied our need to press more fruit at the time, but as the orchards matured I always worried that the press would break down with no backup. So we made the large investment in a belt press, capable of pressing 8-10 tons of pulp an hour with just one operator. We now have six 60,000 gallon vats, plus 100 smaller vats for fermenting and conditioning the cider.

We employ eight people throughout the year, in orcharding, quality control labs, pressing, fermenting and blending, plus an engineer to keep the machines going. The fruit trees are the heart of the business. The success of Knights is in no small part down to its employees, who work together as a team and have grown the company into a medium sized cider maker on the same scale as Westons in just 20 years, whilst other small and medium sized cider makers have been disappearing due to market forces, or taken over by Bulmers and Matthew Clarke. Not long after we got going we started to supply Aston Manor Brewery in Birmingham with cider, which continues to this day - for many years they were our main customer. Over the last five years growth in cider has been static for small producers in the U.K. which has encouraged us to look for other markets, so we have started exporting to Europe and the USA, so expanding our customer base.

6   CIDER SCIENCE

Viscount Scudamore of Holme Lacy, Herefordshire, started to bottle his Redstreak cider in the 1640s using a process pioneered by Sir Kenelm Digby, a fellow of the Royal Society and fellow ciderist. Sir Kenelm's method used a bottle with a wired cork which kept the cider fresh, whilst slow fermentation of residual sugars into alcohol gave off carbon dioxide that was trapped in the bottle imparting a pleasant, natural fizz to the cider, resembling the newly invented champagne wines. The build up of carbon dioxide in the bottle also prevented the acetification of the cider. Bottling had to be carefully timed as, if fermentation had not stopped completely before filling, the bottles could explode. To reduce the risk of explosion during the secondary fermentation the bottles were kept in cool cellars or wells, buried in sand or stood in running spring water.

It was to be another 200 years before the causes of fermentation and acetification of cider were to be fully understood, through the experiments and discoveries of Louis Pasteur (1822-1895). Fermentation was thought to be an entirely chemical process, but Pasteur demonstrated that fermenting solutions contained living organisms: yeasts and bacteria. He discovered that if these organisms were destroyed by heat and new ones prevented from entering the flask, fermentation or putrification of the liquid could not take place. With further research he developed the technique of pasteurisation that prevents the spoiling of liquids by micro-organisms.

Despite Pasteur's discoveries there were still problems with fermentation of cider through reliance on wild yeasts on the skin of the fruit, which could also harbour bacteria that would spoil the cider during fermentation. Successful fermentation relied on the wild yeasts dominating the process by sheer numbers, preventing the growth of other micro organisms.

It fell to Dr. H.E. Durham in Bulmers' laboratories to solve these fermentation problems. Dr. Durham, who's name is perpetuated in the Durham Tube he invented in 1897 for measuring fermentation, was a retired Fellow of the Royal Society when he joined Bulmers as director of research in 1905. He worked out ways of estimating the amount of tannin and sugar in any juice and developed a stable, dominant yeast culture from natural apple yeasts by selective culturing and preservation, so that for the first time control of fermentation became possible.

As a result, filtration of fermented cider through double skinned linen bags was used in the large cider mills to remove excess yeasts, stabilising the cider for bottling and transport. Improved filters made from paper pulp were introduced in the first half of the twentieth century, but these had a limited life and would stop working due to clogging or being holed. To save money, paper filters would be washed, re-pulped and reformed, then replaced on the filtering line.

Samples of filtered cider were tested by placing them in warm room to encourage yeast growth, which could take 42-72 hours. After the Second World War a filter test was introduced that reduced the result time to 24 hours, using a harmless red bacterium *Serratia Marscens* that grew faster than yeast. The cider chemist, Brian Nelson (subsequently chief executive of Bulmers), introduced the use of Colloidal Gold to test filters —the gold is mildly radioactive and a Geiger counter picks up a faulty filter immediately, saving lab and warehousing costs as there is no time-lag between testing and release of the packaged cider to retailers. Geoff Warren of GCW Technology developed a technique in the 1970s using a micro filter taking a drip sample, which was cheaper than Colloidal gold, but just as effective. When an ultra-violet stain is applied to the filter any live yeast absorbs the stain and will fluoresce immediately under an ultra-violet microscope.

Even when successfully tested cider is sent to be packaged, there are still many areas where the process can break down. The filter may be damaged, the lines may not be sterile, containers could be contaminated or bacterium present in the cider could be too small to be trapped by the filter. To ensure stability and freedom from bacteria, pasteurisation can be included in the filling lines to ensure the filtered cider is free of micro organisms before and after being placed in containers. Unlike beer, pasteurised cider does not lose flavour or smell during the heat-treatment process, and as it does not contain proteins it is unlikely to form a chill haze in the container. Cider that has been pasteurised after filtering is hot filled into sterile containers, a process suitable for cans, glass and plastic bottles as the pasteurisation takes place at low temperatures. Glass bottles and cans may be passed through another bulk pasteuriser after filling to ensure both container and contents are sterile.

Scientific analysis now permeates every aspect of cider making. Laboratories test the soil the young trees are planted in for the right balance of nutrients, provide advice on the application of chemicals to ensure good fruit yield and prevent pests and diseases attacking the trees, test the resulting juice before, during and after fermentation and during blending and packaging. Scientific analysis data is even used to blend the cider to the correct proportions of alcohol acidity, sweetness, tannins and colour for each brand, although the final test of success still lies with the experts' taste buds.

Many of the scientists and lab technicians working for the cider industry were graduates or employees of Long Ashton Research Station (LARS). This was founded originally as the National Fruit and Cider Institute in 1903, and many of the tests and processes commonly used in cider making were developed there as part of research projects for the government or industrial sponsors. Andrew Lea graduated in Chemistry at the University of Bristol in 1969, then worked for three years in a tea industry research lab before undertaking an MSc then PhD in cider phenolics chemistry at LARS, after which he became a full member of the Station staff.

> LARS was almost entirely dependent on income from the Agricultural Research Council (ARC) and from MAFF. By the time I joined, the Cider and Fruit Juices Section numbered about 25 people - this was only one-tenth of the total number of Station staff, who mostly worked on a wide range of other agricultural and horticultural topics and had no knowledge of or interest in cider. The local bus drivers still universally referred to it as the Cider Institute, however!
>
> By the mid-70s the Cider Section had become the Food and Beverages Division and no more than half a dozen people were working on cider-related issues as such. From about 1975 onwards with the introduction by the government of direct funding by industry for research work, the purpose of stations like LARS became increasingly unclear and uncertain. In 1981 the ARC withdrew all support from the Food and Beverages Division (since its work was considered to be too 'near market'), and we then had to try to survive through commercial contracts. This was not successful, and the Food and Beverage Division closed in 1985. With hindsight, it was almost inevitable that the whole of LARS would eventually close (in 2002) though it took the best part of 20 years to finally kill it off!
>
> The major contribution of LARS to cider making was about 'understanding' and 'control' and had been made long before I got there, initially by Professor Barker and then, after the Second World War, by researchers such as Len Burroughs, Fred Beech, the section head, and Geoff Carr. On the basis of the Cider Section's

work between 1903 and 1980, the knowledge became available to make any style of cider which we choose (from 'bulk' to 'craft'), and make rational decisions on exactly how to achieve it and the type of result we can expect.

Barker's contribution was about classification of cider apple cultivars, their cider making and orcharding characteristics and unravelling in outline the complexities of the microbiological process that is traditional cider making. I guess another of his contributions was the establishment in the 1930s of the pioneering trials of bush cider orchards, which are now universal in main-stream cider growing.

Beech's contribution was especially about understanding the role of yeast, and in introducing to the industry the idea that yeast could be controlled and managed, and that defined strains of yeast could have a major benefit to a commercial operation. Together with Burroughs, he also promoted the rational use of sulphur dioxide, its relationship to yeast behaviour, and its value to the industry in keeping fermentations clean and controllable. Geoff Carr's contribution was in finally understanding and controlling the role of malo-lactic bacteria in cider making.

A lot of the value of the LARS Cider Section came from its close contacts with similar wine research and horticultural institutes in other countries, and the great cross-fertilizing of ideas that this brought about. That had always been a feature of the Station, even from its earliest years, when strong links were established with French and German labs before the First World War.

Long Ashton Research Station in 1975

My own main achievement at LARS was to finally unravel and understand the nature of cider 'tannin' which had been pretty obscure since Thomas Andrew Knight had described it in 1801, and to elucidate exactly why and how it contributed to the taste and colour of cider. I have to say that although I did the work, the 'achievement' was in one sense waiting to happen, since it depended crucially on two factors, firstly the pioneering work of Eddie Haslam's plant phenolics group at the University of Sheffield, and secondly the commercial development of HPLC (high performance liquid chromatography) as a robust analytical tool.

One of my experiments was a major trial of tree nutrition versus tannin levels. We used a Bulmers' orchard west of Hereford for the work. Thousands of trees were involved and they all had to be statistically randomised. Early in my LARS career, I spent a day with our chief statistician and a large pot of white paint. He and I walked through the orchard - he reading out from a book of random number tables and me marking the trees he indicated with a blob of paint. It was like some bizarre religious rite - the priest and his acolyte marking the sacrificial victims. In fact they were not victims at all, they were the most favoured trees. If any died a substitute tree had to be chosen to preserve the statistical pattern. Later the trees were individually marked with coloured tape depending on the fertilizer treatment they were to receive, and every year we sampled leaves on 10 August (or as close to it as we could manage) from every tree. The bags of leaves were sent off to ADAS for measurement of NPK (nitrogen, potassium and phosphorous) as a measure of the nutrient status. Later in the autumn, all the fruit from each tree had to be individually harvested into labelled bags and taken back to LARS to turn into individual juices and ciders which were further analysed. It was a big programme and it went on for 10 years. I depended entirely on the goodwill of my lab colleagues to help me with this. Andrew's Leaf Sampling became an annual event and we would take an August party up to the orchard complete with picnic. The lab staff enjoyed a day out then - but it was much more difficult to get help in the grey rainy days of November when the dripping wet fruit had to be hand harvested!

Another of my projects was concerned with the sensory assessment of bitterness and astringency in these experimental ciders. The heavy bittersweet ciders were tasted unsweetened and were fierce and tannic to say the least. I needed a tasting panel of at least 20 people for this. I was never popular when recruiting for the panel and had to resort to all manner of bribes to keep the numbers up!

Lab life is fairly dull and there is not much to say about our day to day work but I remember especially the old Cider Tasting Days which took place in May or June every year (although they were killed off in the late '70s because the old small-scale cider makers they were intended to help had virtually died out and the event was becoming a party that had outlived its usefulness). It was fun though, and in some ways it was the highlight of the year. The food and cider was free. All the lab staff would dress up smart for the day (it was the '70s so the young girls were in flowery cotton dresses and the lads like me with kipper ties and flares!). Senior staff would dust off their best suits for the day to look rather less 'boffinish'. A very young and flamboyant Julian Temperley (later to become the pioneer of Somerset Cider Brandy) used to arrive with a crowd of his mates and make quite a splash! Sometimes we were graced with Bertram Bulmer himself arriving in a black chauffeur-driven car, and a large fruit grower whose name I've forgotten who would arrive by helicopter. Retired staff would turn up too.

The day started in a huge marquee - over a hundred people seated at trestle tables with tasting sheets in front of them. The junior staff would pour out the samples as they were announced (just an inch or so in each glass). Fred Beech would describe them from the podium and they would be tasted and commented upon with little nibbles of cheese between each sample. There would always be a theme - for instance, experimental ciders made from dessert varieties of fruit, or those made with different strains of yeast. It was intended to be truly educational.

After the tasting came the buffet lunch, complete with John Llewellyn's best perry. John was in charge of the cider house at LARS in the '70s and was very proud of his perry which was exceptionally good and came from fruit from LARS perry trees that grew in the original orchard planted in 1903. There was always a bit of a contrast between the sharp-suited young men from Bulmers, Showerings and Taunton Cider, who would be talking production volumes and margins, and the old farm cider makers. There was a shabby old boy who turned up every year in a trench coat with deep pockets, which he proceeded to stuff full of pasties, hunks of cheese and anything else he could carry away with him. After lunch there were tours of the labs or the cider house for those who wanted them and the visitors could come in and talk to the lab staff about their projects if they wanted to. We usually put on poster displays in the labs to explain the work we were doing - though it hardly meant anything to the old time farm cider makers.

On 18 December 1981 I learnt from my morning paper that the Cider Section was scheduled for closure. The ARC had kept it a secret and had unforgiveably told the press before they told the staff - my innocence was lost on that day.

Ray Williams joined Long Ashton as a pomologist in 1952, he remembers that:

Ray Williams

Long Ashton was a very academic place to work. In the early days academics were given a lot of freedom about their research. As long as you published a certain amount of papers in scientific journals you gained regular promotion. I was not too keen on the 'blue skies' (for the sake of it) research that this culture produced. I prefer to look at the basics of a problem, tackling it in a scientific manner to produce a practical solution. This was not always well received by the scientific community.

When the Conservative government changed the focus of research from pure science to practical, short term projects for industrial sponsors in 1982, a lot of the academics who were not happy with working alongside industry to secure sponsorship and scientific research funding left the institute. Then my contacts with the national association, local farmers and cider makers stood me in good stead for continuing my research, right until the day I retired in 1988.

The Monday after my retirement I was invited back to the Research Station to work part-time on finishing my research projects, as there was no-one else with the depth of experience able to take on the work. It took me two years to settle up the loose ends, then between 1990 and 2000 I worked as a Consultant Pomologist for the cider industry, providing solutions for intriguing problems, including the selection of varieties and care of trees in organic orchards, analysis of soil conditions and suggesting improvements to pomological practice for commercial growers.

Ray finally retired in September 2000 having spent 50 years serving the cider making industry. On his second retirement he was presented with a gold medal by the National Association of Cider Makers at the Bath and West Show for his many achievements.

Peter Mitchell started cider making as a hobby, but by the early 1980s it had become a line of business. In 1985 he set up an evening course for amateur cider makers and a short block release course for industry at Worcester College Hindlip campus. During the early 1990s the resources at Hindlip were developed and a small scale production unit was installed, including a mill, press and bottling line. The production unit enabled the course to mirror industry and provided students with the same challenges in production, Hazard Analysis and Critical Control Point (HACCP) monitoring, quality control and marketing as they would experience in the workplace. It also enabled Hindlip to provide training and consultancy services for small to medium sized enterprises and employee training courses for the cider making industry which were much missed with the passing of LARS. In 1993 Hindlip produced its first vintage using the new production unit, which was marketed for sale to the public. Previously cider had only been made in small quantities for in-house consumption.

It was becoming clear that the industry was looking for in-depth and broader training, supported by qualifications. A working party was set up with industry representatives to consult on the structure of the course and map out their requirements. This led to the Accreditation of the BTEC Professional Development Certificate in Science (Cider making) Level 4 in 1994. The course covers the main principles and techniques of cider production, from pomology through lab skills, marketing and environmental management, as well as hands on experience of pressing and fermenting cider and tutored product tasting.

In 1996 a laboratory was installed at Hindlip and the college made a bid to the government's Competitiveness Fund to provide support services to the food and drink industry in the west midlands. The bid was successful and enabled the establishment of the Hindlip Centre for Food and Drink Industries which aimed to be a National Centre of Excellence for the cider industry and promote local food and drink producers in the west midlands. The centre opened in 1997 and quickly developed, outgrowing its premises in 18 months. In conjunction with industry partners the centre made a bid to the government's Skills Development Fund to relocate to a purpose built centre at Pershore. The bid was successful and construction started in January 2000. Construction was complete by July and the Core Food and Drink centre launched on 15 September 2000 as a one stop shop for regional food and drink producers, and as a national cider centre. In March 2003, Pershore Group of Colleges converted the CORE building at Pershore into an animal care facility and refocused the role of the Core food and drink department as a mainstream training centre for the general food and drink industry. The cider section has been closed, along with the laboratory and cider production facilities essential for supporting the cider industry and related qualifications.

The environmental impacts of cider making have become central to medium to large scale cider makers in recent years, as Jonathan Blair, who was master cider maker at Bulmers until May 2003, recognizes.

> The company was very concerned to minimise its impact on the environment. We were constantly seeking ways to become sustainable by maximising the reuse and recycling of all resources used during the cider making process: water, steam, heat, electricity, gas, chemicals, yeast, lab testing and transport, and being involved in voluntary schemes that gave value back to the community through volunteering, fundraising, health and environmental improvement projects.

This philosophy was encouraged throughout the company by Head of Sustainability, Charlie Bower. Over the past couple of years Bulmers undertook a review of its operations and relationship with Herefordshire's community against principles of sustainability, which produced a wealth of ideas for the company's Board to consider. The company hoped to achieve a 75% reduction in current environmental impact by 2004, acting as a catalyst for Herefordshire's emergence as a vital and sustainable rural community. For the time being though, these objectives remain no more than stands taken by the company. Charlie Bower acknowledges 'the Board are supportive but they have not yet said "Go and deliver", rather "Tell us more, show us how you can make it work".' It remains to be seen what Scottish and Newcastle's attitude will be.

During the period 2000-2001 Bulmers managed to cut its process energy consumption per hectolitre of product by 4%—well ahead of the industry's 1% per year target under the climate change levy agreement with the government. The company's second biggest source of carbon dioxide and other air pollutants is transport, with outbound goods accounting for some 85% of its total transport emissions; half a million tonnes of finished goods are shipped by road from the Hereford site every year. Bulmers has been testing ways of putting some of that traffic back on the rails. Working with Railfreightline, a consortium of freight companies which recently secured £2.1 million from the Strategic Rail Authority to develop innovative freight solutions with industry partners, and using the railhead still in place at the Moorfields site, the company conducted a two week trial with a new concept of a mini-goods train. This can carry four lorry-loads of freight per journey and accelerates as fast as passenger trains, which should enable it to travel on the rail network during the day. The trial proved very successful. It is expected that a partial switch to rail would be 'reasonably cost neutral' and if implemented, will result in big environmental benefits, with Co_2 emissions per tonne-kilometre being reduced by about 80%.

The company is already doing well in diverting waste from its packaging lines from landfill. Some 95% of its steel, aluminium, glass, plastic bottles and polythene is now recycled, but that leaves all the packaging discarded by consumers of Bulmers' products. The company has been looking at the feasibility of recycling this post-consumer waste by picking up the equivalent in and around Hereford and establishing a local recycling infrastructure. 'We wanted to encourage a different form of inward investment into Herefordshire', said Charlie Bower. 'It was all part of a reappraisal of Bulmers' role in society'.

Pomace is another bulky waste stream, more than 18,000 tonnes of wet pomace is produced by the mill each year between September and the end of November. Most of it is dried for pectin extraction while the rest, around 5,600 tonnes, is sold as cattle feed. The drying process is energy intensive and alternative ways of managing the by-product are being investigated. One proposal is to convert the pomace into compost with straw, so it can then be used as a fertiliser in the company's orchards or sold commercially. Then there is the 1,500 tonnes of apple tree prunings produced in Bulmers' orchards each year. Collecting the material for use as fuel is too expensive so it is currently burned in the field, yet the chipped prunings could be used to grow high-value mushrooms. Professor Ivanka Milekovic, a mycologist at the University of Belgrade, conducted a trial in the summer of 2002 on behalf of Bulmers to establish which fungi will grow on apple wood.

The Bulmer Foundation, a new offspring of the Bulmer family's and company's push towards sustainability could be the body to develop the mushroom project. The Foundation has already initiated Project Carrot, which is aimed at establishing Holme Lacy College near Hereford as a leading educational centre for sustainable agriculture and land management, and developing a replicable regional model for sustainable land use in Herefordshire.

The company's biggest waste problem is its discharge to sewer. Several hundred million gallons of water are discharged each year, along with five million litres of cider recovered from cleaning vats and failure of containers on the canning and bottling lines, plus smaller amounts of solids, apple juice, cleaning agents and other materials. Cedric Olive, former mill manager says 'You could float the *Queen Mary* on the water coming out of the mill'. A project involving lagooning followed by reed bed treatment, and allowing some water reuse, is being investigated by the company.

Such a scheme has already been implemented by Westons Cider in 1994, who introduced a system of combined soil percolation and wetland treatment using reedbeds and rotational coppice management. This exploits plant species which have evolved symbiotic relationships with micro-organisms that are able to both oxygenate and purify water—as well as provide a habitat for rare and diverse species. The alternative would have been to build waste tanks, add acid neutralising chemicals and use mechanical aerators and mixers to treat the waste water. This would have meant a large power supply and both the running and maintenance costs would be high.

The mainly clay soil was puddled to hold water so that the ponds and ditches would not need to be lined, excavated clay was used to form a retaining wall around the whole site preventing seepage into other watercourses, and deposits of limestone gravel on site were used for neutralising the low pH waste water without the need for an expensive chemical dosing system. The whole site is fed by gravity as it is below the level of the mill, so no pumps are required to transport the waste water to the cleaning facility. Cardboard and waste pomace is used, along with spoiled straw bales from the farm, to create a sheet mulch to help establish trees.

The yeast lees in fermentation vessels are not allowed to enter the system but are tankered out of the mill for use as pig feed as it it rich in B vitamins. Allowing this waste to enter the pond would cause foul

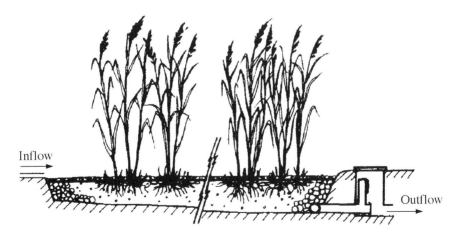

Inflow

Outflow

A simple reed bed system in cross-section. The core of the bed is made of gravel in a shallow sloping depression, its sides supported by larger stones. The outflow has a sampling chamber and weir which can allow for adjusting the water level in the reed bed. The outflow could be to a pond or willow bed

smelling gas to be produced due to anaerobic degradation of amino acids. A Phragmites reed raft covers the whole of the surface of the anaerobic lagoon to preclude any potential odour problems as well as keeping the top 3 or 4 feet of the waste water well oxygenated.

From the pond, the waste water flows through a pipeline to the remainder of the wetland entering a shallow pond with a large open surface area, which enables the deoxygenated water coming from the anaerobic pond to become recharged with oxygen from the atmosphere. It then passes into the first of the swales and so starts to infiltrate the soil. Planted on the swale bank are thousands of acid tolerant, biomass type willow varieties which are coppiced annually to maintain the rapid growth necessary for waste transformation and provide an additional income source from the facility, yielding osiers for basket making and biomass to fuel the mill boilers. The water then passes through a meandering, shallow pond densely planted with reeds and rushes, flowing over limestone gravel which increases its pH, then through three further ponds planted with around 40 species of local aquatic plants, marginal waterplants and reeds, which give the system the capacity to deal with large volumes of waste water during the pressing season. Microbes in the roots of the plants convert the high nutrient load of the waste into minerals whilst the high surface area of the water encourages its evaporation as water vapour into the atmosphere. The site is also planted with 14 different species of coppice wood trees, which are managed to produce a variety of products for use on Westons' farm or for sale. The site has now become a wildlife haven and local conservation officers have remarked that its biodiversity will probably attract SSSI—Site of Special Scientific Interest—status if well managed.

The health giving benefits of apples have been praised for hundreds of years. The Reverend John Wesley's treatise on medicine, *Primitive Physic*, published in 1747, recommends cider as the best cure for asthma and cancers and the juice or flesh of apples for healing the eyes and cystitis. In his book, *Cider and Perry*, C.W. Radcliffe Cooke reveals that having found he suffered from gout in London and having consulted the doctor who prescribed whisky and water, he found no relief. But on returning to Herefordshire and drinking only cider and perry he suffered more rarely from gout. 'I accordingly gave up whisky and took to cider and perry as my staple drinks; and from that time to this I have never once had an attack of gout'. He also notes that regular cider drinkers are not prone to strokes, rheumatism or diarrhoea and have excellent digestions due to cider's quality of prolonging the digestive process, adding greatly to the nutrition gained from the food. However, he qualifies his opinion by stating:

One of the strongest arguments in favour of cider and perry is that, apart from their refreshing and thirst quenching properties they are peculiarly wholesome, possibly the most wholesome of all fermented liquors. In proportion, however as they are adulterated, they lose their wholesomeness ... Cider and perry are in truth wines of low alcoholic strength. Their merit consists in the fact that there is, or ought to be no artificial ingredient whatever in them; that they consist of nothing but the fermented juice of the most whole-some fruits known to man. Like wines they vary in flavour and quality. ... To resort to artificial means to give flavour to the liquor and to use preservatives to prevent acetification or arrest fermen-tation is to result in the production of a beverage which is no longer pure, and no longer, therefore, so wholesome as it would be without the addition of these ingredients. ... A mixture which mostly consists of added water, sterilised by heat, fortified by spirit and when bottled, carbonated to make it sparkle has no dietetic value whatsoever and its sale as English cider ought to be forbidden by law. ... Let consumers insist on a guarantee from the seller that the liquor he supplies them with is pure English cider and perry, made without preservatives and in time the demand for the foreign and inferior article will cease.

Recent research conducted by Dr. Caroline Walker at Brewing Research International, in partnership with the Institute of Food Research Group in Norwich, showed cider to be one of the top alcoholic drinks for health, due to the presence of antioxidants. Antioxidants are thought by nutritionists to protect against cardiovascular disease and cancer by quenching and neutralising the damaging effects of free radi-cals on the body's cells, which are suspected of triggering cancers and speeding up the progression of cardiovascular disease. The absorption of the antioxidants into the bloodstream was shown to be high due to the micronutrients being free in solution, rather than locked into cell walls as in fruit and vegetables, making them easier to absorb through the gut.

Ciders manufactured with added water and preservatives showed fewer antioxidants per 250ml then pure juice ciders, confirming Radcliffe Cooke's opinion that adulterated products have less beneficial value to health. To reach the same antioxidant value as a 100% juice cider you would need to consume ten or twelve pints of the lowest rated fizzy stuff. There are severe health consequences associated with heavy drinking, so the health benefits of cider should only be considered in moderation. Department of Health guidelines recommend two to three units of alcohol a day for women and three to four units a day for men. The number of units is dependent on the alcoholic strength of the drink and the size of the measure, a unit being 8mg of alcohol equivalent to half a pint of cider at 4% alcohol by volume.

Other studies have revealed that Quercetin, a specific antioxidant found in apples has been linked to improved lung function, whilst moderate consumption of alcohol has been shown to reduce the risk of gall stones, osteoporosis and strokes. In 1970 the *Hereford Times*, reporting on the 101st Birthday of Mrs. Fanny Mason, said she put her great age down to a daily glass of cider!

7   WHATEVER HAPPENED TO SCRUMPY?

Writing in the *Hereford Times* in 1936 an old time cider drinker found no comparison between the cider made and marketed by the big cider mills and the rough cider of his youth, which was so dry it was hard to tell the difference between the cider and the vinegar barrel:

> When I was a young man at home in Gloucestershire, we kept cider about the premises in casks. It was good cider and I was fond of it. Early in life I learnt to tell the cider from the vinegar by the label on the cask - it was the only way one could tell, as I said before it was good cider though unsweetened.
>
> The art and practice of drinking cider has certainly declined in the cider apple counties. ... The continuous advertising of great firms such as Messrs. Bulmers, Godwins and Westons have educated the public to appreciate the virtues of fermented apple juice, but this is not the cider of my youth. All the advertising in the world would not educate a Cockney or a Yorkshire man to appreciate the stuff we drank then, it would take them half a life time to learn to distinguish it from vinegar. Nevertheless we drank the stuff, it suited our palates and our stomachs yearned for it. Here's to the good old days when the man who couldn't go his daily dozen quarts was a departure from custom likely to cause talk amongst his neighbours!

The larger U.K. cider mills have aimed to produce a consistent and uniform cider with a high alcohol content, aimed at drinkers as an alternative long drink to beer or lager. Customs and Excise regulations define cider as being fermented from apple juice, with an alcohol content between 1.2% and 8.4%. Regulations permit the use of sodium dioxide, carbon dioxide, sugar and sweeteners in the fermentation and blending of the cider, and labels on the produce must show the common name of the food (cider or perry), if it is sweet, medium or dry, its alcoholic content in %, the quantity contained in the pack in metric (the minimum size of pack is 6 cl), the name and address of the producer (a postcode is sufficient) and if the cider contains artificial sweeteners. Natural sugar, artificial colours or other additives, or the amount of juice used in fermentation, or a best before date, is not required to be declared on the label at present. Natural additives such as herbs, fruit or fruit juices (other than apple or pear) used to vary the flavour or colour of the product are prohibited. Cider which has been combined with these natural additives are taxed as fruit wines whatever their alcoholic strength and attract a higher level of duty. Cider makers using the symbols of the Soil Association or other organic schemes must be certified and registered with those associations. At another level, EU regulation PGI (Protected Geographical Indication) protects designation marks, and 'Herefordshire Cider', for instance is audited by Trading Standards who confirm the source of the raw ingredients are as stated on the label. Low alcohol (under 2%) ciders are classified as food, rather than alcoholic beverages and as such must state all ingredients, but do not need a best before date.

According to the National Association of Cider Makers (NACM), cider and perry contributed more than £370 million in duty and VAT to the Treasury in 2000. Duty in the U.K. on cider is at least 34 times greater than that in France and, because of the small size of the cider sector (at 5% of the total alcoholic drinks market in the U.K.) the retail price of

The image of making scrumpy. In fact this is the 'west country way' depicted in 1883, where the pulped was packed between straw before pressing

cider in pubs remains consistently 15 to 20p a pint higher than the price of beer. In 2000 the U.K. had 53.7% share of the European cider and perry market, with the second largest being the French with 13%. 11% of people drink cider compared to 50% who drink beer.

The policy of the large cider mills to subsidise the growing of selective varieties of cider fruit has further strengthened the uniformity of taste in their products. The use of sulphur dioxide to kill wild yeasts and spoilage bacteria before fermentation, replacing the natural yeasts with cultured stable strains also affects the taste of the cider. Sugar can be added during fermentation to increase the specific gravity of the fermentable liquor and reduce the amount of fruit juice required to reach a specific ABV— Alcohol By Volume. Some brands of cider may contain as little as 16% fruit juice. The liquor is fermented out to full dryness, then sugars, saccharine and malic acid are added to sweeten and flavour the cider, plus artificial colour and cloud may be added to produce a cider pleasing to the eye of the drinker. Filtering and pasteurisation before and after blending prevent the cider refermenting if sugar rather than non-fermentable saccharine is added, as residual yeasts are removed or destroyed. Sparkle is provided by artificial carbonation before packaging. Since the 1980s the introduction of draught keg cider has increased the consumption of branded cider, leaving farmhouse products struggling to survive with only 2% of the U.K. market.

Genuine farmhouse cider, be it rough, dry, medium or sweet has a flavour and natural potency unknown to draught keg cider. 'Perhaps they dips an apple in it' opinionated one scrumpy-imbibing native in 1963.

The name scrumpy derives from scrumpies, the apples the cider was made from, which was used to describe small, underdeveloped fruit and was also sometimes applied to a small person or animal, he being 'only a scrumpy little thing'. An inference could be drawn that cider made from scrumpies was of inferior quality, but anyone who knows anything about cider making will tell you this is far from being the case. Indeed, farmers pride themselves on their vintages and would happily tell you at length about how each variety of apple had been carefully blended to obtain the subtle flavour. The proportions of fruit were anything but haphazard, but perhaps the word scrumpy was originally applied as a derogatory term to that cider which was made from fruit picked too early, or at random, for the purpose of making a cheap and inferior cider.

Mike Edwards grew up in Cleeve Prior near Evesham helping his father make cider. They gathered their fruit from several orchards including one at Holden Lane, the apples of which were renowned for the quality of cider they produced, then took it to The Ivy Inn, North Littleton, to be milled and pressed, carrying the juice home in barrels on the back of the lorry. At home the juice was piped off the lorry into four 40 gallon barrels in the outhouse. Each cask had 20lb of brown sugar, dissolved in hot water, added to it before fermentation which made the cider 'quite strong'. Mike's father, Len Edwards, preferred to ferment the cider in rum barrels, but Mike says he favours whisky or brandy as rum 'hung over the top of the cider' and spoilt the flavour by 'reaching the nose before the tongue'.

> Every third year father would buy one or two new barrels from Richard White's, the coal merchants, who also stocked spirit and wine casks. When I was old enough father gave me the job of going to buy the casks, the foreman at the yard would always offer you a wine cask first, you had to ask him for a spirit one for cider. When they brought out the barrel you took out the bung and breathed into it, as this built up the pressure inside and you could tell by the strength of the fumes if it was a good un. Then you tipped it up to look inside, letting the light in. If the light reflected off the wet wood the barrel was OK, you knew the cider would fetch the spirit out of the wood and add to the strength of the brew. It was strong stuff, not like the pop they sell today. Some people added rum to make the kind of stuff you would sell to Indians in tin bibles, but you didn't drink it in large quantities so it usually did you no harm. Sometimes a barrel went bad, just like vinegar and nobody could drink it.
>
> My grandfather would never change a barrel, he scoured out his empty ones every year with boiling water, but time and time again it was poor because he hadn't changed the barrel. Grandmother would invite me into the house for home made lemonade and cake (no one could make cake like my grandmother) but to keep in with grandfather you had to go to the shed for a tot of cider. On the whole grandmother's lemonade was the better of the two!

Terry Watts remembered a cider drinker from Devon who bought his cider regularly from a farm, in small casks. He told him:

> 'Sometimes it were good and sometimes not so good. I drink a good one ever so quick 'cos I can't wait to get another. But a bad one - cor I drink it even quicker so that I can go back and get a better 'un.'
>
> Science intervened to ensure we did the right things in the cider industry; when you have a vat containing a million gallons you can't afford for things to go wrong! Of course, this technology is available to small makers too, so there is no reason why they should produce a bad batch any more.

CAMRA (the Campaign for Real Ale) formed APPLE (the Apple and Pear Liaison Executive) in 1975 to promote traditional draught cider and perry and ensure outlets were recorded in CAMRA guide books. APPLE's committee needed to decide what it meant by 'traditional draught cider', and in 1980 CAMRA endorsed the following definition:

> Traditional draught cider is made from a primary fermentation of the juice of cider and dessert apples, with a dominant yeast derived from a natural apple yeast. Sugar may be added. Natural conditioning may be introduced by the addition of further amounts of yeast and sugar prior to casking, and there must not be total filtration or pasteurisation. The cider must be dispensed without the use of extraneous carbon dioxide.

This definition has parallels to the description of cider introduced in 1931 by the Board of Trade as part of the National Mark Scheme, which aimed to install quality and uniformity in British food and drink. With the onset of the depression the National Mark became part of the Buy British Campaign. The scheme insisted that cider must be made from apples grown in England and Wales, and so was immediately crippled by the failure of the English crop of cider fruit, which made the use of imports and concentrated juice unavoidable. It never really caught on with the big cider mills and died a natural death in the Second World War, leaving the cider manufacturers to set their own standards and methods of cider production.

A similar fate almost befell APPLE at the CAMRA A.G.M. in 1977, when some campaigners proposed that 'cider has no place in the campaign', but the motion was defeated. The following A.G.M. saw APPLE strengthen their position by winning a motion to include the symbol for real cider in CAMRA's national guide, on the basis of both good real ale and traditional cider. APPLE then grew in strength, especially after the publication in 1988 of David Kitton's *Good Cider Guide*. A motion to that year's A.G.M. succeeded in getting APPLE a budget to set up as a campaign group.

The next edition of the *Guide* appeared in 1995, edited by CAMRA staffer Ted Bruning. Ted Bruning is also editor for the CAMRA newspaper *What's Brewing* and supported APPLE's cider campaign with the launch of the *Cyder Press* in 1995, a quarterly supplement on cider, aimed at cider lovers and cider producers. 'I realised cider was in a world of its own and conceived of the *Cyder Press* supplement as a way to strengthen campaigning for traditional cider. There was a revival of interest country wide in cider which seemed promising, so I hoped that the supplement would become self-funding'. Sadly there was not enough advertising forthcoming from cider producers to continue the publication. At first *Cyder Press* was produced quarterly, and then reduced to three times a year, then two, as it became clear it was losing money. Finally, in 1999, it was pulled, with cider features moving back to the main body of *What's Brewing*, with a special 'cider month' of features in October.

Over time CAMRA has sought to promote the wider availability of high quality draught ciders and perries, celebrating the diversity of regional differences in both the drink and the fruit used in its production. It encourages producers to produce and the retail trade to stock and distribute traditional ciders and perries. It encourages the production of such ciders and perries free from the use of concentrated juice, artificial sweeteners, artificial colouring materials, extraneous carbon dioxide and other superfluous additives, and aims to ensure that labelling gives reliable information as to the contents and production methods used.

To fulfill its aims, CAMRA initiated cider bars at its beer festivals, run by volunteer cider enthusiasts. One of these was Mick Lewis who, along with his friend Jon Hallam, had set up a cider supply company that provided traditional cider in 5 gallon polycasks. According to Mick:

> It was missionary work, later cider suppliers may have seen it as a way to make a fortune but it isn't, the main market for traditional cider and perry is now CAMRA festivals and cider only festivals like Brogdale in Kent (September) and CAPE (Cider and Perry Exhibition) again run by CAMRA activists. CAPE would not have happened without APPLE, but the fourth exhibition lost money, then the possibility of running another also suffered from lack of suitable venues in London. We tried a local cider festival in Hereford in 1998, but really CAPE needs to be in London to attract enough cider drinkers and publicity.

Alongside the cider bars CAMRA also provide experts to talk to the media about traditional cider and perry, put producers in contact with technical services for cider makers, and have a network of representatives across the country who liaise with local producers, keeping APPLE up-to-date with developments in the industry and new producers.

CAMRA created the Champion Cider and Perry of the Year Competition, and also present The Pomona Award each spring to any person, company or 'thing' (someone once nominated a cider van called Fly) who has done excellent work in promoting cider and perry within the previous 12 months. Past winners have included Peter Mitchell at Core, Brogdale in Kent and Kevin Minchew, master cider and perry maker in Gloucestershire.

Recent years have seen much debate in APPLE about what is, or is not, real cider, a debate also causing dissent in industry groups such as the National Association of Cider Makers. Although the two sides may never agree, NACM being focused on producers' needs and APPLE for the consumer, Mick Lewis has a definite view of what is, and what is not, cider. In a historic debate during an APPLE meeting about the difference between category A (traditional cider), category B (some concentrate used) or C (keg ciders) Mick stated:

> We all know what real cider is, it is made from fresh juice with no added yeast, sugar or water, and is allowed to ferment naturally till dry. The only thing that should be allowed is a sweetener to make it medium or sweet. Keg cider is so obvious that I needn't go into it here. But, then you have some ciders that use concentrate instead of juice, others kill off the natural yeast and add their own, others add sugar to ferment above strength, then dilute with water. Some are filtered, some are pasteurised and hot filled. None of these ciders should be called real, but clearly they aren't keg either. Given no choice you would certainly recommend them above keg cider, hence the reason for category B, not as good as A, but far superior to C.

The *Good Cider Guide* became the bible for cider drinkers and enthusiasts keen to find traditional cider straight from the farm, or in local outlets. The first edition of the book emerged from David Kitton's diaries of working east to west across England, seeking out local cider makers during the hot summers of 1976 and '77.

> It took a lot of leg work, as the cider makers were reluctant to reveal their secrets or sell cider to strangers at that time. I broke down the barriers by drinking with them, showing a knowledge of cider which gained me respect. I must have been doing about 25 miles to the gallon (of cider) those first few years!
>
> It was clear most of the smaller cider makers relied on local, regular customers, plus a few tourists to sell their cider. Cider making was an added extra to the farm income, ambition was lacking to grow the business any bigger than the 1,500 gallons customs and excise free of duty limit, they were quite happy with their sales and production as it was.

CAMRA's third good cider guide was launched in May 2000, edited by Dave Matthews, a writer, journalist and cider enthusiast (later maker) from Wales. On the whole it remains a very useful reference book for the cider enthusiast—and is still the most recent.

Not all cider makers welcome CAMRA's efforts, seeing them as townie busybodies with no interest in the real countryside or the economic viability of the product, and that APPLE do more harm than good, but this is a tiny number in comparison to the producers who support CAMRA's campaign. Denis Gwatkins is one of those supporters who believes in making good, traditional ciders and perries. Denis feels that the group 'have done a brilliant job on the shows. Cider will never rival beer in sales, but there are more people drinking cider now and APPLE have helped in converting people to the real stuff, but it still needs a higher profile with more articles in *What's Brewing* telling people where to get it'.

One of the economic problems for small cider producers is the Customs and Excise duty on cider and perry. Cider was not taxed in the 20th century until 1917, when duty was imposed as a war time measure—in 1923 this tax was abolished. In 1956 the government decided they could no longer allow strong cider and perry to be sold without duty in competition to British beer and wine, and imposed duty on all ciders and perries above 8.5% alcohol. As a result most producers reduced the strength of their cider below the rate at which duty became payable. In 1976 the government imposed a 22p a gallon duty on all cider and perry, unless production was below a limit of 1,500 gallons, when no duty is payable (since altered to 70 hectolitres, equivalent to 1,540 gallons). In response most farmers reduced the output of cider and perry made on the farm to the 1,500 gallon limit. The imposition of duty caused sales of cider across the country to fall, hitting all cider makers in the process, and reducing output in big mills as well as small. Speaking to the London *Evening News* in February 1978, Brian Nelson, then managing director of Bulmers, said 'we could have absorbed the duty bit by bit, but not in one chunk which was indigestible to both the industry and the consumer'. Smaller makers described the duty as 'inflation through taxation' and many gave up altogether rather than deal with the extra red tape of paying duty, or gaining an exemption certificate from Customs and Excise. Efforts to raise the exemption level to help small makers were blocked by the NACM with the backing of Bulmers, Taunton and Coates/Gaymers.

Pete Smithies of Priding Farm, Saul, got an unexpected increase in his free of duty limit when Jasper Ely died. 'The Excise license for the cider transferred to me along with the name of the cider. Customs got the certificate wrong, they wrote 15,000 gallons instead of 1,500 gallons! They wrote within a week to say it should read 1,500, but it is still wrong—they never sent me another certificate and I've still got the wrong one'.

If a maker produces even just 10 gallons over the 1,500 gallon limit he has to pay duty on the whole batch. Ray Hartland of Flat Farm fell foul of Customs and Excise for supposedly infringing the duty free regulations and got a visit from the Excise man. Ray was a genial man with a great sense of fun, who enjoyed life and could make a joke out of any occurrence:

> He asked about my personal consumption allowance, said Ray, and I said I drank a gallon a day. 'Impossible', they said. After I'd drunk four pints they sort of believed me! Anyway, I said 'That'll be 365 gallons a year, but don't forget I shall expect an extra gallon every leap year mind'. They laughed a bit then.

As consumer acceptance of duty on cider increased, so did annual growth for the big cider mills. In 1990 the EEC announced that Britain's cider makers would be allowed to keep their 1,500 gallon free of duty allowance when the single market came into force in 1992. In 1996 the government imposed a rise in duty on all ciders over 7.5%, but below 8.5%, in response to market growth of alchopops, originally a lemon brew of 8+%, but now including flavoured ciders often with added spirits. In 1997 the EEC ruled on the sale of UK produced Lambrini Perry being 'passed off' as Italian Lambrusco, increasing the duty on sparkling, bottle conditioned ciders to wine levels, causing a slump in the sales of all ciders and perries. In 2002 the government, for the first time after 25 years of duty increases, reduced the duty on cider by 2p a pint following a pledge from NACM members in March 2000 that 'cider makers will reduce their prices by the corresponding amount if cider duties were reduced and will encourage their wholesale customers to pass on the reduction to the consumer'. However, like many such promises, although the duty cut has been passed on to the consumer by the small makers, medium to large mills have chosen not to pass on the bonus and their prices at the bar actually increased by 15p in the following three months.

The reduction in duty on cider was, in some small part, attributable to the Parliamentary Cider Group started by Hereford's MP Paul Keetch. As a parliamentary candidate Paul had visited the Strangers Bar at the House of Commons with Simon Hughes MP, and on asking for cider was offered Dry Blackthorn from Somerset. He spoke to Colin Shepherd (then MP for Hereford) and the chair of the House of Commons Catering Committee, but still could not get decent, Herefordshire cider stocked in the House.

> It became part of my election campaign, putting Herefordshire on the map'! Cider is a traditional industry for the county, but it is disadvantaged due to government policy of equalisation of duty based on alcoholic content. Local cider makers are badly hit

*MPs Shona McIssac and Paul Keetch sampling cider
in the bar in the House of Commons*

economically as cider has higher alcohol than beer, this makes little
difference to the lager or beer drinker, but the cider drinker is
paying far more duty per pint and this reduces cider sales. At that
time Bulmers were making people redundant due to higher duty,
which had led to improved production facilities to absorb the costs.
As the second key employer in the county this was disadvantageous
to Herefordshire I felt that cider was not being listened to by
government.

I mentioned in my maiden speech that I would like to set up a
Parliamentary Cider Club, like all-party groups already established
for beer and Scotch whisky. These groups represent their industries
at government level and lobby for better legislation, fair duty, taxation, exports and trade.

The first meeting of the Parliamentary Cider Group was announced
on 6 November 1997, 35 all party MPs supported the meeting, enabling
the group to comply with the all party group rules which state that the
group must have at least ten members from the majority government
party, along with at least ten members from the other parties, six of
whom must be from the official opposition. These numbers may include
members of the House of Lords. As a result the group was able to publish
its aims and elect officers. Paul Keetch (Lib Dem, Hereford) stood as

chair, Robert Syms (Conservative, Poole) as Treasurer and Shona McIssac (Labour, Cleethorpes) as Secretary.

> The group hold two meetings per year, summer and winter, and are now 60 MPs strong and growing. Meetings include an exhibition of products from NACM members, large and small, which amaze MPs with the range and diversity of cider styles. Mostly MPs only think of cider as the recognised, commercial draught products, not the premium bottled brands, bottle fermented cider, U.K. cider brandy or traditional draught ciders. Coming to the group increases MPs knowledge and awareness of the industry.
>
> The achievements of the Parliamentary Cider Group have included getting [Bulmers] Scrumpy Jack into the House bar in 1997, followed by Strongbow and Westons Stowford Press (in bottles). Being able to introduce foreign guests in the House to Herefordshire cider is a great delight to me. Recently the Senior Financial Advisor to President Putin of Russia was drinking a pint of Stowford Press!
>
> By us raising the awareness of cider with MPs the industry now feels someone is listening to them. The NACM newsletter distributed to Member MPs and the industry have made both aware of the need for PR in the House for cider producers.
>
> Since the group formed cider has not been disadvantaged against beer when the Treasury has increased (or lowered) taxation. Cider has been treated equally and cider makers now have access to the House and MPs who understand their industry.
>
> The Parliamentary Cider Group cannot help individuals, we are bound by regulation to listen and respond to NACM and other large groups. I urge individual makers to join NACM to get their voice heard, they can then visit the House and exhibit at our meetings twice a year.

Geoff Warren of GCW Technology feels that small cider makers are in a similar degenerate state to some of the Spanish and French winemakers just after the Second World War:

> Much of the wine from the south was poorly made with the minimum application of technology, leading to the EU wine lakes and the distillation of wine for road fuel. The French wine research Institutes got to grips with some of the problems and they were helped by the 'Flying Winemakers' from the New World areas of Australia, South Africa and California. This resulted in an increased application of technology, better understanding by the local makers and a huge increase in quality. The academic institutions working on cider in the UK are the now defunct Cider and

Fruit Juice Research Unit of Bristol University's Long Ashton Research Station and, latterly, Core Food and Drink.

They have made it possible for small makers to improve on their knowledge, although many makers consider the courses expensive and time consuming despite the fact that they are making a food product which they are going to sell to the public. In my opinion they have an obligation to the consumer to become as expert in their craft as possible. For many small makers the income from cider is 'jam on the bread', a simple cash boost from a product sold at the farm gate, and its production is not taken seriously. There are a number of exceptions, like Jean Nowell at Lyne Down Cider whose name occurs very frequently in competition winners' lists, but they are not that numerous. The attitude is often that it works now, that's the way we've always made it, they buy it, so why mess with it? Even though the resulting cider may be acetic, taste of nail varnish or pineapple/banana, have 'mouse' taint and go black after being poured out into a glass. All these faults have been seen at the Putley Big Apple cider competitions over the last few years, and yet you would expect that the ciders entered for a competition would be the best that can be made! The small makers cannot compete with the big makers or make their ciders as cheaply and many suffer a lack of awareness of just how much their cider actually costs them.

The commercial makers will contract fruit growers to intensively produce and deliver it to them. The cider may be made with some imported concentrate and with added fermentation sugars, helping to make significant savings. It is rumoured that some 'bottom shelf' products contain less than 25% juice, but not all cider and perry makers are members of the National Association of Cider Makers. They also have the economies of scale available through owning their own efficient and up-to-date plant and machinery. They are also aiming their product largely at a non-traditional, urban market and are able to sell the product at an across-the-bar price of £14 a gallon, as a premium drink helping to cover all the costs involved in the retail chain and licensed premises.

The small maker does not have the economy of scale. He probably owns and manages his own standard orchards, which may give less than half the crop of intensive orchards, picks the fruit himself, has decided to make the product from 100% juice by hand, although he has the freedom to do otherwise, packs it himself and labels it with home-produced labels, and puts considerable time and effort into production. Yet, he only gets £4 to £6 a gallon from the cider drinker, for a product sold in a plastic jerry can at the farm gate. His cider may be acetic due to poor equipment or hygiene and it may be unstable if sweetened with sugar. Smaller makers could use non-nutritive sweeteners such as saccharin, aspartame or Acesuiphame-K but generally choose not to. The product has a short shelf-life, is often poorly presented and so does not appeal to the trade.

So, to improve it he must sterilise, filter or pasteurise it, which costs money, or can co-operate with other makers to use a small-scale bottling plant like that until recently at Core Food and Drink. He can invest in a decent bottle and better presentation, aimed to appeal to the interested and enlightened cider drinker. Then he has the costs of marketing it, so that the consumer knows it is available, but a much better return can be made, perhaps £3 to £3.50 per bottle. The up-marketing of properly made traditional, 100% juice, ciders is the only way that the smaller makers can establish a niche for themselves. Far more co-operation between smaller makers could help public awareness of their premium products. The adoption of some EU schemes, such as Protected Geographical Indication (PGI—available for Herefordshire, Worcestershire and Gloucestershire only so far), would also instil confidence into the consumer.

Added to the small maker's woes is that the consumer has come to expect ciders to be sweetened to some degree and sweetening sugar is an added expense. Bulmers Number 7 had no added sweetening and was a quality drink for the *cognoscenti*. Weston's Oak Conditioned Extra Dry has $1/4\%$ sugar just to balance the acidity and natural astringency of traditional cider fruit, but very few consumers will drink absolutely dry ciders.

Peter Mitchell, whilst a tutor at Worcester College at Hindlip and at Core, led the way for small cider makers to eradicate poor quality cider and 'scrumpy' image:

> I feel cider is a tremendous product with huge potential. It is important for cider makers to take care and do it properly, to use science appropriately - good cider is an artisan product, which modern technology can help and complement to raise the quality and marketability of the drink.
>
> It is frustrating to me to come across poor cider that has been made without effort or care. Rather than directly criticise the maker I prefer to encourage them to improve, to see the faults not as problems but as challenges that can be overcome. There is always a way round. The problems often lie with a lack of understanding, technical knowledge and skills. Everyone can make a top quality product and find a market for it, if they pay attention to detail.
>
> Technically the most important factors are hygiene and an understanding of the fundamental science behind the cider making process. For example, a main spoilage problem is acetifi-

cation caused by aerobic bacteria. By eliminating oxygen content through careful use of air locks and carbon dioxide or nitrogen gas, the micro organisms are unable to grow and spoil the cider. Contamination can also be controlled through the use of sulphur dioxide - the Romans used to do it so it is not a new technology and should be seen as traditional. As long as it is used in managed amounts it is sometimes the best option for controlling the fermentation process.

Jean Nowell retired to Lyne Down Farm with her husband Terry in 1984. Cider had been made at Lyne Down before the Nowells arrived, originally using the stone press that still stands in the cider house attached to the main farmhouse, fruit later being milled using a vintage hand scratter converted to mechanical power by a young Ivor Gwatkins.

Terry kept rare breed poultry and I made the cider. The poultry was not that successful so we started to concentrate on the cider making and let the poultry go. When Terry died my brother Michael started coming up from Plymouth to help with the cider making, it was always a family affair. My father had made cider at Ross (he was a market gardener) when we were children. It was a nostalgic trip in a way, a second childhood, but better than the first!

Jean Nowell of Lyne Down Farm with some of her produce

My philosophy on making cider is due to the 1,500 gallon limit. It is not worth me treating the cider making commercially, nor does that interest me, but 1,500 gallons is worth making an effort over to improve the quality and preserve the tradition of farmhouse cider. I think we need as many people as we can to come into cider making at this level. It can help save the life of older cider trees by bringing in a small income for farmers with orchards, making it worth their while to

Feeding the scratter at Lyne Down, 1989

keep them rather than dig them up. Small scale cider making is a huge benefit to local farmers, and the cider making industry. If small makers' cider is decent it improves the image and quality of the drink and keeps the big firms interested in producing quality cider, as they keep an eye on the small makers as a benchmark to quality and market trends. In the past decade the standard and marketability of farmhouse cider had gone up tremendously, £3 for a 70cl bottle of farmhouse cider would never have happened five years ago.

The old orchard at Lyne Down Farm is planted with Yarlington Mill, Dabinett, Kingston Black and Stoke Red.

A lot of the best trees were grubbed out by accident when we came to the farm. We had marked the trees to be removed, but the farmer removed the unmarked trees. The new orchard contains 20 varieties budded from odds and ends that I hope will make a nice blend. I also buy in some local fruit - one particular orchard of which I am very fond is planted on deep red clay. The specific gravity of the juice from this orchard is always consistently higher than other crops. In 2000 my perry pears came from the Monks Walk at Hellens. I prefer fruit off the old trees. All of the fruit I use is grown within 2 to 3 miles of Lyne Down Farm. Old fruit trees produce better and tastier juice of a higher quality than young trees which produce fruit of a lower gravity. The people who pick my fruit do it by hand, only picking the best and discarding the rest, they will leave what is not good enough because it is rotten or unripe. I can wait for the fruit to be ready, unlike the big makers who need a continuous supply for their mills. My father had a lot of rubbish to say about cider making, but one thing he said was true - 'more bad cider is made by using unripe fruit than for any other reason'. I advise anyone setting up or making cider for the first time to have good fruit. It is very forgiving on your mistakes, you can still produce good cider, but with poor quality fruit you start off wrong and head further into disaster.

Two old screw presses at Lyne Down Farm, the one on the left with a compressed cheese, whilst the other shows the runnel around the base used to collect and feed the juice out of its spout

I mill what is really ripe at the time regardless of variety. Single varieties are nice and interesting, but I prefer a balanced cider, which you can only get from a blend. I start blending after the pressing is all finished and first fermentation has started, each time I rack off the ciders I blend them together. Acidity is my first consideration, I look for sharpness in my blends to give interest to the cider and help the vintage keep well. I keep a record of the fruit and the date of pressing plus what barrel the juice is fermented in - each of my barrels is named. As I'm blending I move the labels (or a copy of them) onto the fresh barrel, this helps me in tracing any faults and keeps me right for claiming Herefordshire on my labels, which is a protected geographical location in the EU.

The name of the place was a gift for marketing the cider. A nephew (I think) sent me a postcard which read 'Lyne Down - the only way to take it', and I drew the lady under the apple tree to go with it. For me, she sums up the charm of cider, a happy drink.

Jean took retirement in 2001, selling Lyne Down Farm to a new owner who intends keeping the cider making tradition there alive. In her time at Lyne Down her ciders and perries won many awards in both the CAMRA and Cider Museum Competitions, but none more outstanding than her 1st for Perry and 1st for Cider at the Big Apple Cider Trials in 1999.

8   21ST-CENTURY CIDER

Dereck Hartland's cider house at Tirley Villa is a haven for Gloucestershire traditional cider and perry, served from the wooden barrel. The white lined walls display the awards Hartland's have won for their cider and perry, alongside pictures of Flat Farm where Ray Hartland, Dereck's dad, first started making cider. In the drawers of a small table are more pictures and press clippings, along with the treasured cider making diary of Ray, which records the result of his fruit collecting and the volume of resulting juice, along with notes on that year's vintages. It may be an unspoiled idyll of what a farmhouse cider shed should be, however Dereck is stoical about the real world challenge of selling his cider:

> Cider still suffers from the smocks and straw image whilst the word scrumpy conjures up thoughts of cloudy cider with bits floating in it. I feel traditional is a better word for my cider, it does not carry so many negative images for the customer. Everyone wants organic nowadays. Though our orchard and fruit are not sprayed they are grazed by two cattle for manure and no artificial fertilizers are used, but I can't call it organic. Certification is too expensive for small makers like me and the Bulmer's organic scheme is too limiting on my production. I couldn't afford to sell my cider to supermarkets—they'd screw me to the floor! I feel that bottles have sparkled up traditional cider's image in the eyes of the customer. They are the way forward for the future. I think that the smaller maker should be able to produce 1,500 gallons tax free and then pay tax on anything above that limit.

Geoff Warren feels that it is the media who must take much of the blame for perpetuating the scrumpy myth. Very few drinks writers ever take the trouble to investigate and comment on cider on a regular basis, as they might beer or whisky.

At Bulmers we would hold occasional open days for journalists. They would be brought down from London by train, be shown the Moorfields Mill and the Ryelands Street vat house and then I would be wheeled out as the acceptable cider scientist, at the time being Technical Manager and responsible for product development as well as having a strong interest in the history and past technology of the industry. The visitors would be shown an audio-visual presentation about modern cider making, have a tutored tasting and then lunch, each course accompanied by a different Bulmer cider, starting with Number 7 as an *aperitif* and ending up with Sweet Pomagne or still Special Cellar with the desert course. There were very few serious articles to come out of these events, enjoyable as they were. Cooking features in women's magazines were quite well represented but the mainstream journalists still latched on to the rats in the vats and country yokel themes, if they wrote about us at all.

George Thomas joined Bulmers in 1978 as Bulmers' public relations manager, with the job 'of bringing cider into the 20th century, never mind the 21st'.

Cider is soaked in heritage and history which we must not lose sight of, but for it to survive in modern times it must develop and move forward into the future.

In the 1920s cider was little known outside of the West Country. Salesmen for Bulmers, when expanding trade outside of the traditional cider making and drinking areas, often had to explain to publicans what it was. Publicity for cider was unsophisticated. A 1936 slogan read 'A for Apples, B for Bulmers, C for Cider' whilst an advertisement showed a rosy cheeked county lass pouring a stream of rosy apples from a sack. Adverts in women's magazines for Pomagne were aimed at

persuading women that cider was a more ladylike drink than beer. with slogans like 'Every woman knows that mineral salts in apples keep the complexion clear'. This was followed by adverts suggesting that strong, dry cider was a drink for he-men.

The launch of ITV in 1955 saw Bulmers seize the opportunity to advertise on the screen, hiring the Beverley Sisters to promote Bulmers cider with this song:-

> Bring out the Bulmers cider
> That's the cider I adore
> Bring out the Bulmers cider
> I couldn't ask for more
> See how it sparkles like my eyes
> pour me the cider I idolise
> Bring out the Bulmers cider
> The cider that satisfies ...
>
> Bring out the Bulmers cider
> It makes me feel so bright
> Bring out the Bulmers cider
> We'll have a ball tonight.

In 1960 a new brand, Strongbow, was launched by Bulmers aimed at men in the 18 to 24 age group, who were now earning higher wages and had more disposable income. By the 1970s, point of sale floor standing panels showed a group of young women in fashionable short skirts clamouring for Woodpecker cider, clearly targeting a modern young woman and moving away from promoting cider as a drink for farm workers with straws in their mouths and West County accents. George Thomas continues:

> By promoting our cider to the 18 to 24 age group we walked a tightrope between tradition and the demands of the modern consumer. Today's market is fickle and competitive. Consumer pressure groups like CAMRA and APPLE, run by hobbyists and enthusiasts who are fired up by traditionalism are fine, but we are running a drink business with a commitment to our 7,000 shareholders and our work force. APPLE would have us produce only traditional dry cider such as Number 7. It was a great traditional cider but few people would drink it today. But, we have not forgotten our traditional roots, we still make cask conditioned cider and will continue to do so, but to survive we have to make styles that suit today's drinker and fashions. Very, very dry ciders are not to current tastes in the wider market. Cider is part of the long drinks market and as such must compete with all the other drinks in that market. When a consumer looks at the bar fonts the choice is extensive. Cider is no longer small scale, it is part of the big picture. In the summer of 2002 Strongbow was placed eighth in the long drinks chart, the only non-beer on the list. Sales have more than doubled in volume due to our commitment to developing modern long drinks that appeal to the 18 to 24 age group, which are available on draught in almost every pub in the U.K. alongside our biggest competitor - lager.
>
> When I joined the company cider was dry or sweet and came packaged in a big brown bottle with a hand applied label. Now we produce diverse styles of cider with packaging aimed directly at specific consumers. Drinking is a fashion accessory. The young go out wearing their best clothes, hairdos and make up, and they are looking for products and packaging that make a statement about themselves and their peer group. Bulmers' packaging is fashionable, modern and contemporary, a critical factor in sales. Consumers at the bar buy with their eyes, scanning the dozen or so fonts on the bar and buying by mood rather than knowing what they want before they get there. An attractive font design catches the eye and sells the product.
>
> The exceptions to these rules are brands aimed at older customers who know what they want. Bulmers Original still stands on the bar presented with a wooden cask font, and Traditional with handpump, the cask being hidden in the cellar or displayed as a five gallon polycask within a built in tap on the bar. When we

relaunched Scrumpy Jack as a premium cider in 1989 we tried a handpull pump on the bar to reflect its links with tradition, but it needed a more modern marketing approach. The original Scrumpy Jack was a traditional, rough cider which would not have sold in the modern market, but it was a good name that could be utilised for a new quality product, made from 100% English cider apples. CAMRA objected to the handpump as false marketing as the cider was served carbonated from a keg and was not cask conditioned. The older market we were aiming at were confused, so we changed the bar font to a bright, contemporary one. Scrumpy Jack is now the number one premium cider and is a huge success.

The industry was in a period of growth until 1984 when the increase in Excise duty created a decline in sales. In 1989 the Bulmers Board took the initiative to double marketing, spent up to £11 million which meant a drop in profits for shareholders, but enabled us to build brand awareness. Innovation became a key plank in the company's plan. Top of the agenda was, and still is, to compete with lager. We recognise that other cider makers are not our competitors, we are all in the same fight against the dominance of lager in the long drinks business. In innovating we have tried all sorts of things: Schnapper (peach schnapps and cider), Strongbow Smooth (a nitrokeg cider with a creamy head), Strongbow Ice, Black Cider (cider with stout). Some worked, some did not, but we still aim to innovate. Our aim is to make cider less challenging as an introduction drink for young people.

People's palates have changed over the years and the generations. We have to keep one step ahead and produce a brand that each succeeding generation will enjoy. It is no use presenting a young woman with the same Woodpecker cider brand that her grandmother used to drink, she is looking for something much funkier and modern to impress her friends with her sophisticated tastes. If she later finds out that granny enjoyed Woodpecker as a girl as well that's fine - it is bringing the generations together.

British drinking habits have changed. Once Pomagne was the common sparkling party drink - the party popper, a poor man's champagne promoted by the Pop a Pomagne TV ad in the late 1960s. Pomagne has now been overtaken by cheap sparkling wines from around the world at under £2 a bottle. Pomagne was a nice drink for £1.50 and genuine quality for the price, but you can't say the same for all the cheap sparkling wine! It all comes down to the image of what will impress your guests.

In the supermarket, cider is not an established purchase. When shopping in the drinks aisles with all the competition provided by wine, beers and spirits, it is often an impulse buy, so point of sale promotions are essential along with consumer offers and in store competitions. Young people are often already established drinkers of our brands through pub promotions, in the supermarket we are targeting the older customer who may be reminded of a special event, holiday or a visiting relative or friend who enjoys cider. We have to use every marketing trick to get the attention of this impulse buyer.

The small makers such as Westons, Gwatkins and Dunkertons, who have a commitment to the tradition of cider yet are also participating in the modern marketing and production of cider as small scale craft makers, deserve tribute from us. They are important for the mythology and methodology of cider making, reflecting cider's heritage and as visible proof that cider still has its roots in rural Herefordshire. The small cider companies success depends heavily on the amount of promotion we give our brands and our success as the market leader. We spend millions a year on TV ads, then they pick up their share from incremental purchases as they do not advertise or have the resources to promote their brands on the same scale as Bulmers.

Keith Knight of Knights Cider has found the aggressive purchasing power of the supermarkets to be a problem to all cider makers.

They are always pushing for cheaper cider, which affects the quality of the product consumers buy. If you follow their lead you are in danger of producing an industrial product with very little apple juice in the process, mainly sugar and water. Aston Manor was our main customer until three years ago. We made a variety of different styles of cider for them, also flavoured alchopops on a cider base, our best seller being lemon. We saw others go into decline because of capital investment in alchopops, which was a factor in making us decide to get out of the cheap, white cider market and concentrate on our core business, producing a quality cider from English bittersharp and bittersweet cider fruits. The big producers can afford to offer incentives that are not economic for

154

smaller makers, so the market for traditional, quality cider is very small, perhaps it is only there because it is not profitable to the large players. Still, I would like to be remembered for using the great British Bittersweet and hope maybe one day the U.K. cider industry will be proud to use this term to fend off the cheap imported cull concentrate products that any cider maker using traditional apples and 100% juice to ferment a cider to 6% alcohol by volume cannot hope to compete with.

Roger Jackson is Sales Director for Westons Cider, who market their products with very little advertising, preferring to trade on tradition.

> Westons' cider is a traditional product made with traditional skills and our ciders taste of apples. We market to the top 10% of cider drinkers who are looking for a quality product, a market niche that Bulmers and Matthew Clark cannot fill, that only represents 1% of the cider sold in the U.K. We like to believe that Westons sells through the name rather than the brand.
>
> Packaging is a strength, it is something we can be both pro-active and reactive to as a small company, giving us an edge over our competitors. Old Rosie and Herefordshire Perry in 2 litre clear flagons are unique in the industry and have won five gold medals from CAMRA. In 1994 our strong (8.4%) Double MM cider was being sold in an innovative, clear bottle which marked it out from beers on the shelf, but it still had a paper label. In 1998 we found that the paper label interfered with the light passing through the bottle and showing off the clarity of the contents in the new illu-minated chiller cabinets being used in pubs. So we switched to a clear label, with a picture of apples on and renamed the cider Marcle Millennium. In 1999, 2000 and 2001 it won the best Premium Cider Award in the International Cider and Beer Festival at the International Food Exhibition, yet the cider inside the bottle was the same as we had sold in 1994. Staying true to what we believe in we were one of the first cider makers in the U.K. to produce an organic cider in 1997, which went on to win the *You* and Soil Association Organic Food Award for an alcoholic drink in 1998.

Ivor and Susie Dunkerton first tried selling their cider in local pubs in north-west Herefordshire, but soon found that the restrictions placed on publicans by brewery loans and the tied-house system meant they did not get very far, so instead they packaged the cider and marketed it to shops.

> We were aware of cider's down-market and cheap image and were also concerned about drunkenness amongst young people, so we deliberately set out to create an up-market image with corked,

elegant bottles with an illustration of Adam and Eve on the label, pushing the cider more to the middle classes where nobody else was and creating our own niche market. For a long time Dunkertons' cider was sold mostly through specialist retailers, food halls, wholefood shops and draught in our own farm shop.

When we first made cider we were novices. One year we bottled a new cider in June when fermentation appeared to have stopped and sold the cider to the House of Fraser in Cheltenham. They put it on a shelf below the whisky - as the summer got hotter the corks in the bottles began to rise, pushing the shelf above into the air. A lesson learned about a late malo-lactic fermentation!

We are still presenting an old fashioned still cider in bottle and on draught. Because most of our produce is sold in the bottle, all but the driest of the ciders is now pasteurised. We have tried other methods, only to have filtered all the taste out of them. It's not always pasteurisation that gives a cider a cooked flavour but often the use of apple concentrate. Bulmers and Matthew Clark have

established the idea in the consumer's mind that all cider is sweet and carbonated, so in the early days some of our bottles were returned by customers because, in their eyes, the cider had gone flat. In order to expand our market we have had to carbonate our products and are very pleased with the results. Cider is often a lost memory for the

156

older consumer and I dearly wish we could sell more still dry cider, but the market will not accept it.

Presentation is what sells our cider to new customers, so we have recently created a new look for a younger market - Black Fox with a simple direct label. Our Premium Organic label was devised after looking at all ciders on display in supermarkets. You could not tell they were cider, there were lots of pictures of apples but no obvious word 'cider'. So we went the other way with a big 65 x 68 mm label saying 'cider' in big type. It certainly attracted many new buyers.

Along with pure juice content and high alcohol duty, such presentation costs more to put together than if we had chosen a basic farmhouse cider image. We soon realised that if we were going to grow the business we would have to deal with the super-markets. Waitrose know their business and have been very good. Dealing with them has been instructive and good business, as being small and specialised we have been able to stay in control.

We have not really found a local market, although the visitors to our shop and to the Cider House Restaurant which Susie opened in 1994 have contributed enormously. The 400-year-old oak barns that form the restaurant were dismantled and re-assembled at Hays Head. We started the restaurant because people were always asking where they could drink our ciders in the area, but the Cider House is also a showcase for local, organic Herefordshire produce and cider and perry is used in most of the cooking. Susie took over as

The old barn re-erected at Dunkertons to form The Cider House Restaurant which uses their cider, and much other local, organic, produce, in its varied menu. A pleasant couple of hours can be had tasting cider and then relaxing over lunch or tea

head chef in 1999. The restaurant is quite fun - essential to the business and has helped enormously to raise awareness of our cider and perry to individual customers.

Dunkertons are just one of the cider outlets on Herefordshire Tourism's *Herefordshire Cider Route* leaflet. First published in 1996 and revised every year since, it is an essential guide to finding cider producers in Herefordshire that has led the way for other cider making counties to produce their own trails. Some of the outlets offer sales from shops, others from the farm gate along with additional attractions such as orchard walks, local food, mill tours and, in season, an opportunity to see cider being made.

Broome Farm, in Peterstow, Herefordshire, has been part of the cider route since the latter's inception in 1996. The farm also offers bed and breakfast, cream teas and dinners in the evening. New in 2003 is a small herd of Alpacas, the first 'baby' to be born was named Perry, for obvious reasons! Mike Johnson says:

We value our regular customers, their small purchases soon add up. Customers who buy a gallon a week on a regular basis soon empty a barrel. We started bottling for off licenses and shops then were listed on the cider route, which has been a great help, having many people visiting daily who are following the route. We found there is a limit to what people are willing to pay for cider and perry, even in a well presented glass bottle. The prices hadn't risen for 10 years, in 1989 it was 50p a pint and still the same in 1999, now we charge £1.50 a litre (in your own container) and bottles are £3 each. As we are VAT registered the price had to also reflect this. In 2003 we expanded above the duty exemption limit and are now called Ross-on-Wye Cider and Perry Co. Ltd. The reason for expansion is simply the realisation that I was depending on Bulmers for my main income and due to their problems over the last 12 months, needed to make more of my own cider.

Robin Haig at Dewchurch Cider, in Much Dewchurch, sells most of his produce at the farm gate.

We are deliberately not on the cider trail because we are a pretty small-scale concern. We've only ever made under 1,500 gallons of cider and perry, and last autumn made just 600 gallons of cider and 100 of perry. Although we sell most of our production from the farm, we are selling increasing amounts through farm shops and the cider specialists in Leominster, Orchard Hive and Vine—and naturally we drink quite a lot ourselves. The cider we sell through retailers is normally bottled in half litre bottles.

It is interesting to experiment with blends of different apples, and by far my favourite cider is made from Stoke Red apples, either as a single variety or blended with a small proportion of another variety such as Dabinett. Stoke Red apples produce a wonderful cider with a clean, slightly honeyed flavour. Beats Kingston Black hands down in my opinion. It is not a common variety and it's not easy to grow, but we have enough to make a few barrels each year.

Our cider usually comes out at about 6% or so, although our first year's production, matured in former rum casks with a bit of rum left in the bottom, was quite a bit stronger! The regulars in our local pub, the Black Swan, have been known to hold Dewchurch Cider drinking competitions, and of course you can't drink too many pints without feeling a bit the worse for wear, even if it hasn't got rum in it.

Geoff and Sue Morris set up Orchard Hive and Vine in the Buttercross, Leominster, in August 1997 after extensive local research. Geoff was seeking a market for his mead (Meads of Mercia), he was finding it difficult to get onto the shelves of independent off-licenses and could not produce the quantities required by the supermarkets. Geoff had also started making Cyser (fermented apple juice and honey) which also required a market. With the help of Peter Mitchell at Hindlip, Geoff was put in touch with the Three Counties Cider and Perry Association. Through the Association Geoff discovered that a lot of cider makers had the same frustrations, along with English wine makers and local brewers who would also be keen to supply bottled beers. Janet Mackay of Putley approached Geoff with her Jus apple juice, and it was also decided to stock the honey from Fosse Way Honey that goes into Geoff's mead.

To select the first stocks of local cider a massive tasting was held with Geoff's friends in Walsall, West Midlands, where the favourite drink turned out to be Robin Haig's James Grieve Apple Juice! Geoff took early retirement from his job as a chemistry teacher and the small amount of capital he and Sue had, was used to open Orchard Hive and Vine in Leominster.

Orchard Hive and Vine aims its range at customers who are disappointed or disillusioned with mass-market ciders available from Bulmers and Matthew Clark. The shop is promoted through tastings, boards out on the pavement, adverts and editorial in specialist press and local papers, joining in local celebrations by providing a stall at street markets, festivals and street promotions, by entering national competitions and having a listing in the Herefordshire Cider Route leaflet.

> Customers hear about the shop and come to find us, many clutching the cider trail leaflet. We do a lot of business by centralising the stock in one place, but visitors also like to see where the cider is made as well. So if they don't have a leaflet we give them one and encourage them to visit one of the makers on their way through the county.

The shop also has an e-commerce website and a mail order catalogue.

> It took a while to find a reliable carrier, as firms appeared to either drop or drink it! So now we charge £8 for delivery, and are much more confident it will arrive safely.
>
> When we are selling cider and perry we try to maximise its appeal to the consumer by talking about the cider makers as local characters. We feel it is essential to sell them as well as their products as each craft cider or perry is unique and each cider maker has their own approach. They are making cider their own way because they feel everyone else is doing it wrong, so to sell their produce you have to sell the craftsman too.
>
> More farmers in the three counties are turning to cider to provide extra income and added value to their farm produce. They have realised that cider does not need a lot of technical expertise, only some basic equipment. A lot of people could set up cider making and a market would still be there for a quality product. It is important for farmers to have these added value products, but they must produce packaged products, not just raw materials to benefit from the venture.
>
> How the cider is packaged affects its perceived quality by the consumer and also its shelf life. Presentation is crucial, but price is also a factor. The cider maker has to decide who he is producing his cider for, what their personal taste might be and what they will

expect in the way of packaging and presentation. He must deliver the right message to attract the customer - like the cider makers every cider or perry has its own character and market. Customers looking for traditional cloudy ciders buy draught cider which is filled into litre PET bottles. The cider is delivered to us in 15 litre manucubes, a bag in a box system which preserves the cider perfectly, provided it is stable.

Denis Gwatkins' new colour label showing the horse-powered stone mill is more up-market than his previous neat home-made labels. It may attract a different customer, though the high quality of the product remains the same.

Kevin Minchew's smart label of a Celtic tree with twisted roots is wonderful, it sums up the quality and care taken with the produce in the bottle and what a good cider or perry should be, made from quality fruit from trees planted in good soil (and dependent on it). The packaging looks good and attracts customers seeking a premium product who are willing to pay more,

Minchew's

7.4% Vol.   75cl.

Still Perry

Dumbleton Huffcap

Minchews Real Cyder & Perry, Ashchurch,
Gloucestershire GL20 8HX

or those that know about Minchews.

Ivor and Susie Dunkerton's landscape label with Adam and Eve shows the time and trouble taken to get the product right. Also the organic mark is very attractive at the moment, a classic.

Small cider makers often ask us for advice on how to bottle their products for sale in the shop. There are two options: filtration and pasteurisation to extend shelf life. Filtered cider will last up to a year on shelf. But if cider is pushed through a filter at high pressure, this appears to effect the taste. There is no scientific explanation for this and the taste and aroma comes back after two to three weeks in the bottle, although the resulting clear product is not to everyone's taste. It is a compromise for shelf life, you have a loss of yeast and fruit particles, but the benefits far outweigh the problems. Using coarse filtration makes a difference so small as to be unnoticeable, unless it is pasteurised, which can caramelise the flavour of the cider, a fault that is even easier to pick up in perry.

Producers are beginning to invest in their own bottling and filtration equipment, to continue the momentum built up over the last few years with the demand for quality, well presented, still ciders and perries.

The Three Counties Cider and Perry Association was begun in July 1993, as a result of an idea proposed by small cider makers during the Putley Cider Competition that spring. The association aims to represent its members with local and national government, with the press and media at all levels and at shows and exhibitions. As well as promoting the transfer of technical knowledge between its members, it contributes to research by being a member of the National Association of Cider Makers. Jean Nowell says:

> The Association has been very useful. It has helped to distribute lots of information between large and small cider makers. The experience of the bigger makers, legislation and technical stuff, filters down to the small makers and improves our practice. It is a supportive organisation but the main advantage is that it has helped us to get to know each other, we can phone each other for advice when problems arise and co-operate on marketing initiatives, reducing the cost of packaging, publicity and promotion by acting as a group.

In 1997 Jean Nowell and Kevin Minchew went to the NEC in Birmingham to tell people about real cider and perry. While they were there an idea formed to create a Guild of Craft Cider Makers. They were soon joined by Geoff Warren and Peter Mitchell on the technical side. Three Counties Cider and Perry Association members were surveyed about the idea and the juice content of their ciders. Most were using 100% juice which was adopted as a benchmark for Guild membership.

Geoff Warren acknowledges that the Guild of Craft Cider Makers hit problems in agreeing standards for craft ciders with juice content less than 100%. The NACM, for example, no longer have a minimum standard for juice content due to the difficulty of monitoring and policing it. A number of very different methods for estimating juice content have been attempted but the variability between apple varieties, and within one variety grown under differing conditions, has made it impossible to make absolute and impartial judgements. Declaration of techniques to an industry neutral, or to Trading Standards, have been greeted with scepticism and suspicion by large and small cider makers alike. The fear is that commercial confidences would be compromised. Strangely enough, monitoring of records by Trading Standards for the purposes of Protected Geographical Indication (PGI) registration has not hit the same problems.

Geoff Morris soon became involved in the Guild.

> While we were trying to decide on standards for all craft cider makers we found that the counties of Devon and Cornwall had similar ideas, but were ambivalent about the word 'traditional'. They felt that their ciders should be made from bittersweet or bittersharp apples with no culinary fruit allowed. We wanted to be inclusive to all craft cider makers, so adopted a draft standard as a quality scheme that allows for the culinary fruit used in the traditional cider making counties of Kent and East Anglia. This could have been got over by registration of specific techniques for countries or areas, as is the case with the PGI rules.
>
> As 95% of commercial cider is sold carbonated the Guild could not force makers to produce a still cider, which possibly would not find them a large enough market. Just still cider would also have excluded a number of excellent products made from 100% juice that were seeking to compete with mainstream ciders and provide a stepping stone for cider drinkers between carbonated products and traditional still cider and perry. In the end a limit of three atmospheres of Carbon dioxide was agreed upon, which permits and encompasses bottle conditioned products and champagne style ciders and perries. So, the decision whether to carbonate or not remains with the cider maker.
>
> Our members are all committed individuals with their own cherished secrets, ideas and tricks, as well as being characters who are reluctant to pool abilities and knowledge if it will assist a poorer competitor. There is not much common ground between them. This resulted in the collapse of the organisation in 2002. To succeed the members of the Guild needed to subdue their self interest and act in a co-operative manner. The Bath Agricultural Society (1890s-1900) should be our benchmark for co-operation. They were gentlemen who were able to separate self interest and commercial rivalry for the good of the industry, they pooled knowledge and conducted experiments for the benefit of the group.

The Guild also hoped to raise the profile of craft cider and perry with the media. Geoff Warren again:

> It has always been difficult interesting journalists in cider and perry due to its rural image, or because of the ubiquitous bland commercial brands. Beer and wine writers are unaware and uninterested in craft cider and do not write about it as being a varied product of differing qualities and flavours, they prefer to portray the drink as a yokel product whilst wearing a straw behind their ears.

163

Kevin Minchew's appearance on BBC Heart of the Country talking about Gloucestershire perry making, resulted in increased orders at Orchard Hive and Vine and direct to the public on Kevin's stand at the Three Counties Show in Malvern. This proved the media can help educate consumers without talking down to them, inform them without being on high or on a clichéd hobby horse. It is to be hoped that in the future we could raise the profile of fine, traditional craft ciders and perries and promote the Wine of the West to a more sophisticated and discerning drinker through column inches in the Sunday papers and intelligent reporting on the national media that breaks the stereotypical image, making the general public aware that craft cider and perry can easily rival fine wines.

9 THE PERRY REVIVAL

Perry, made the same way as cider but with perry pears, is a strong, clear, still and usually dry drink, free from acidity and with a heavenly floral scent and taste. It leaves you wishing for more than a glassful, despite the locals' gleeful warning that 'perry goes in like sunshine, round and round like thunder, then out like lightening'.

Perry pear trees are taller than apple trees and twice as long lived, sometimes surviving for up to 300 years. They occur as boundary markers on the edge of parishes and as avenues to big manor houses in many parts of the three counties. The biggest trees flourish in the gravelly, red sandstone soils along the Welsh Marches, giving rise to the local saying that 'perry pears flourish only within sight of May Hill'—the views from the summit encompass the counties of Herefordshire, Gloucestershire, Monmouthshire and Worcestershire.

The perry pear tree is a magnificent feature in the landscape. In the winter the bare branches soar high into the sky, their boney fingers making the tree easy to identify. In spring the branches are covered with a cascading froth of white blossom two to three weeks before the cider apple trees come into bloom, and in autumn the tree is weighed down with the small, hard pears whose tannic, bitter flesh discourages young boys from scrumping them for eating. Yet, once pressed, the juice of these pears is sweet and rich, producing two to four hogsheads of perry from one tree in a good year. Perry maker Kevin Minchew of Aston Cross says:

> Although my father made cider and perry I took no real interest in it as a child. I considered picking up the fruit in the autumn a bit of a chore, but the smell of perry pears in hessian sacks never really left my nostrils and even today that autumnal scent floods me with memories of the pear orchards whose immense trunks and canopies brought together an almost religious awe, similar to the feeling one gets when amongst the columns of our churches, abbeys and cathedrals.

Andrew Knight was the first to record the virtues of the perry pear in his *Pomona Herefordiensis* (1811), which includes illustrations of five varieties of perry pear, including the Holmer Pear he had found growing in a hedge at The Moor in Holmer on the outskirts of Hereford. Many of the trees recorded by Knight had been planted in the 17th century and by 1910 they were dying. Yet no young trees had been planted to replace them as farmers needed a guaranteed crop to sell to the new cider mills, and perry pears with their slow rate of growth and maturity were uneconomic. C.W. Radcliffe Cooke called for a revival of planting using the perry pear collection at the National Fruit and Cider Institute in Bristol to save esteemed varieties of perry pears such as Barland and Taynton Squash being forced into extinction. His appeal to farmers had some success, including the extension of perry pear planting into Somerset for the first time.

In the 1920s Dr. Durham of Bulmers carried out an extensive survey of perry pears in Herefordshire, recording the great wealth of varieties found in the county and trying to sort out the great confusion of names, which were often purely local. He was the first to emphasise the importance of the shape and growth of the tree to identifying varieties, and established a collection of 40 of the best varieties at the Bulmers' nurseries at Broxwood as a reference for future researchers.

Dr. Durham's research helped Ray Williams of Long Ashton Research Station in his search for perry pears in the 1950s. There were a number of perry trees in the Long Ashton Cider Fruit collection when Ray arrived.

> I grew up in Longhope, Gloucestershire, on the northern border of the Forest of Dean and made perry with my grandfather at home as a boy. I had studied at Long Ashton as a post graduate student and having a knowledge of perry pears, I noticed that one or two trees in the collection had been wrongly identified or labelled. As a student I was shot down by the Professor [Barker] for pointing out these mistakes, but later I also found out Knight's *Pomona* also had some inaccuracies. Once I got my research job at the Institute, I felt we should have our varieties properly named and described.

A then recent Ministry of Agriculture survey contained a census of fruit trees, including perry pears. Using the information in the survey, Ray located the farms that had perry pears then, being a keen cyclist, visited each farm, collecting fruit and the local names of each variety. Many of the farmers he visited thought he was from the Ministry and were distrustful at first—they held bad memories of the war time years when Ministry men had forced them to plough up grazing land and orchards for arable crops against their wishes, and didn't want anyone snooping around their pear trees.

> When I arrived they often looked puzzled as I didn't have a car and was not wearing a suit and polished shoes. It helped a lot that I had local knowledge of the prices of pigs and that at Gloucester market, which helped to break down the barriers and explain my eccentric interest in perry pears.

Ray was glad he had his bicycle. Often the farmers would give him a sample of the perry made on the farm whilst reminiscing about the old days, frequently necessitating a quiet rest by a hedge on the way home.

Some of the farmers in Taynton remembered another man coming round on horseback 50 or 60 years before Ray, also to look at perry pears. This turned out to be Dr. Durham, Bulmers' chemist. Dr. Durham was also a keen photographer and had documented the trees during the 1920s, along with descriptions of their locations. His work had never been published, but he donated his albums to the Woolhope Naturalists' Field Club. Ray traced one of these albums to the Royal Horticultural Society Archives in London and found it to be of great help in identifying lost varieties and spotting trees in the Herefordshire, Worcestershire and Gloucestershire landscape. In 2000, Charles Martell later traced the other volume of Dr. Durham's album to the library of the Woolhope Club.

As well as thoroughly documenting the trees and their fruit, Dr. Durham had marked good specimen trees with an ornamental lead label. At first Ray had some difficulty finding the labels until an old farmer, who remembered Dr. Durham from when he was a lad, explained that to stop the labels going missing as souvenirs for young boys the doctor had stood on the back of his horse and nailed them high up on the tree's branches. Because of this many of Dr. Durham's lead labels remain in place on surviving perry pear trees today.

The identification and documentation of perry pears by Ray enabled Long Ashton to locate supplies of high quality fruit for their cider house, notably the varieties Winnal's Longdon (first identified by Dr. Durham) and Hendre Huffcap, which can be blended without production problems. These became the standard varieties for Long Ashton Perry. Long Ashton published Ray's research identifying perry pears in memory of Professor Barker who was the first director of the Fruit and Cider Institute.

Charles Martell has dedicated his farm at Dymock to preserving local distinctiveness. Rare breed Gloucester cattle graze the orchard and produce milk for Gloucester cheeses made on the farm and sold around the world, including his award winning Stinking Bishop named after a perry pear and washed in perry made from the trees in the farm's orchard. The Three Counties Perry Pear collection grew out of Charles's work to identify local varieties of perry pear to grow in his orchard:

When I was a lorry driver delivering to local farms, a lot of the farmers would talk to me about the perry pear trees. I noticed they were unique to Gloucestershire and magnificent trees in the landscape. As years went on a lot of the perry pear trees were lost to gales and not replaced. I recognised that no-one was planting them for the future and wanted to prevent them dying out or being lost through neglect, or due to modern living which had eliminated the need and market for perry pears.

In 1990, I approached the Three Counties Showground as a site for a national collection, as I did not know if I would still be at my farm in 5 or even 10 years as we were struggling to survive. The Three Counties site was perfect as I knew it would be around long after I had gone and would provide a library of varieties for future generations to revive or continue to preserve for horticultural and historical interest. The Three Counties Agricultural Society saw the value of my idea and to my surprise said yes. So then I had to get to work identifying trees and provide grafted specimens for the collection. My main point of reference to identify the trees was Ray Williams' book *Perry Pears.*

Ray Williams remembers that one of the problems he faced in helping Charles establish the collection was the arrival of fireblight in the UK. Fireblight (*Erwinia amylovora*) attacks pear and apple fruitlets, causing rotting of the fruit and of extension fruiting spurs. Fireblight is a bacterial infection which can spread from local hedgerows, the greatest risk being when fruit trees are carrying heavy blossom. There is no effective chemical cure and the infection can kill young trees. Mature trees usually survive the attack, but can become a source of infection to other trees, so it is advisable if a fireblight attack is confirmed, to grub out the trees and burn them.

The disease was probably brought into the country on imported ornamental nursery stock then was spread along hawthorn hedges edging roads and motorways. Caxton Superb pear (a culinary variety) along with a number of Canadian and American varieties were found to be immune to fireblight. Virus free stem builders of these varieties were developed at Long Ashton in the hope that the immunity would be passed to the budded or grafted branches, or at least stop it spreading to the stem. These stem builders were used to establish the Three Counties Perry Pear collection, but by this time fireblight had run its course and disappeared.

To find the varieties for the collection, Charles carried out a fresh survey during the 1990s. During this survey a number of varieties mentioned, but not described in Ray's book came to light, in addition to a number of varieties 'new to science'. Most of the perry pears originate in Gloucestershire but because of the difficulty in deciding which varieties are indigenous to the county, all known varieties from Gloucestershire, Herefordshire and Worcestershire are included. There are now 75 varieties of perry pear planted at the Three Counties Showground at Malvern. Charles says:

> To find the old varieties you have to go and ask the old boys what is in their orchards. Many of the trees are named after the place where they came from or after local people who developed the varieties—they form a link to local history and tradition that is held by those old boys.

Charles happily admits he gets very excited if it looks like he has found a lost variety. His search for the Dymock Red perry pear took him all over the three counties:

> The Dymock Red pear was first recorded at the White House in Dymock but was lost from there. I was really worried about it, could not find it. I got so frustrated and worried! I spent three weeks solid going round looking for clues and discovered that the last place it was known at was Blaisdon. I went to the right farm but it was gone, then I looked in the next farm and there it was, a distinctive tree, like an ash, tall and slim with a bit of a bush on top and the bark serrated into postage stamp sized squares. Miles up there I could just see some fruit. There was no way of reaching it as there were no low branches, it was right at the top, so I flung things up in the air. I flung a log and it came down and hit me on the head, but no fruit. Then the old farmer came out and he had a walking stick, so I flung that up and it got stuck there, it was his best stick! That scuppered that. Anyway, eventually I got a fruit down and his stick too. I could see it was a Dymock Red and I was really pleased, so exciting to find something like that. I took it to Ray Williams and he positively identified it, then we had it grafted for the collection. I have also returned a Dymock Red perry pear to the White House in Dymock, which I planted with Robbie Oxley (then aged 10) who is looking after it for future generations. They say if you plant a perry pear tree you 'plant it for your heirs' as they take so long to mature, so it is important that young people plant them today for their grandchildren.

One variety has eluded Charles through ten years of searching: the Late Treacle, identified in Ray's book, but which has lately vanished. Charles never gives up hope that it will be rediscovered. There have been a couple of near misses—one discovered by Kevin Minchew in South

Gloucestershire and another by Charles near Much Marcle, both of which turned out to be a Treacle but not Late.

> The fruit has got a reflexed eye, the sepal flexes right back into the basin of the fruit revealing the stamen, pubescent (hairy) leaves and the stem of the fruit is fat and lumpy. The tree is tall and straight with rectangular strips of bark, it should be grafted low down on the stem and have some die back near the graft. To identify the tree you need to take the fourth leaf down from a non-fruiting spur—it is very distinctive, and always taking the same leaf helps you be consistent.

The discovery of Dr. Durham's photographic survey of pears compiled in 1926 helped Charles to identify three lost perry pear varieties at Hellens in Much Marcle in the autumn of 2001.

> It was like striking gold. Hellens has a magnificent avenue of old perry trees along the Monks' Walk, many of which are nearly 300 years old, but the names of the varieties of trees were mostly lost. It was assumed they were all Hellens Early. When I looked at the plates in Dr. Durham's book it appeared that some of them had been reversed by the printer, so I had them scanned into a computer and flipped over. Then it was back to Hellens to compare the pictures to the trees. Two of the pictures matched exactly, revealing for the first time the varieties Hellens Green and Water Lugg. Nobody alive had ever heard of Water Lugg—perhaps it was named after the River Lugg. It is a magnificent vintage tree, still bearing fruit almost 300

The Monks' Walk of Perry pear trees at Hellens

years after it was planted. The trees have since been scientifically described and saved from certain extinction.

Another picture showed a tree at Brinsop near Hereford called Stoney Way. Robert Hogg, the early pomologist, had seen the same variety at Colwall near Malvern, but a visit some years before had not found it. By reversing this picture the tree was tracked down to the very spot in a field at Brinsop where, according to local legend, St. George slayed the dragon.

Dragon's blood is also part of the folklore of The Plough at Elmley Castle near Pershore, for that is what the locals called the cider made there by Fred and George Webber until the mid 1980s, when the pub closed. Kevin Minchew remembers The Plough as he used the press there to make his cider and perry; Fred would charge you 50p a gallon for pressing juice into your own barrel. At the family smallholding in the parish of Ashchurch near Tewkesbury there was always a barrel of cider and perry in the stable.

> Cider was like currency then—and can be now. It would be traded for things you needed. Father once swapped a bottle for a goose that lived in the orchard for many years, and I recently swapped five gallons for a TV and four tyres! As a young man cider was cheaper than beer and as a poor apprentice I became aware of the cider houses dotted around Bredon Hill. Each had its own unique brew. It was possible to visit the Yew Tree in Conderton for Lanchbury's (now a Westons' house), Elmley Castle for Dragon's Blood and the Monkey House at Woodmancote for a final half, or even a pint, before winding one's way home, very merry but with change in one's pocket. It was like one big brotherhood—once you were accepted it was 'all right Bro" with your own mug behind the

A general view of Kevin Minchew's works

bar. Everyone there was working the land and drinking cider was their solace in the shed.

I operate between the Cotswolds and the Malverns, from Broadway to Upton St. Leonards. I drive round in the spring and look for the blossom on the perry pear trees, then go back in the autumn to try and pick them. I try to ask the landowner's permission if I can, but it is sometimes difficult to know who owns the tree, so I climb it and start to pick, hoping to catch the attention of the owner, then when they turn up offer to buy them. Sometimes they're OK, other times they pull a shotgun on you, just depends. Not everyone accepts payments, some like to keep the fruit for themselves, others claim they make perry but let the fruit rot. As I go around I'm always on the lookout for new varieties to add to my orchard at the smallholding or to the National Collection at Malvern Showground.

Ray Williams and Charles Martell approached me about the Three Counties Perry Pear collection. I helped with the search for varieties, knocking on doors and identifying trees. They were excited that another individual was 'tagging' trees while harvesting. The collection has varieties in it that you would never see anywhere else, preserved for the future, ensuring a broad gene pool.

When the Plough at Elmley Castle shut down I sourced my own kit. I am an engineer by trade so I made my own press and reconditioned an old scratter. Now I have two presses, a hand press and

A screwed down press at Kevin Minchew's pouring forth juice

a hydraulic press, which uses the ram of an earth mover and a tail-lift of a truck to apply the pressure to the cheese. If I have lots of fruit I use both presses, but for small quantities, such as the perry, I use the screw press because I want to get every drop of juice out. I've only had a roof on the press shed two to three years. People had asked 'How much water do you put in'? 'Well if it rains, some'.

My cider sheds are precast concrete ex-council garages. My father bought them as pig stys, then when the pigs went I made them into cider sheds. One of

A line up of barrels at Kevin Minchew's

them is the old village shop my gran used to run, it still has the steel enamel advertising signs on the walls and over the years some have been used to repair the roof. I make single variety ciders and perries, producing a bench mark for everyone on that year's vintage fruit. I believe it is very important to be selective about fruit and maintain good hygiene. I make by hand in small batches, quite an expensive way of doing it. When it comes to pressing, the ripest fruit gets priority. My fruit is sorted before and after picking, removing all bad or rotted specimens, then washed. One bad fruit can spoil a whole barrel. I may be too fussy but I do not use sulphur dioxide in my juice, the only sulphur dioxide in the produce comes from the equipment and cloths—they are 100% clean and kept sprayed with sulphur dioxide in solution. Tests show only six to nine parts per 1,000 parts per million sulphur dioxide in my finished products, the legal limit is 200/1,000, so it is very low. It can take up to 3 months for the cider or perry to mature in wooden barrels in the shed. I use air locks and keep them topped up with solution in hot weather to prevent spoilage. I won't bottle until all fermentation has stopped. The result is my ciders and perries keep well, an open bottle is still good three to four days later, a part barrel three to four weeks later.

I feel that cider makers with a premium product, who take care over the production and presentation should charge more. The low price for perry from Gloucestershire was encouraged by ship-pers of port and madeira in Bristol and London, who would use it to stretch out the wines. British cider has suffered from farmhouse producers selling cheap, acetic cider to tourists. With quality improving, the consumer started to realise that cider did not have to be acetic to be strong, but they switched to 'white ciders' from commercial makers whose quality may be dubious. Perry does not have the same stigma, it can be used to introduce good cider to new imbibers.

When I first set up I was offered £1 a gallon from a wholesaler for my cider, but it was not enough for the time and effort involved. I've found once people know my product or have an interest in quality, they come and find me. I ask £1 a pint (duty paid) so I am one of the most expensive around.

I feel the consumer has a right to know what is in the bottle. My new labels show the ingredients and I believe I'm the first to do this in the industry. I just want to sell everything I make, with two bottles a day for me, but I can't make any money out of it. The problems for small makers are just the same as 200 years ago: distribution, taxation and politics all favouring the bigger concerns. Customs and Excise limits set the strength of cider to under 8.5%, this means I have to water some of my products up to 10% to keep within the law. I don't agree with it but I have no choice. Making perry is our culture in Gloucestershire, if I (and others) were not doing it we would all be drinking with the Magnates. You can always buy bread, cheese will keep, and as long as you have cider you don't need anything else. It's all about quality of life.

Worcester and Worcestershire are also connected with pears and perry. Since the middle ages local place names such as Perrywood and Perry Court reflect an ancient association with pears. On her visit to Worcester in 1575 Queen Elizabeth I saw a pear tree laden with black pears that had been transplanted from the gardens at White Ladies to honour her entrance through the city gate. Recognising the appropriateness of the pear to Worcester, she directed the city to add three pears to its coat of arms, which acquired the term Black Pear from the sable of the escutcheon. When the county of Worcester was set up in 1888/1889 an official coat of arms could have been applied for, but it was not until 1936 that this occurred and a formal coat of arms, incorporating a Worcester Black Pear tree laden with pears, was eventually granted to the county in 1947. The pear tree logo is still in use for the county today.

The Worcester Black Pear is the oldest cultivar of a type of culinary pear known as a Warden or Warndon pear first recorded at Warden Abbey in Bedfordshire in the 13th century and is possibly the same as the French cultivar de Livre. At the start of the 20th century Worcestershire's orchards were flourishing, due to good transport connections and an expanding market for fresh fruit in the prosperous industrial midlands. The land at St. John's in Worcester was particularly suited for orchard fruits due to the river sands and gravels of the River Severn. Most of the fruit grown was culinary, but a number of varieties of perry pear were also grown,

The emblem of
Worcester City

The emblem of
Worcestershire
County Council

including Squash, Huffcap, Barland and Linton. Over the past 50 years at least 70% of Worcestershire's traditional standard orchards have been lost. As Worcester expanded, its orchards were cut down for housing, including veteran specimens of the Worcester Black Pear, so that few old and historic trees remain. Worcestershire County Council has included the Black Pear tree with other fruit trees of local origin in their fruit tree initiative, and since the late 1980s over 400 Black Pear trees, grown at Pershore College, have been replanted in the county as a result of the scheme.

A good number of fruit trees survived the destruction of Worcester's orchards as isolated trees in back gardens or in public spaces. Fruit from these trees and orchards was identified by Ray Williams at the Royal Horticultural Society Autumn Show in September 1998, uncovering that the city council's orchard at Aconbury, just behind Nunnery Wood, contains the rare Chancely Green perry pear, described as critically endangered by Ray, along with a mystery variety of perry pear which is small, round and yellow with a red bloom. The discovery of these rare varieties led to an orchard survey of Worcester being conducted, with three or four surviving fruit trees of over 40 years old being counted as an orchard. The survey revealed 22 possible orchard sites of which 20 could be surveyed.

One of these sites, Barlom Orchard, matches the boundaries of the 1753 Manor of Claines owned by the Bishop of Worcester. Seven trees have survived, two in the grounds of St. Barnabus School and five in a remnant of orchard to the rear of the school grounds. All are Barland Perry Pears. John Doharty's map of Claines Manor in 1753 shows the orchard to have been densely planted, and the remaining veteran trees have girths of over 100 inches at breast height, suggesting they could be as much as 300 years old. The land is now owned by the city council and includes access via a public footpath. The council plans to restore the orchard with new plantings of Barland Pear.

The results of the Worcester City Orchard Survey were published in October 2000, and encouraged the formation of a group to help care for Worcester's orchards and use their fruits. Known as Worcester Orchard

Part of John Doharty's Map of Claines Manor of 1753 showing orchards amongst the other features

Workers (WOW), the group are supported by Worcester City Council's Green Space Project Officer Rory McLure and meet regularly through the year. They maintain the perry orchard at Aconbury, which was saved from development in 1990 and has recently been planted with young perry pears between the established trees of Blakeney Red, Barnet and Chancely Green. WOW are also restoring the neglected orchards at the

RNIB College in Worcester which had been left to go wild. In June 2001 plans were being made to plant a new community orchard off Bromwich Road, near the River Severn, with local Worcester varieties.

In October 2000 the Worcester Orchard Workers collected their first fruit from the Aconbury orchard, which had previously been left for the wildlife. Assisted by master cider maker Tim Munslow and his scratter and press, a group of eight enthusiasts picked, pressed and fermented their own Worcestershire Perry. A tasting event was held in Spring 2001 to assess the results, when some of the perry was declared by Tim to be very promising. But all were too early to drink, needing to ferment for longer. Fruit collection now commences in September, to catch the early ripening fruit, with a pressing day in October, now using the group's own scratter and press, which is also employed at public exhibitions and demonstrations in schools.

Up until 1960 perry remained a craft product. It is a difficult drink for commercial cider makers to produce, due to problems of handling the fruit, which bruises, squashes and rots easily due to the fast ripening of perry pears, and the risk of bacterial infection during fermentation. Perry does not blend well, it can suddenly turn opalescent or 'ropey' throwing a protein/pectin haze which clumps together in the bottle or glass, making it unattractive to consumers. These factors mean it is difficult to produce a standard product for a wide market.

These drawbacks were not such a problem on farms where the ripening, pressing and fermentation could be tightly controlled. It was convenient for smallholders, as the making of perry fitted well in-between other crops and farm activities. The farm perry maker could easily cope with single varieties of pear that ripened at different times— early pears like Thorn in September, Moorcroft and Taynton Squash in November and Rock as late as January, any of which in an off year may only produce small quantities of juice for fermentation.

It was not until Francis Showering of Somerset perfected his technique of juice handling to produce Babycham in the late 1950s that perry production was considered possible on a large scale. Perry orchards had suffered like cider fruit from neglect, so Showerings were unable to source a reasonable sized crop for annual mass production. They therefore tried developing perry orchards in Somerset with the help of Ray Williams. Francis Showering set up a test orchard of 50-60 acres in Bradley, West Somerset, using sample varieties grafted from a list of farms provided by Ray. Showerings later planted 500 acres of bush perry inter-planted with standards, with the intention of taking out the bush trees once the standards began to bear. 60% of the trees planted were Hendre Huffcap. The orchards, however, came to nothing for Showerings had selected grade 1 agricultural land for the orchard, but perry pears are not often found on good soils—records from as early as 1600 say that pears would thrive in poor soil. The trees grew rapidly in the good soil. Within 12 to 14 years they were massive, but the crops were very poor as the trees were too vigorous.

The well known Babycham label

Showerings tried severely pruning the trees to check growth and encourage cropping, but silverleaf fungus immediately attacked the freshly pruned Hendre Huffcap and quickly spread to other varieties, killing huge numbers of trees. Lighter pruning of small branches was also tried, but by this time fireblight had established itself in England and the majority of the young trees were highly susceptible, sounding the death knell for Showerings' orchards and forcing the company to use imported pear concentrate to produce Babycham.

Bulmers also made perry, but quantitatively it was only a small element of their production, less than 7% of their fruit consumption. They now do not produce any perry at all. George Thomas, Public Relations Manager at Bulmers, says:

> Perry is under great threat. Bulmers have not made perry now for 3 to 4 seasons. Modern consumers find it a bit sweet and the drink is very regionalised. Demand for Bulmers perry was falling. It appeared better to let Westons have the market for perry and the limited amount of fruit that was about rather than be in competition with each other for a dwindling market. The key problem is lack of orchards, and the loss of the 'girlie' market tapped by Showerings for Babycham. In the early 1960s women were just starting to go into pubs, but were not allowed to drink pints of beer or cider with the men as they wanted to appear ladylike. Babycham with its cute bambi logo and little bottle arrived in time to fill that gap and was a great success. But I doubt many women drinking Babycham presented in a champagne bowl with a cherry on top realised they were enjoying perry! Now women have lost that inhibition and drink what they like in pubs so Babycham's key market has gone.

Roger Jackson, Westons' Marketing Manager feels that:

As perry makers, we need to raise consumer awareness and get the product recognised on the bar and shelf to increase sales and outlets. Generic marketing is needed to educate the consumer as to what perry is, without deliberately passing it off as a cheap party type drink or as cheap wine. Anyone who tries our traditional perry becomes an instant convert, but the demand this creates is very hard to satisfy. Winning CAMRA awards for our perry has raised the public awareness of both Westons' Herefordshire County Perry and perry generally, but promotional efforts are thwarted by a shortage of raw materials. We have our own orchards, some of which are truly ancient, and we have loyal contract growers, but finding new sources of supply is very hard as it is not a commercially viable fruit crop for growers, even at a premium price per ton.

The same pressing problem of sourcing perry pears from local growers troubles Ivor Dunkerton.

The quality of the fruit is key, it has to be absolutely perfect - we have planted an avenue of Thorn and Moorcroft perry pears but we always need more; frost can catch the early perry blossom which then limits the crop and varieties available. I think there is an awareness in the middle class market which could lead to a revival in perry drinking. Waitrose is now a stockist.

Paul Hands of Bees and Trees Trust, a charity which teaches children and communities to value local distinctiveness and preserve local varieties of apples and perry pears, was shown some perry by Jean Nowell, that had thrown rope on being carbonated. The texture of the perry, which smelt and tasted fine, just slowly dripped from the bottle. The perry reminded Paul of a child called William who attended an adventure playground in the West Midlands where Paul was a play leader. 'William always had two long strings of snot dripping from his nose, sometimes reaching to his navel. As one string went up the other would come down, like a grandfather clock's winding mechanism—totally reminiscent of Jean's ropey perry problem!'

Another charity, Farms for City Children, provides for children from cities all over the Midlands and beyond to live and work for a week at Wick Court Farm in Arlingham in Gloucestershire. The children and their teachers get to learn how to look after the land and the animals and how food is produced. Every October the children help collect the perry pears from the ten acre orchard and press them into juice, using an old stone mill in the cider house. The ripe fruit looks unappetising, and stimulates comments such as: 'Ugh! They're too scabby, birds have nibbled them and there is a worm in this one!'—any such moth maggot is eagerly examined by all the children. Squishy brown rotten fruit is sorted out during collection and thrown into to the hedge for hibernating insects and butterflies, but the children don't like touching it so tend to kick it into the hedge, though one young lad liked putting them in his pocket 'for later'. Some children like to play a trick on their mates, telling them that the fruit are sweet to eat and watching their faces as they screw up in disgust at the tannin in the fruit.

The cider house at Wick Court is too small for the farm horse to move round the circular stone mill safely, and the smaller rare breed Gloucester cattle who live on the farm are not keen on the cobbled floor of the cider house as their hooves slip on the wet stones, so the children push the mill wheel round themselves, taking turns to squash the ripe perry pears to a pulp. The cheese is built on a single screw hand press for pressing out the juice, then the juice is transferred to one of two wooden barrels. The children declared perry making to be great fun but hard work, but worth it for the perry at the end, though 'I prefer my warm house with a TV in the city to the hard work, cold and wet here'! The children get the opportunity to try the juice, but the perry is not ready for drinking until the following spring when it is sold at the Wick Court Elizabethan Fair in June, and later at Wick Court Wassail in January.

The youngest perry maker at Wick Court is young Tom Crump who started helping his dad, Jonathan Crump, the farm manager, make perry when just 2 years old. Tom, now aged 7, is already an expert not just on perry making but on tasting and giving constructive criticism to any master cider makers who dare to let him near their cider sheds or produce. With such young experts around it is hoped that perry will not become a legend to the next generation of cider makers.

Eric Freeman lives in Taynton, home of the Taynton Squash perry pear which is reputed to make perry equalling, if not exceeding in quality, the finest champagne. Taynton Squash pears ripen early, often when the weather is still warm, so the juice is troublesome to ferment, but in a good season will well repay the care given to it. Eric told me the tale of Farmer John of Taynton:

> He made very good perry. People used to come from miles around to drink it, but Farmer John also had a wicked sense of humour. After the drinkers had supped a pint or two he would sew up the back of their braces to their shirts and gaiters, so when they were caught short with the purgative effects of the perry on their bowels, they would find they couldn't get their trousers down and would have soiled themselves before they solved the mystery!

10   A CIDER ALMANAC

Throughout the year in the three counties cider makers and local communities celebrate the local customs and traditions associated with cider and perry. Pressing the juice starts in late September or early October depending on the ripening of the fruit. Around the counties many small orchards and single trees are picked by hand by small scale cider makers, often using the traditional panking poles, an ash pole with an iron hook on one end, to shake the fruit from the trees. It is very much a community activity with the cider maker being helped to crop the orchard by friends and family who then muck in to assist with the scratting and pressing.

Cider making goes on in the most unexpected places, not just on farms and smallholdings. The Apple Tree pub in Worcester started producing its own cider and perry in 1997, made from local fruit by the landlord, Hamish Lothian. Hamish had been a regular at The Plough at Elmley Castle, which had inspired him to try making cider and perry and selling it over the bar of the pub. In 2000, the pub garden acquired two vintage pieces of equipment: a scratter with stone rollers dated 1854, powered by a stationary steam engine, and a four screw Victorian press. For two years the pub regulars used the mill and press to help Hamish make the

The Apple Tree pub in Worcester's Lowesmoor

181

cider and perry, which was then fermented in the pub's cellar, but production stopped in 2001. At a location in Hereford city, a cellar in a private house has been fitted out as a cider factory, complete with an hydraulic press and electric mill, that produces cider and perry using fruit 'scrumped' from single trees and under-cropped small orchards around the city boundaries. During September to January fruit regularly appears at the back door in sacks from anonymous (and not so anony-

mous) donors who later benefit from the produce of the cellar.

Visitors to the three counties who do not know of a local cider maker, but want to see how cider is produced, can also join in the fun. In Gloucester, the Gloucester Folk Museum present a cider making demon-stration on the third Saturday in October in the cider house alongside the yard at the back of the museum, which also includes a reconstructed apple loft which provides a great vantage point for children to watch the cider making. It is the only time of the year that the equipment is used, although the cider house is open all year round for viewing and the museum has a good collection of drinking horns and costrells.

Local farmer Eric Freeman brings along one of his heavy horses to push round the stone mill wheel, ably assisted by engineer Albert Wrixen who restores farm machinery and carts, including a steam powered trav-elling cider maker's tack from the Forest of Dean, which is often seen at fairs and rallies around the U.K. A good group of adults and children squash themselves into the cider house to watch Eric crack jokes with Albert about old cider making traditions whilst explaining the way cider making was done, and answering questions about fermentation of the juice. Apples are provided by the museum and are mainly all culinary fruit. After crushing in the horse mill the must is juiced in a wooden single screw press.

Every October half-term, Shortwood Farm at Pencombe, near Bromyard in Herefordshire, makes cider and perry watched by chil-dren visiting the farm. Cider and perry has been made here by the Legge family for more than three generations. Janet and David Legge who run the farm, which is one of Herefordshire's visitor attractions, carry on the tradition. The history of Shortwood Farm is on display in the visitor centre, along with photographs of the Legge clan. Janet Legge recalls that grandfather Legge had 17 children, one of which was her father-in-law.

All grandad Legge ever drank in his life was rough cider. When he was in his 40s he became ill, blood poisoning or something like, so the doctor advised him to stop drinking for a bit until he got better. So he drank tea in his old ceramic cider mug instead. After six months he declared that was enough of that and went back to drinking cider; he never touched tea again! I can just remember him, sitting in his big armchair sipping cider from his big jug and eating an enormous rice pudding from the bowl it had been cooked in.

In Worcestershire, the County Museum at Hartlebury Castle invites a cider maker to make cider using its cider house or his or her own travelling press on the first Saturday of October. In Worcester City, Worcester Orchards Workers gather fruit on the second Saturday in October then press it on the third Saturday.

As well as pressing the juice for fermenting into cider and perry September and October are busy months for identifying local fruit, and for displaying apples and pears grown locally.

The local traders of Leominster, in north Herefordshire, organised the Leominster Fruity Affair in 1997, which showcased local fruit, vegetables and produce along Broad Street, along with cider making demon-

Janet Legge's father-in-law, raising a glass of Perry-to-be as he and his horse take a rest from the tasking of milling perry pears

strations by Brian Jones of the Great Oak Cider Company, Eardisley. Unfortunately, the fair was not held in 1998 due to lack of bookings from traders, but the following year its place was taken by the Leominster Apple Fair initiated by the Leominster Green Party. 'Although the event is non-political it does meet the group's objectives of promoting locally grown food, local employment and local traditions such as orcharding and varieties and uses of local fruit', says organiser Felicity Norman.

The Leominster Apple Fair is held in the Lion Ballroom, a community venue in Lion Yard behind Broad Street. Although on a much smaller scale than the Fruity Affair, the event was so successful that it has become an annual event. The fair is bursting with interest for the apple enthusiast or the general visitor. Central to the fair is an enormous display of local cider and culinary fruits gathered by local experts, enthusiasts, growers, nurserymen, greengrocers or donated by members of the public. The volume of apples on display on the tables down the centre of the Ballroom light up the hall with their glowing colours and impart a delightful fragrance to the room. As the fair has become established the attractions offered have grown to include local crops, local foods made with apples, apple games and contests, and displays about orchard preservation and management, along with local apple juice and cider provided by Orchard Hive and Vine. It is hoped in the future to include outdoor displays in Lion Yard or Broad Street, including a travelling cider maker, reviving the lost attractions of the fruity affair.

Ray Boddington of Marcher Apple Network identifies apples brought to the fair by the public. The Network also hosts a number of displays and identification events during the autumn, including an apple fair at Croft Castle near Leominster and a display of apples with tastings at Berrington Hall also near Leominster. The Network also appear at local food festivals including the Royal Horticultural Society Autumn Show at the Three Counties Showground, Malvern, displaying traditional fruit varieties and running an identification service. The R.H.S. alternates each year between a vegetable and an orchard fruits display. Their next fruit display will be in 2004, coupled with an identification service. The Marcher Apple Network also participates in the Big Apple which is held in the seven parishes around the Much Marcle Ridge in south Herefordshire every October.

The first Big Apple event was held in 1989 as part of the Year of Food and Farming. Apple growing is part of the traditional history of the parishes along the Marcle Ridge, where orchards produce dessert, culinary and cider apples. Since the success of the first Big Apple the event has evolved and changed but has remained true to its aim of bringing people into the area to enjoy the fruit and learn about orchards and

A line up of ciders at the Big Apple event

apples. Within two years a national tourism award was won, followed by a European prize—fourth place in the *Village que j'aime* Award in 1990. As this was a major prize, bringing with it 5000 euros, the group became a proper Association so as to manage the funds, functioning as an educational group who provide information on apples, varieties, orchard preservation, standard orchards and orchards in the landscape. Local groups also raised funds through the Big Apple, the Women's Institute by providing refreshments and cookery demonstrations and the local church at Aylton through its flower festival. The festival has been able to run at nominal cost due to volunteers who are flexible and open to new ideas, and using the team of Jackie Denman (who developed the initial idea when working with the Community Council of Herefordshire and Worcestershire, now Community First), Janet MacKay and Jean Nowell as a sounding board. The culinary fruit event in September was gradually dropped as visitor numbers fell, now the event happens the weekend before National Apple Day (21 October) so as not to split audiences or visitors with other local apple events.

Within the Big Apple event are guided walks through orchards, demonstrations of rural crafts, and apple teas, as well as plenty of cider. The Royal Oak in Much Marcle hosts a massive display of culinary, dessert and cider fruit. There are cider making demonstrations at Lyne Down Farm and Westons is open for tours and purchases from the shop and cider house restaurant. An important activity over the weekend is the Enthusiasts' Day, which gives an opportunity for up to 25 people with an interest in cider making to learn how to make their own cider. From picking up the fruit in the orchards, to milling and pressing in the afternoon, all the processes are carried out by the enthusiasts themselves. By the end of the afternoon the juice is ready to sample and be compared to the previous year's production of cider.

An interested audience usually watches the fun, so there is an element of education for all concerned. At the end of the day the enthusiasts take away some juice to ferment at home, supported by expert advice and knowledge of college courses, competitions and associations who can help them develop their cider making skills.

Until 2001 the enthusiasts' day was hosted by Jean Nowell at Lyne Down Farm. Jean says: 'I've run quite a number of enthusiasts' days now, or tutored local cider makers on the farm. Those that have gone on to make their own cider I call "my brave boys". Some still use the equipment at Lyne Down to make their cider and some have set up on their own'. Bob Cooke is one of those brave boys.

> I grew up in Warwickshire but have lived in Herefordshire for 25 years. My grandfather and father both grew apples and liked cider, but mother disapproved! I used to go with my father to visit cider makers in Evesham and May Hill. It was great fun watching the cider being made, but the result was often awful! It was mostly Bramleys and very acidic, you couldn't drink it but felt obliged to buy a gallon while you were there to take home. I started making cider after being a student on one of Jean's enthusiast days. She's a very good teacher, meticulous and very keen on hygiene, with very high standards.
>
> I collect apples and pears for myself and Jean with the help of my brother-in-law, Paul. Two of us picking can do more than Jean on her own. We then mill and press both Jean's and our fruit in October. I have a small electric mill and an old beam press at home for making small quantities, but it is not as efficient as Jean's kit and as we do the picking and pressing for ourselves and Jean it is a fair trade.
>
> The most exciting time for me is seeing the fruit in the autumn, thinking and hoping for a good crop which will make a vintage cider. I'm just starting with making perry. I'm very excited as I've lots to learn and it is more difficult than making cider. You are always learning! I often think 'What if I had started 20 years ago?' or 'I wonder how many more years I'll be making cider?' as it is quite physical and I'm not getting any younger. You have to make the mistakes first to be really good, all the really good makers have made mistakes and learnt from them.

Since Jean retired from Lyne Down Farm the Big Apple enthusiasts' day is being hosted by one of her 'brave boys'—James Marsden of Gregg's Pit. James bought Gregg's Pit in 1992 and takes his fruit from the traditional orchard that has been there since 1785 and is home to the Gregg's Pit Perry Pear. The orchard has been restored in the past ten years with the help of a countryside stewardship grant and the expertise of the former owner, Bill George, who was able to name several of the 150-year-old trees that could not be identified on the orchard plan. James also collects fruit from orchards in and around Much Marcle, specialising in single variety perry, including one made from Gregg's Pit. James only produces 200-300 gallons of cider and perry a year, saying 'I don't do it to make money, I do it because I want to, because I feel it is important to maintain the old varieties of perry pears for future generations'.

In January 1999 the Big Apple Association initiated the Much Marcle Wassail, held at Lyne Down Farm. The celebration involved the residents of the Marcle Ridge parishes, plus many enthusiasts of Jean's ciders and perries from wider afield, with the entertainments and ceremony being led by Leominster Morris. Leominster Morris developed from the Breinton Morris (now disbanded) who danced in Hereford City from 1978. In 1983 two members of the Breinton Morris wished to try different dances and celebrations so formed a new side. Most of the members of the new side lived in the Leominster area, so dance practice moved from Hereford to Leominster and the Leominster Morris name was established.

Finding an identity for the side took a little longer. A side which had been active in Leominster before the First World War had left some traces in local memory of the dancers having worn print jackets, but there were scant written or photographic references. When the new side first started there was no set costume, dancers and musicians improvised from what they had available. Gradually the side evolved a costume of decorated top hats and print jackets along with black trousers and braces. The decoration of the hats varies with every appearance, using fresh flowers and foliage available from the local hedgerows that adds seasonal interest. In summer—May Day to Halloween—the side wear white shirts, in winter black shirts are worn along with traditional Border Morris blackened faces. The side also has the unique figure of a Ram as its totem, representing the local Leominster Ore, the wool from the Ryelands sheep that made the town of Leominster rich. The Ram has supplanted the Mare or Mayr commonly seen in Welsh Border Morris made of a cow's skull with a long cloak of black fabric, who traditionally walks abroad at Twelfth Night and Halloween, trotting round the streets and houses, driving away evil spirits and bringing good luck to all who meet her. The Leominster Ram costume was commissioned for the side by Westons Cider from a local artist who created it as a cloak sewn with strips of soft leather forming a multi-coloured fleece topped with a 'hat' of a sheep's head.

Leominster Morris' Ram costume

Leominster Morris have held Wassails since January 1984, first at private orchards, then Symonds' cider works at Stoke Lacy and Westons in Much Marcle, now the side choose each year where they will dance. They also appear at a number of apple related events, including Blossom Time (see below), the Big Apple weekend, May Day on Bache Camp near Leysters in Herefordshire and of the birthday of William Wordsworth on 7 April at the Poets Stone in Leysters. The dances of the side are not specific to the apple, mainly they are drawn from the Welsh border tradition in winter, whilst in summer the side increase the number of Cotswold dances in their programme.

The format of the Leominster Wassail has been collected from diverse sources, including the writings of local folklorist Ella Mary Leather of Weobley who wrote of the Herefordshire Wassail in her book *The Folklore of Herefordshire*. Mrs. Leather revived the Weobley Wassail in 1907 with the assistance of the young people of the village, a festivity which included a mummers' play, local songs, a Wassailling cup and the 'antics of Morris dancers' according to the *Hereford Times* of that year.

These antics can be found reflected in the present day ceremony along with further embellishments. When the audience have gathered at the appointed place, either a farmhouse or pub near the orchard to be Wassailed, the side hand out fire torches to the crowd. The fire torches are made of a wooden pole with an empty baked bean can screwed to the top which is filled with firelighters. The musicians and dancers lead the audience with their lit firebrands to the tree that has been chosen to represent all the trees in the orchard, and which is surrounded by a ring of 12 unlit bonfires, 30 to 40 feet from the trunk of the tree beyond which the onlookers gather. Only the dancers and musicians are allowed within the ring of fires during the ceremony. A small fire has also been built about halfway between the tree and the ring of fires.

The ceremony begins with a piece of toast being soaked in cider by one of the dancers and placed in the fork of the tree as an offering to the guardian of the orchard and the tree spirits, then the rest of the cider is poured around the tree roots as a libation, to encourage it to produce a good crop the next year. The dancer leading the procession then lights the Herefordshire Lantern, a cage made of dry branches of hawthorn stuffed with straw. The lantern represents the coming back of the sun from its long winter journey, and as the lantern burns the assembled company sing *The Apple Tree Wassail* to the tune of *Lily White Pin*:

> Our lily, white lily, Oh lily white pin
> Please to come down and let us come in
> Lily, white lily, Oh lily white smock
> Please to come down and pull back the lock
>
> *Chorus*
> *Our wassail, jolly wassail, joy come to our jolly wassail*
> *How well they may blow, how well they may bear*
> *So we may have apples and cider next year*
>
> Oh master and mistress, Oh are you within
> Please to come down and pull back the pin
>
> *Chorus*
>
> There was an old farmer and he had an old cow
> And how to mill her he didn't know how
> He put his old cow down in his old barn
> And a little more liquor won't do us no harm
> Harm me boys harm, harm me boys harm
> And a little more liquor won't do us no harm
>
> Oh the ringles and the jingles and the tenor of the song goes
> Merrily, merrily, merrily
> and the tenor of the song goes
> Merrily
>
> Hatfuls, capfuls, three bushel bagfuls
> Little heaps under the stairs, Hip, hip
> Hooray

When the lantern dies out, the central fire under the tree boughs is lit. This fire is known as the Judas Fire and represents the dying of the old year, it can also be said to represent the 'dark' 13th moon of the Celtic calendar, when evil and dangerous spirits were believed to be abroad seeking to harm men, beast and crops. The fire is stamped out quickly once it is alight, then a shotgun is fired into the air banishing the dark spirits to the underworld. Using their fire torches the audience then lights the 12 fires around the tree, representing the 12 months of the coming year. The side then performs two or three dances under the tree, whilst cider is taken round the audience by several of the men.

The wassail bowl is often made of carved wood, traditionally sycamore or 'white maple' with a scalloped lip, known as an Elwood lip to enable drinking without dribbling. There is no set design for wassail bowls, which can range in size from two pints to over a gallon capacity, but wooden bowls usually have a lip or groove around the base to hold decorative ribbons. The bowl is filled with old cider or brown ale, which may be mulled with spices and have baked apples floating on top, when the drink is known as 'lamb's wool'. In many wassail customs the leader of the procession first offers the bowl to the farmer and his or her partner, with a toast of 'Wassail' (old English for 'be thou whole') which brings with it blessings for the coming year. The cup may be passed around the company, a toast being proposed to each person in turn, young or old. Following such toasting and dancing the audience may be led three times around the tree then back to the cider house or pub for refreshments and the mummers' play.

The mummers' play performed by Leominster Morris involves the whole side and is based on traditional sources, along with the addition of local characters and references that have been added as the play developed over the years. The theme of the play is the death of the old year

Leominster Morris wassailling in an orchard

and resurrection of the new, symbolised by the battle between the Turkish Knight (night) and St. George (day). The players take different roles each year. Thony Handy, the side's archivist, says: 'It is the spirit of the play that counts, the characters change to incorporate topical news and modern political references to local people or places, and also references to local folklore. The character Hob-of-the-Hops is also unique to Herefordshire, he is a local faerie who lives amongst the hop yards, orchards and fields'. Hob-of-the-Hops is best described in his own words:

> Here I come, young Hob-of-the-Hops
> Lord of all the harvest crops.
> The pears and apples, they're all mine
> The hops as well, upon the bine.
> The barley, rye, the oats and wheat
> Are gathered in, now all's complete.

Other characters are Beelzebub and his imps, who help St. George to defeat his foes, Friar Tuck, Robin Hood, Boneparte (*sic*) and the Turkish Knight, Widow Quill—wife of the Turkish Knight, and the Doctor, who revives all the fallen with his potion:

> Here I am the man you need
> With powders, spells and potions pure.
> I'll see this man who lies down here
> And find for him a certain cure.
> So lady, do not weep and wail
> I've never known this bottle fail.

In Gloucestershire the Lassington Morris led by Eric Freeman as the Sweeper perform a similar play around the pubs in the city, and have also revived the 17th-century Newnham-on-Wye mummers' play. In Gloucester the part of the Mayr is taken by a kangaroo, and as well as resurrecting the dead the Doctor cures the Widow's toothache by removing a giant molar from her mouth. In Newnham-on-Severn the battle is the main focus of the play, though a fresh topical element was improvised in 2000, when the mummers' play coincided with a local fancy dress party themed on Rock and Roll Heroes. A phalanx of eight Elvises were in the pub, so the Turkish Knight was revived by the King of Rock and Roll!

The performance of the Wassail also varies in Gloucestershire. 'The Butler', who dresses up to show that he is a figure of authority, blacking his face and wearing formal evening dress complete with hat and decorations of his calling, directs the ceremonials. He leads the company out to the orchard followed by the dancers and musicians, then the audience with their lit firebrands, places the toast in the tree and pours the liba-tion. It is his duty to pass the Wassail cup sunwise around the company, proposing the toast to each person in turn, young or old. The Butler also presents an honoured female guest, or the farmer's wife, with a tray on which are arranged yew branches, nuts and a lighted candle, announcing to the company that the yew is for long life, the nuts for fertility and the lighted candle for the love she brings.

The *Gloucestershire Wassail* song is sung to a traditional tune wishing good fortune and good health to the farmer and his beasts. Additional traditional songs, the *Farmer's Boy* and *God Speed the Plough* are also sung on return to the farmhouse.

Gloucestershire Wassail
Traditional; first verse is also the chorus

1. *Wassail, Wassail, all over the town!*
Our toast it is white, and our ale it is brown,
Our bowl it is made of the white maple tree;
And a wassailing bowl we'll drink to thee.

2. So here is to Cherry and to his right cheek,
Pray God send our master a good piece of beef,
With the good piece of beef that may we all see;
With the wassailing bowl we'll drink to thee.

Chorus

3. And here is a Dobbin and to his right eye,
Pray God send our master a good Christmas pie,
And a good Christmas pie that we may all see;
With our wassailing bowl we'll drink to thee.

Chorus

4. So here is to broad May and to her broad horn,
May God send to our master a good crop of corn,
And a good crop of corn that we may all see;
With the wassailing bowl we'll drink to thee.

Chorus

5. And here is to Fillpail and to her left ear,
Pray Good send our master a happy New Year,
And a happy New Year as e'er he did see
With our wassailing bowl we'll drink to thee.

Chorus

6. And here is to Colly and to her long tail,
Pray God send our master he never may fail,
A bowl of strong beer; I pray you draw near,
And our jolly wassail it's then you shall hear.

Chorus

7. Come, butler, come fill us a bowl of the best
Then we hope that your soul in heaven may rest;
But if you do draw us a bowl of the small,
Then down shall go butler, bowl and all.

Chorus

8. Then here's to the maid in the lily white smock,
Who tripped to the door and slipped back the lock!
Who tripped to the door and pulled back the pin,
For to let these jolly wassailers in.

Chorus

Cherry and Dobbin are horses, Broad May, Fillpail and Colly are Gloucester cows living at the farm of Eric Freeman of Taynton, who has also revived a number of Toasts to the Tree from Gloucestershire, used during the wassail ceremonies:

> *The Taynton Toast*
> Here's to the old apply tree
> Whence thou mayest bend,
> And whence thou mayest blow.
> And whence thou mayest bear apples enough.
> Hats full, caps full, bushel, bushel sacks full
> And a little heap under the stairs.

In the village of Maisemore (who revived their Wassail in 2001) the Butler says:

> Old apple tree we Wassail thee,
> And hope that thou will bear,
> For Lord doth know where we shall be,
> Till apples come another year.
> To bloom well and to bear well,
> So merry let us be,

> Let every man take off his hat,
> And shout out to thee.

To which the wassailers respond:

> Old apple tree we wassail thee
> And hope thou will bear
> Hats full, caps full, three bushel bags full
> And a little heap under the stars.

At Dymock in Gloucestershire the wassailing ceremony includes Tickling the Ox. A large cake is provided with a hole in the middle. After the main ceremony the company are invited into the cattle barn, where the cattle are toasted by name by the farmer in cider from the wassail bowl. This being done the cake is ceremonially produced and placed on the horn of the largest beast, who is then tickled to make him toss his head. If the cake falls in front of the beast it belongs to the men of the company, if behind to the women.

A wassail is an opportunity for the company to gather together in the dark days of winter, forget their differences and past grudges and wish each other good health for the coming year.

As the blossom starts to set on the trees in late April, cider makers in the three counties are carefully checking their cellars for the best vintages to enter into cider competitions. On the weekend nearest May Day, the Big Apple Association as part of their Blossom Time event hosts the Putley Cider and Perry Trials. Jean Nowell suggested the idea of spring cider trials to the Big Apple Association in autumn 1990. The autumn events held by the Association were awkwardly timed for makers, as they were busy pressing the fruit and making the cider, but a spring competition was felt to be more attractive. Jean says:

> I felt that we had an unique opportunity to create a competition run for cider makers by cider makers. A lot of the small, non-commercial makers felt that the judges of other competitions did not fully understand what we were trying to achieve. There were a lot of prejudices about 'Expert Judges', 'bottled products' and cider having to be bone dry to be judged good by other small makers. Since them we have broadened our views!

The first Blossom Time was held in 1991 centring around the cider competition and cider tastings, along with guided walks through orchards in blossom, demonstrations of rural crafts and apple teas. Organisation of the event was handled by Janet MacKay.

At first the cider competition was slow to be accepted. People were dubious about the idea of a 'blind' judging, self-judging of flagons where names had been replaced by numbers so that it was difficult to pick out your own. People tried using distinctive corks or flagons, so now we watch the flagons. Of course, some cider makers can pick out their own or other's ciders by taste, that is fair enough. In the early days some of the makers (and visitors) got somewhat inebriated but now the competition is taken seriously. The cider makers enjoy the contest and it is a social event. The competition mostly attracts small makers who make the odd barrel, so the public can learn about the different styles, palates, bouquets and production methods of small scale cider and perry makers direct from the horse's mouth.

Peter Mitchell who has judged a number of cider competitions explains that: 'Judging is always a controversial role, it can raise a lot of hot air! You have to ignore your personal preferences and try to be objective, looking for established criteria, such as freedom from off flavours, balance, attractiveness and repeat drinking potential'. Robin Haig of Dewchurch Cider thinks 'The competitions have stimulated interest in cider, it's amazing how many entries there are. Most of the people who win are amateur cider makers who have not made before'. The first year Kenelm and Michael Johnson at Broome Farm made cider then entered it in the Cider Museum Competition— 'Just for fun'. They were awarded a First and Supreme Champion for their cider, 'The biggest shock of my life'! says Kenelm. Michael adds: 'Since then I've done well entering the competitions, especially Putley. I find it keeps you interested and striving for better quality, you know that others are also improving and have to keep up'. Jean adds:

> The small makers now have a better appreciation of their products due to comparing them to others in the competition. They have also increased the quality of the product and have benefitted from exchanging views, values and techniques with other small makers.

Held a week after the Putley Trials, the International Cider and Perry Competition at the Cider Museum attracts both local entries and submissions from outside the UK. It is just one of the special events held at this year round attraction. The creation of a museum in Hereford to house artifacts and articles relating to cider and perry was first suggested in the October 1966 edition of Bulmers' employee magazine, *Woodpecker News*, by the then editor, Bill Matthews, who had been appointed by Bulmers to collect and catalogue relevant information or old pieces of equipment brought to his notice by Bulmers' employees or the general public. Early donations included a wooden tunpail, a cider drinking horn and a bottle of Pomagne from 1929 which had been found bricked up in a wall of a Bridlington Hotel. In 1969 Bertram Bulmer wrote to every parish priest in Herefordshire inquiring about local cider mills and presses that were then surveyed by a local fruit buyer and some of his men. The farmers trusted them as they knew them from buying the fruit each year, so were very honest, also the fruit buyer knew where the mills might be hidden as he was familiar with the county's orchards. The survey produced 220 replies and was a great success. As a result the idea of setting up a cider museum at the Ryelands works was seriously taken in hand by Bertram Bulmer on his retirement from the firm.

Donations for the museum from local farmers and cider makers started trickling in some years before the museum had premises. A beam press arrived from France that is now in the main display, but local presses were hard to find. Farmers realised they were worth something with the boom in antiques prices.

Michael Quinion, the new curator for the collection, tried to complete a second survey of cider artifacts in 1978, with the help of Manpower Services. But those employed to carry out the survey were strangers to rural life and cider making and were told fine tales by some farmers who enjoyed leg pulling town dwellers. 'Those blokes in pinstripe suits and polished shoes doing that survey, you can tell 'em anything and they believe you' was a typical Herefordian attitude to strangers poking around where they were not wanted. As a result the survey was a disaster.

The Hereford Cider Museum was formed into an independent trust in 1973 and opened to the public in 1981, housed in the old offices and champagne cellars of Bulmers' Ryeland Street Cider Mill. It cannot afford to purchase exhibits, so most of the acquisitions in the museum have been donations from the public. To raise revenue the museum levies an entrance charge and also has a shop selling cider related items, including its own King Offa Cider Brandy, named after the Mercian ruler who is believed to have organised the building of Offa's Dyke along the Welsh border.

Bertram Bulmer obtained a license from Customs and Excise in 1984 to distill cider for educational purposes. A 1905 pot still from Normandy was imported to Hereford and installed as a working exhibit in the museum, with the aim of selling the brandy to supplement the revenue from entrance charges. The first case went on sale in 1987, but not before Bertram had battled Brussels to be able to call his product 'cider brandy'.

I printed thousands of labels proclaiming it as King Offa Cider Brandy, then they told me that it must be produced from French grapes to be called brandy, and suggested calling it 'cider spirit'. Cider Spirit! It sounds like something you run a moped on! I have written back saying I intend to ignore their silly directive.

Bertram also enlisted the British government and Ministry of Agriculture to make a special plea against the ruling, supported by other countries who wanted to retain names such as Cherry Brandy. As a result, Bertram won his appeal.

HEREFORD

CIDER BRANDY

©

5
years old
from
THE KING OFFA DISTILLERY
HEREFORD

40% vol   70 cl

The first bottle of King Offa Cider Brandy was given to Queen Elizabeth II, who had donated an oak tree from Windsor Great Park to be made into cider brandy casks. Prince Charles donated an oak from his Duchy of Cornwall Estates, and so was presented with the second bottle. In 1988 the original 1905 pot still which distilled cider was retired, to be retained as an exhibit and can still be seen in the outside viewing window of the distillery. In 2002 the museum released the brandy matured in the Queen's cask in celebration of Queen Elizabeth II's Golden Jubilee.

Margaret Thompson has been working at the museum since the doors opened in 1981 and is the current museum director.

I had ceased working in the Bulmers offices in 1982 and Bertram came to see me and asked if I would like to work from home, doing the museum accounts for the trust. I was happy to help as this fitted in well with my family. However, with Bertram there was always a sting in the tail. He also suggested I take control of the distillery and blend the cider brandy. I had no practical experience of this part of the business and was not so keen on this aspect of the job, and told him I did not feel qualified. He asked, 'Can you make a cake?' When I said yes he replied, 'Then you can make cider brandy; all you need to do is follow the recipe!' So it was settled.

The King Offa Cider Brandy works with the old pot still towards the top right

The Museum commenced distilling in 1984 and released the first bottle of cider brandy in 1987. Initially the distillation process proved very challenging as there were no other UK producers to refer to for advice. The smell of toffee apples filling the Museum during distillation is delicious and during the early years our bottling methods were primitive compared to those of Bulmers itself which by then were fully automatic.

Choosing the right wood for our maturing casks was also a challenge. We tried casks of Hereford Oak, but it was too fresh and the brandy came out coloured green! We also tried American white oak but didn't feel it imparted a pleasant flavour. Now we use whisky barrels with heads of Hereford Oak. Our maturing barrels of brandy are stored in the old cellars at the Wickwar Cider Company in Gloucestershire. Blending and bottling is done at the museum. We don't try to be consistent with our vintages—each has its own particular character, which we hope will appeal to our customers. We have found that customers tastes are very subjective, so if they don't like one vintage they may enjoy another. There is a batch number on each bottle so it is possible for a customer to request the same brandy from us again, if any remains in stock.

In 1987 we were given some perry to distill. As we didn't know what it would be like, we just produced two small barrels as a trial. In 1995 we tasted the results and it was fantastic, with an excellent nose and flavour. We bottled one barrel and hoped to be able to keep the other maturing for future blending, but demand was so high that both barrels were sold. We still get requests from interested customers for more, but we have not been able to get any more perry for distilling since. We hope to distill more perry but the vintage will take 7 to 8 years to mature, and we hope that it will turn out as well as the last batch. But we can only hope that there will be enough surplus perry to distill in the future.

The galleries at the cider museum take the visitor through the cider making process from pip to cask. The entrance hall contains the 300-year-old beam press brought to Hereford from Honfleur, Normandy, in 1980. The next gallery recreates an orchard, giving information on apple and perry pear cultivation and conservation; at the end of the orchard is a reconstructed farm cider house and smallholding, including a travelling cider maker's 'tack', used by David East of Yazor, Herefordshire, until the 1920s. The walls of the gallery describe how cider is made and some of the infections that can be a problem to the cider maker. The next gallery displays items relating to the tax on cider; Devonshire colic, identified by Exeter physicians to be caused by lead in old mills and scratters; plus a range of traditional drinking vessels, including horns and costrells. The Pomona Room houses three original *Pomonas*, those of

Looking across an old screw press and stone mill in the Cider Museum, Hereford

Farmhouse bottling display at the Cider Museum, Hereford

Thomas Andrew Knight (1811), The Woolhope Society (1875-1889) and Bulmers' own *Pomona* (1987) including original, beautifully detailed water colours of cider apples, perry pears, their blossoms and leaves. The original Board Room of the Bulmer empire, complete with furnishings has been preserved and is still used by the museum trustees for their board meetings. A collection of advertising, bottles and drip mats from many countries around the world line the corridor down to the champagne cellars, which explain and display the equipment imported from France which was used to make Pomagne cider. Further along the cellars the presses of Godwins Cider Works, Holmer, are preserved along with a mural showing presses at Evans Cider Works, Widemarsh Common, in action. Sharp eyed visitors may spot granny busy at her typewriter in the old accounts office. The cooper's shop is tucked between the presses and Vat house. During festivals and special events a cooper can be seen making and repairing casks used for King Offa Cider Brandy, using traditional tools. The vat house displays oak vats which would have held up to 500 gallons of fermenting cider, along with a Bamford engine which until 1929 used to generate power for Knights' Cider Works of Gloucestershire. Walking through the next gallery shows how bottling was done in the early 20th century, most of the process being labour intensive and done by hand. The galleries continue up the stairs into the

King Offa distillery where can be seen a travelling French still, as well as the original Normandy copper pot still. The shop offers tastings of King Offa Cider Brandy, Apple Aperitif (apple juice and brandy) and Cider Liqueur (cider and brandy) as well as gifts and souvenirs. Margaret Thompson says:

> Visitors to the museum peaked at 29,000 in the late 1980s. Since then we have lost the advantage of being a new attraction to other heritage sites, so we have to work harder to get people to visit us. We are always seeking new alternatives. Our committee and active board of trustees and volunteers are always developing new ideas to stimulate people to come back.
>
> We also provide a venue and organise educational talks for cider makers as well as social events for the Friends of the Museum and an educational resource for the general public related to cider and cider making. A lot of individuals come to visit the museum who are hoping to make cider on a small scale, often using old equipment found in a barn. I always warn them that it is advisable to make a trial batch and have it tested as much of the old machinery does not meet modern hygiene or health standards, and may contain metals or other contaminants that can be a risk to health.
>
> In October 1999 we started a cider making festival. It began with an invitation to Ralph Owen, a cider maker in Radnorshire, to bring along his travelling cider press for a demonstration in the museum yard. Soon the weekend had grown to include local craft makers, apple displays and local beekeepers. It was a great success and increased our visitor numbers, on that weekend, from the normal 63 to 623. Within one or two days after the festival a coach party had already booked for the following year. The festival is now an annual event and has grown to include activities for children, games, local cider makers selling their wares in the museum yard, and displays and activities that reflect the local heritage of cider making in this area. The event is organised and staffed by the friends, employees and volunteers at the museum, who all donate their time for free on the weekend. We hope that in time it will become a major event for Hereford, reflecting the heritage of the locality.

The cider museum in Hereford is a natural starting point for visitors to Herefordshire interested in exploring the cider making heritage of the three counties. While there (or at any tourist information centre) you can pick up the latest copy of the *Herefordshire Cider Route*, promoted by Herefordshire Tourism. As well as providing a circular tour of the county, the cider route map points you towards eight cider producers who welcome visitors, including details of their history and opening hours, plus seven outlets, two of which stock cider and perry in their specialist shops, plus five small producers who will sell at the farm gate by prior arrangement. When visiting during the pressing season of late September to late November visitors will see cider being made on the farm, whilst in the spring the orchards are filled with blossom.

Herefordshire Tourism also promote the Flavour of Herefordshire Awards, with cider outlets, producers and chefs using cider and perry being amongst the winners. Orchard Hive and Vine in Leominster have won awards in several categories. Owner Geoff Morris says:

> Flavours of Herefordshire is a wonderful scheme and should be used by every county to show off its food and drink. Herefordshire is well placed in this respect: it has good cider, perry, vineyards and hops, plus some innovative food producers. The brochure produced by Herefordshire Tourism is in all the tourist information centres and along with our entry in the cider route brochure brings us extra business from visitors to the county, but somehow we also need to convince local people that local food is good and worth seeking out. Everybody who promotes or produces food in the county should enter. Our motto is 'We don't sell local because it's local, we sell local because it is good'! Everything that comes into the shop is tested by us first.

The mystery and magic of cider making and cider drinking is still to be found alive and well in the three counties of Herefordshire, Gloucestershire and Worcestershire. It beckons to us, stranger and local alike, from the eaves of the apple orchard and farm cider shed, or we may catch a glimpse of its reflection in the shining stainless steel fermenters of the modern cider mills. To experience the magic for yourself, visit the three counties at any time of year, but especially in the spring and autumn when the orchards are at their most glorious. Take home some of our cider and perry to share, along with your memories— and return for more!

Directory

Cider Producers

Broome Farm Cider   Kenelm and Michael Johnson
Broome Farm,   01989 562 824
Peterstow,
Ross on Wye,
Herefordshire

When open: Sales at any reasonable time

Products: Draught dry cider and perry. Bottled medium and dry cider and dry perry.

Bulmers (part of Scottish and Newcastle Breweries)
The Cider Mills,   01432 352 000
Plough Lane,   enquiries@bulmers.com
Hereford

When open: Office Hours

Products: Bulmers Traditional (medium or dry), Bulmers Original, Strongbow, Scrumpy Jack, Woodpecker, White Lightning.

Orcharding Services: Bulmers Growers Scheme, locally grown cider fruit trees supplied with stakes and guards (wholesale).

Cheyney Lodge Cider Company   Mike Henney
Cheyney Lodge,   01531 640 159
Bishops Frome,
Herefordshire

When open. By appointment only, please ring for wholesale orders.

Products: Bishops Frome Herefordshire Dry Cider (Flagon), Cheyney Lodge Dabinette, Cheyney Lodge Bramley single variety ciders.

CIDER IN THE THREE COUNTIES

Dewchurch Cider and Perry
Hill Farm,
Much Dewchurch,
Hereford

Robin Haig
01981 540 247

When open: By appointment only.

Products: Draught Dewchurch dry cider and perry. Still Dry and Sweet cider in bottle, Sparkling Medium Cider in bottle.

Dunkertons Cider
Hays Head Farm,
Luntley,
Pembridge,
Herefordshire

Susie and Ivor Dunkerton
01544 388 653

When open: Cider sales all year Monday to Saturday 10 to 6 (5 in winter). Cider House Restaurant closed from 2005.

Products: Draught Organic traditional dry cider, medium dry cider, medium sweet cider and sweet cider. Bottled Organic dry, medium, medium sweet and sweet cider. Black Fox Cider, Improved Kingston Black, Court Royal, Perry (some subject to availability)

Great Oak Cider Company
Roughmoor,
Eardisley

Brian Jones
01544 327 400

When open: Telephone before visiting.

Products: Great Oak Cider and Perry.

Gregg's Pit Cider and Perry
Gregg's Pit,
Much Marcle,
Herefordshire

James Marsden
01531 660 687

When open: Telephone before visiting.

Products: Draught or Bottled Greg's Pitt Perry, Greg's Pitt Cider.

Gwatkins Cider
Moorhampton Farm,
Abbeydore,
Herefordshire

Denis Gwatkin
01981 550 258

When open: Tuesday to Sunday 9am to 6pm, closed Monday.

Products: Ciders: Dry, medium, sweet, Stoke Red, Yarlington Mill.
Perries: Thorn, Oldfield, Malvern Hills, Blakeney Red, draught or
bottled. Golden Valley Cider in bottles only. Single Varieties subject to
seasonal availability.

Hartlands Farmhouse Cider
Tirley Villa,
Tirley,
Gloucestershire

Dereck Hartland
01452 780 480

When open: All year, but call first and bring a container.

Products: Hartlands traditional dry, medium and sweet cider. Hartlands
traditional dry perry.

Jus, Aylton Cider and Perry
Glebe Farm,
Aylton,
Ledbury,
Herefordshire

Janet MacKay
01531 670 518

When open. On request, please telephone before visiting.

Products: Single variety apple juice, Aylton Dry Cider and Perry on
draught (subject to availability).

Knights Cider
Crumpton Oaks Farm,
Storridge,
Malvern,
Worcestershire

Keith Knight
01684 574 594

When open: Farm shop 10.30am to 5pm Saturdays and Sundays only.

Products: Knights Cider, dry, medium or sweet in PET or bottles.

Minchews Cider and Perry   Kevin Minchew
Rose Cottage,   0797 403 4331
Aston Cross,
Tewkesbury,
Gloucestershire

When open: On request, please telephone before visiting. Farm gate sales wholesale only.

Products: Single variety ciders and perries, occasional blends. The range varies from year to year depending on the availability of fruit. Bottled or draught.

Olivers Cider and Perry   Tom Oliver
Stanksbridge,   01432 820 569
Ocle Pychard,   oliversciderandperry@theolivers.org.uk
Herefordshire

When open: Draught products wholesale only. Bottled cider and perry available from Orchard, Hive and Vine (for details see p.ADD).

Products: Sweet, Medium Sweet, Medium Dry and Dry Perry, Medium Dry Cider, Bottle fermented Cider and Perry, Coppy single variety perry (subject to availability and season).

Shortwood Organic Farm   Janet Legge
Shortwood Farm,   01885 400 205
Pencombe,
Bromyard

When open: Easter to the end of October from 10am. Feeding Tours 2pm every day and 11am in school holidays and at weekends. Groups by arrangement. A working organic farm and family friendly visitor attraction. Cider and perry making with stone mill and horse in October half term. Entry to farm £4.50 adults, £2.90 children (2003 prices)

Products: Farm Shop stocks Shortwood Farm Cider.

Tiddly Poms   Pete Smithies
Priding,
Arlingham,
Gloucestershire

When open: No phone, drop by on the weekends but not too early on Sundays! Bring a container.

Products: Tiddly Poms cider and perry on draught.

Westons Cider   Rosemary Manns
The Bounds,   01531 660 233
Much Marcle,   www.westonscider.co.uk
Ledbury,   Scrumpy House Restaurant: 01531 660 626
Herefordshire

When open: Shop, Museum and Henry Weston's Garden open: 9am to 4.30pm Monday to Friday, Saturdays 10am to 1pm, closed Sundays. Mill Tours by prior arrangement. Restaurant: Lunch: 11.30am to 2.30pm Monday to Sunday. Dinner: Thursday, Friday and Saturday only from 7pm.

Products: The shop stocks the full range of Westons products, in addition to Westons souvenirs and cider related crafts by local makers. Products include: Draught: Bounds Brand, GWR, Traditional Scrumpy, Stowford Press, Scrumpy Supreme, Old Rosie, Herefordshire Country Perry. Bounds Brand, Old Rosie, Traditional Scrumpy, 1st Quality, Organic Draught Vintage ciders and Herefordshire Country Perry and are also available as a 20 litre 'Cider in a Box'. Bottles and flagons include: 1st Quality, Special Vintage, Westons Organic, Organic Vintage, Henry Westons Vintage Reserve Cider, Oak Conditioned Cider, Marcle Millennium, Westons Vintage, Stowford LA, Organic Spritzer, Cider and Ginger, Cider and Lemongrass, Cider and Elderflower and Original Perry.

Wick Court Farms for City Children   Heather Tarplee,
Wick Court,   01452 740 117 (Office Hours)
Arlingham,
Gloucestershire

When open: Call for details of educational visits for children.

Products: Double Gloucester Cheese, Wick Court Cider and Perry.

Specialist Shop

Orchard Hive and Vine   Geoff and Sue Morris
4 The High Street,   01568 611 232
Leominster,
Herefordshire

When open: Monday to Saturday 9.30am to 5.30pm (closed for lunch 1.30 to 2pm).

Products: Wide range of craft ciders and perries produced in the Three Counties for sale, plus local beer, wine and spirits, mead and cyser. Also available by mail order, call for catalogue or visit www.orchard-hive-and-vine.co.uk

Cider Pubs

The Apple Tree Real Cider House
54 Lowesmoor,   01905 613 132
Worcester,
Worcestershire

When open: Noon to 11pm Monday to Saturday, Noon to 10.30pm Sunday.

Products: Westons Old Rosie and Bulmers Traditional.

Three Tuns   Lucy Powell
Belmont Road (on the corner with Bridge Street)
Hay on Wye
Powys (just!)

When open: Noon to 3pm and 6pm to 11pm daily, or as trade demands. An unspoilt gem.

Products: Westons draught cider from the polycask, Westons perry in summer.

Bulls Head, Craswell

On a minor road south-east   01981 510 616
of Hay on Wye. OS 278360

When open: 11am to 11pm Monday to Saturday, Noon to 4pm Sunday.
Renowned for its fine cider and good food, the Bulls Head also offers a
campsite for those who have trekked there from afar.

Products; Westons 1st Quality, Old Rosie and Herefordshire Country
Perry (in summer) plus local guest ciders including Gwatkins Golden
Valley Cider in bottle.

The Barrels

69 St Owens Street,
Hereford

When open: 11am to 11pm weekdays, Noon to 10.30pm Sundays.

Products: local guest ciders, Bulmers Traditional, Westons Stowford
Press and Scrumpy Supreme. Charity beer and cider festival every
August Bank Holiday with extensive cider and perry bar.

Brewers Arms

Eign Road,   01432 273 746
Hereford

When open: Noon to 11pm weekdays, noon to 10.30pm Sundays. A no
frills backstreet 'local'.

Products: Westons Cider on handpump.

House in the Tree

Haydens Elm,   01242 680 241
Cheltenham,
Gloucestershire

When open: 11am to 11pm weekdays, noon to 10.30pm Sundays. Just
off the A40 west of Cheltenham, this atmospheric thatched pub stocks a
huge range of draught and bottled ciders.

Products: Bulmers Traditional, Addlestones and Thatchers Dry on
handpump, and Draught Westons Stowford Press, Old Rosie and Henry

Westons Vintage in bottles. Rolls are available in the front bar and the back bar offers a full menu, including an all day Sunday Lunch.

The Volunteer   Stella Forden-Cove
Harold Street,   01432 276 189
Hereford

When open: 11am to 11pm weekdays, noon to 10.30pm Sundays. A friendly local with a wide range of local ciders and perries on hand-pump, draught and in bottles.

Products: Westons, Bulmers and local producers including Gwatkins and Olivers. Food served at lunchtime.

Cider and Cheese

Stinking Bishop Cheese   Charles Martell
Laurel Farm,
Broomsgreen,
Dymock,
Gloucestershire

A unique soft English cheese, named after a perry pear and washed in perry, which gives it a pungent rind. Wholesale orders only. Available locally from Mousetrap Cheese shops in Leominster and Hereford, and D. Waller Butchers in Ledbury.

Museums and Festivals

Hereford Cider Museum   Margaret Thompson
21 Ryelands Street,   01432 354 207
Hereford

When open; April to October 10am-5.30pm everyday, November-March 11am-3pm Tuesday to Sunday, closed Mondays. Groups and Tours by prior arrangement. Museum Shop, sales of King Offa Cider Brandy, Cider Making festival third weekend in October, International Cider and Perry competition first week in May.

Big Apple Association   Janet MacKay
Glebe Farm,   01531 670 518
Aylton,
Ledbury,
Herefordshire

The Big Apple Association run the Spring and Autumn festivals in the parishes of the Marcle Ridge in Herefordshire, along with the Putley Cider Trials each May.

Leominster Fruity Affair   Felicity Norman
The Folly,   01568 780 886
Luston,
nr. Leominster,
Herefordshire HR6 0BX

The Leominster Fruity Affair is held on the third weekend in October at the Lion Ballroom, Leominster. Ring for details.

Hartlebury Museum
Hartlebury Castle,   01299 250 416
nr. Kidderminster,
Worcestershire

When open: Monday to Thursday 10am to 5pm, Friday and Sunday 2pm to 5pm, Bank Holidays 11am to pm. Closed Saturdays and Good Friday.

Preserved cider house, cider making festival each autumn.

Gloucester Folk Museum
99-103 Westgate Street,   01452 396 467
Gloucester

When open: Tuesday to Saturday 10am to 5pm. Closed Sunday and Monday.

Reconstructed cider house and apple loft, interesting collection of cider drinking horns, cider making demonstration in the cider house third week in October.

Associations

Three Counties Cider and Perry Association   Mike Henney
Cheyney Lodge,   01531 640159
Bishops Frome,
Herefordshire

Support group for cider makers in the Three Counties.

Campaign for Real Ale (CAMRA) APPLE Chair: Gills Williams
230 Hatfield Road,   Editor *Whats Brewing*: Ted Bruning
St. Albans,   01727 867 201
Hertfordshire

Campaign for Real Ale Headquarters, APPLE campaign, cider articles
for *Whats Brewing*, Alma Books publish the CAMRA *Good Cider Guide*
2000 - ISBN:1-85249-143-4, which is being updated for 2004.

Community Orchards

Marcher Apple Network   Sheila Leitch
Wye View,   01497 847 354
Glasbury on Wye,   www.marcherapple.net
Powys via Hereford

Coordinator for Marcher Apple Network, information on activities and
events, museum orchards, fruit identification, visiting experts and
network membership.

Brogdale Horticultural Trust
Brogdale Road,   01795 535 286
Faversham,
Kent

When open: Every day 9.30am to 5pm from Easter to Christmas,
national collection of fruit trees.

Common Ground
Gold Hill House,   01747 850 820
21 High Street,
Shaftsbury,
Dorset

Coordinate National campaign for Community Orchards and Apple Day (21 October).

Bees and Trees Trust   Paul Hands
Whitton Cottage,   01547 540 374
Leintwardine,
Shropshire

The Bees and Trees Trust runs educational workshops for children and communities on orchards and orchard fruits in the West Midlands.

Conserve Our Orchards, Gloucestershire   Anna Jones
Environment Branch,   01452 425 679
County Environment Department,
Shire Hall,
Gloucester

Information on Orchard Trees and Grants in Gloucestershire.

Gloucestershire Orchard Group
109 Orchard Way,   www.orchard-group.uklinux.net/glos
Churchdown,
Gloucester GL3 2AP

Founded in 2001 to conserve, promote and celebrate traditional orchards in Gloucestershire. Has information on restoring and recreating traditional orchards, where to source trees, costs and grants. Also on local orchards and fruit collections, local varieties of fruit, markets, cider and juice tastings, local training and events. Members receive the booklet *Restoring Gloucestershire Orchards*, a twice yearly newsletter, advice and updates of information.

213

Charles Martell Collection of Cider Fruit
Alan Watson, County Arborculturalist   01453 794 920
The Malt House,
Standish,
Stonehouse,
Glos. GL10 3DL

Can supply graftwood from the Gloucestershire County Council Mother Tree collection.

Herefordshire Council schemes   James Bisset
Parks and Countryside Service,   Partnership Project Officer,
PO Box 41,   01568 797 305 /798 320
Leominster,
Herefordshire

Information and application leaflets for the council's Environmental Improvement Grant scheme and the council's Fruit Tree Kit scheme, which runs between April and October.

Worcester Orchard Workers (WOW)   Rory Mclure
Orchard House,   01905 722 500
Farrier Street,
Worcester

Local group restoring cider orchards in Worcester city. Educational visits for schools.

Worcestershire Orchard Forum   Rachel Daplin
Worcester Countryside Centre,   01905 766 493
Wildwood Drive,
Worcester

Orchard preservation and surveys, grants, fruit tree scheme, *Orchard Newsletter* (biannual).

Cider Making Equipment and Consultancy Services

GCW Technology   Geoff Warren
2 Berrington Drive,   01568 797 278
Bodenham,
Herefordshire

Cider consultancy

Vigo Ltd
Dunkeswell Airfield,   01404 890 262
Dunkeswell,
Honiton,
Devon

Cider making equipment suppliers.

All Party Parliamentary Cider Group   Paul Keetch MP
House of Commons,   Secretary - Helen Jones:
Westminster,   01432 341 483 10am to 3pm
London

Member for cider, Chair and founder of All Party Parliamentary Cider Group.

National Association of Cider Makers   R.D. Price
Food and Drink Federation,
6 Catherine Street,
London

Trade body for cider makers.

Wassailing and Mumming

Campaign for the Revival of Wassailing
   (CROW)   P. 'Butler' Symonds
The Patch,
Coverham Road,
Berry Hill,
Coleford,
Gloucestershire

Reviving Wassailing in the Three Counties.

Lassington Oak Morris Side   Bill Taylor
                                        01452 422 447

Traditional Cotswold Morris in Gloucestershire.

Leominster Morris Side (Bookings)   Tony Lowcock
                                        01544 388 686

Herefordshire wassailing and mumming.

Cider index

This index is organised around various headings: apples (which covers items to do with the fruit and varieties), cider (which covers general items to do with cider), cider making (which includes all aspects of the process), cider brands / types, Inns, and orchard management.

Also from Logaston Press

Camping on the Wye
ISBN 1 904396 05 4   Price £9.95

In 1892 a group of four undergraduates from University College, London, set off on a boating and camping trip on the Wye. Two of the four were medical students, one the future father of the actor Marius Goring, and the other from a Jamaican 'Plantocracy' family whose tradition relates that a direct antecedent was Willy Goffe, one of Cromwell's major-generals, a signatory to the death warrant of Charles I and who had fled after the Restoration to the new colonies of North America. The third member of the party was a 'dabbler in art', whilst knowledge of the fourth friend has faded with time. They hired a skiff from Jordan's in Hereford, took it by train to Whitney with all their stores and embarked—watched by a small crowd on the bank.

The journey was recorded in a sketchbook and diary, here brought together. With a dry sense of humour it tells of various campsites by the river, of visits to riverside inns and places of interest, of splendid sunny days, of sheltering from wet weather, of battles with bugs and insects, of nosey cows, of highs and lows of a river journey.

What is particularly intriguing is how little some things have changed, yet how others have altered markedly. The friends appear to adopt the kitchen sink mode of travel, whilst now such trips would be done with the minimum of clutter. The number of riverside inns and farms with their own 'cyder' are far fewer. Yet the immediately suspicious nature but innate warmth of country people remains the same, and the day to day concerns of people are what they have always been. It is also strangely gratifying to see that our forebears adopted the same tricks now used on current generations when visiting distant lands. When the travelling companions were camping at Goodrich Castle, one local tried to interest them in artwork supposedly undertaken by King Henry IV (and featured in this book), just as we're now offered ancient coins and artefacts outside tourist traps abroad!

Herefordshire's Postcard Past
by Tim Ward   ISBN 1 904396 00 3   Price £9.95

This is the fourth book of old postcards of Herefordshire compiled by Tim Ward. The book contains almost 200 images largely from the first two decades of the 1900s with a fairly even spread across the county. But perhaps it is the events, rather than the places that are depicted which are of greater interest. Included are early flying machines landing in the county, sheep shearing, a bus tackling the Fromes Hill hill climb, volunteer reservists undergoing training, the opening of a new church, the Church Army at work, saw mills in operation, a chemical works, former shops, pubs, post offices and railway stations—even an eviction from a country cottage.

Accompanying each of the more than 200 illustrations Tim Ward provides some background information to set the scene, and as you dip into the book—or read it from cover to cover—you'll also gain an appreciation of the work of the photographers and postcard makers of the early twentieth century. Finally the book contains a list of all the known producers of postcards featuring the county.

Also from Logaston Press

The Pubs of Bromyard, Ledbury & East Herefordshire
by John Eisel & Ron Shoesmith   ISBN 1 873827 63 6   Price £9.95

Covering the towns of Bromyard and Ledbury and the villages that lie in east Herefordshire, this book continues the series that details the history and social background of the hotels, taverns and inns that have existed in the county. All existing hostelries are included, along with many that have come and gone, including the Frenchman's Inn, which now appears just to be a pile of stones, and the insalubrious sounding The Swill—which perhaps deserved its fade into obscurity.

The information given details not just the history of the buildings themselves, but also of the landlords—some upright characters and others just staying sufficiently within the law to retain their licences. Many landlords had other jobs besides—as farmers, wheelwrights, carpenters, even running post offices, which puts into perspective the fact that some of the pubs are once again acting as the village post office. Few, however, would welcome the return of Inland Revenue offices to their local!

Pubs provide a wealth of social history, and this book contains some wonderful stories—of circus elephants kept at the back of one pub which ate not just the cakes from the local shops, but also people's clothes hanging on their washing lines! Of a piglet offered to one sullen landlord who told his customers that he couldn't supply a ham sandwich. Of landlords that banned all local organisations meeting on their premises, but of many more that encouraged them. Of glasses marked with the pub name on the bottom so that when hop-pickers left the area glasses they had 'borrowed' could find their way back to the right pub—with proof of ownership.

One pub was a venue for the rock band Black Sabbath, whilst another currently provides 'jamming sessions' on a Tuesday evening for locally-based bands and musicians.

Various groups of people can be associated with moderate to heavy drinking— be they amateur sportsmen, those out on a pub crawl or Morris men. But whereas the latter failed to drink sufficient to keep one local going, less expected are the stories of the activities of bell-ringers in a number of hostelries. One pub which made its own cider and perry offered a regular challenge to anyone to try and drink three pints and remain upright. If anyone felt that they'd succeeded, they were requested to walk home—the fresh air on exiting the pub would often prove to be the last straw.